Analyzing Syntax through Texts

EX·LIBRIS·SUNE·GREGERSEN

Edinburgh Historical Linguistics Series
Series Editors: Joseph Salmons and David Willis

The series provides a comprehensive introduction to this broad and increasingly complex field. Aimed at advanced undergraduates in linguistics, as well as beginning postgraduates who are looking for an entry point, volumes are discursive, accessible and responsive to critical developments in the field.

Individual volumes show historical linguistics as a field anchored in two centuries of research, with a rich empirical base and theoretical perspectives, and one tied tightly to all areas of linguistics. Fundamentally, though, the series shows how historical linguists approach language change. Every volume contains pedagogical features such as recommendations for further reading, but the tone of each volume is discursive, explanatory and critically engaged, rather than 'activity-based'.

Series Editors

Joseph Salmons is Professor of Germanic Linguistics at the University of Wisconsin

David Willis is Reader in Historical Linguistics at the University of Cambridge

Titles available in the series:

Analogy and Morphological Change
David Fertig

Analyzing Syntax through Texts: Old, Middle, and Early Modern English
Elly van Gelderen

Analyzing Syntax through Texts
Old, Middle, and Early Modern English

Elly van Gelderen

EDINBURGH
University Press

Edinburgh University Press is one of the leading university presses in
the UK. We publish academic books and journals in our selected subject
areas across the humanities and social sciences, combining cutting-
edge scholarship with high editorial and production values to produce
academic works of lasting importance. For more information visit our
website: edinburghuniversitypress.com

© Elly van Gelderen, 2018

Edinburgh University Press Ltd
The Tun – Holyrood Road, 12(2f) Jackson's Entry, Edinburgh EH8 8PJ

Typeset in 10/12pt Times New Roman by
Servis Filmsetting Ltd, Stockport, Cheshire,
and printed and bound in Great Britain by
CPI Group (UK) Ltd, Croydon CR0 4YY

A CIP record for this book is available from the British Library

ISBN 978 1 4744 2037 2 (hardback)
ISBN 978 1 4744 2038 9 (paperback)
ISBN 978 1 4744 2039 6 (webready PDF)
ISBN 978 1 4744 2040 2 (epub)

The right of Elly van Gelderen to be identified as the author of this
work has been asserted in accordance with the Copyright, Designs and
Patents Act 1988, and the Copyright and Related Rights Regulations
2003 (SI No. 2498).

Contents

List of Figures and Tables — viii
Series Editors' Preface — xi
Preface — xii
Acknowledgments — xv
List of Abbreviations — xviii

1 Introduction — 1
1.1 The History of English in a Nutshell — 2
1.2 Functions and Case — 4
1.3 Verbal Inflection and Clause Structure — 6
1.4 Change: How and Why — 8
1.5 Sources and Resources — 11
1.6 Conclusion — 12

2 The Syntax of Old, Middle, and Early Modern English — 14
2.1 Major Changes in the Syntax of English — 14
2.2 Word Order — 17
  2.2.1 The subject and the verb — 18
  2.2.2 The position of other elements — 19
  2.2.3 After Old English — 20
2.3 Case on Nouns and Pronouns and Agreement and Tense/Aspect/Mood on the Verb — 21
  2.3.1 Nouns — 21
  2.3.2 Verbs — 23
2.4 Demonstratives, Pronouns, and Articles — 28
  2.4.1 Pronominals in Old and Middle English — 28
  2.4.2 Some paradigms and change — 30
2.5 Clause Boundaries: Punctuation, Word Order, and Conjunctions — 32
2.6 Dialectal Variation in the Time Period — 37
2.7 Conclusion — 42

3 Old English before 1100 — 45

- 3.1 The Script — 45
- 3.2 Historical Prose Narrative: *Orosius* — 47
  - 3.2.1 The text — 47
  - 3.2.2 Analysis — 47
  - 3.2.3 Stage of the language and dialect — 55
- 3.3 Sermon: Wulfstan on the Antichrist — 56
  - 3.3.1 The text — 56
  - 3.3.2 Analysis — 56
  - 3.3.3 Stage of the language — 64
- 3.4 The Old English Gospels — 65
  - 3.4.1 The texts — 65
  - 3.4.2 Analysis — 69
  - 3.4.3 Broader view and dialectal differences — 79
- 3.5 Poetry from the *Exeter Book* — 80
  - 3.5.1 The texts — 80
  - 3.5.2 Analysis — 82
  - 3.5.3 Status and dialect — 92
- 3.6 Conclusion — 93

4 Early Middle English 1100–1300 — 96

- 4.1 The *Peterborough Chronicle* — 97
  - 4.1.1 The text — 97
  - 4.1.2 Analysis: from the beginning to the end of the *Peterborough Chronicle* — 100
  - 4.1.3 Status and dialect — 106
- 4.2 *Seinte Katerine* — 107
  - 4.2.1 The texts — 107
  - 4.2.2 Analysis — 107
  - 4.2.3 Status and dialect — 112
- 4.3 *The Owl and the Nightingale* — 113
  - 4.3.1 The text — 113
  - 4.3.2 Analysis — 113
  - 4.3.3 Status and dialect — 118
- 4.4 *The Lion* — 119
  - 4.4.1 The text — 119
  - 4.4.2 Analysis — 119
  - 4.4.3 Status and dialect — 124
- 4.5 Richard Rolle's *Psalter* Preface — 125
  - 4.5.1 The text — 125
  - 4.5.2 Analysis — 126
  - 4.5.3 Status and dialect — 132
- 4.6 Conclusion — 133

5 Late Middle and Early Modern English 1300–1600 — 141

- 5.1 *Cleanness* — 142
  - 5.1.1 The text — 142

		5.1.2	Analysis	142
		5.1.3	Status and dialect	147
	5.2	Chaucer's *Astrolabe*		148
		5.2.1	The text	148
		5.2.2	Analysis	151
		5.2.3	Status and dialect	153
	5.3	Margery of Kempe		154
		5.3.1	The text	154
		5.3.2	Analysis	155
		5.3.3	Status and dialect	159
	5.4	Caxton's *Morte d'Arthur*		159
		5.4.1	The text	160
		5.4.2	Analysis	161
		5.4.3	Status and dialect	165
	5.5	Henry Machyn and Queen Elizabeth		166
		5.5.1	The texts	166
		5.5.2	Analysis, status, and dialect	169
	5.6	Conclusion		171

Appendix I   Summary of All Grammatical Information 175
    I.1   Syntax in General; Dialect 175
    I.2   Nominal, Adjectival, and Pronominal Inflections 176
    I.3   Verbal Inflections 178
Appendix II   Background on the Old English Texts That Are Discussed, Alphabetically 180
    II.1   Old English 180
    II.2   Early Middle English 181
    II.3   Later Middle English and Early Modern 181
Appendix III   Keys to the Exercises 183
Glossary 187
References 194
Index 199

Figures and Tables

Figures

Figure 1.1	Changes in the analytic/synthetic nature of English	3
Figure 1.2	Universal Grammar and the acquisition of grammars	9
Figure 2.1	*Caedmon's Hymn*, from the 'Moore Bede'	15
Figure 2.2	Periods/points in the beginning of *Beowulf*	33
Figure 2.3	The *Peterborough Chronicle* for the year 1066	34
Figure 2.4	The beginning of Layamon's Caligula version of *Brut*	35
Figure 2.5	Hamlet's Soliloquy by Shakespeare	36
Figure 2.6	Old English dialects	38
Figure 2.7	Middle English dialects	39
Figure 3.1	Insular and Carolingian script	46
Figure 3.2	*Orosius*, Tollemache MS	48
Figure 3.3	Wulfstan, first page	57
Figure 3.4	Wulfstan, second page	58
Figure 3.5	Wulfstan, third page	59
Figure 3.6	From the beginning of the Lindisfarne *Matthew*, leaf 30r	66
Figure 3.7	Rushworth Glosses	67
Figure 3.8	West Saxon Gospels	68
Figure 3.9	*The Wife's Lament* from the *Exeter Book*, f. 115r and v	81
Figure 3.10	*The Wife's Lament* and a transcription	82
Figure 3.11	The first lines of *The Wanderer* from the *Exeter Book*, f. 76v	84
Figure 3.12	*The Wanderer* and a transcription	84
Figure 3.13	*The Pastoral Care*	94
Figure 4.1	The Gothic script	96
Figure 4.2	The Introduction to the *Peterborough Chronicle*, Laud Misc. 636, f. 1r	98
Figure 4.3	*Peterborough Chronicle* for the year 1130, Laud Misc. 636, f. 87v	99
Figure 4.4	*Peterborough Chronicle* for the year 1137, Laud Misc. 636, f. 89r	100
Figure 4.5	*Seinte Katerine*, Bodley 34, f. 3v and f. 4r	108

Figures and Tables ix

Figure 4.6	*Seinte Katerine* and transcription, Bodley 34, the last part of f. 3v and first part of f. 4r	108
Figure 4.7	*The Owl and the Nightingale*, Cotton Caligula A IX, f. 233	114
Figure 4.8	*The Lion* in *The Physiologus* or *Bestiary*	120
Figure 4.9	Richard Rolle's *Psalter*, HM 148, f. 23	126
Figure 4.10	Last entry in the *Parker Chronicle* for the year 1070, f. 31v and f. 32r	134
Figure 4.11	*The Owl and the Nightingale*, MS 29, f. 156r	136
Figure 4.12	*Havelok*, Laud Misc. 108, f. 208r, lines 722–811	137
Figure 5.1	The secretary hand	141
Figure 5.2	The italic hand	141
Figure 5.3	*Cleanness*	143
Figure 5.4	Chaucer's *Astrolabe*, MS Eng 920, f. 5v	149
Figure 5.5	Chaucer's *Astrolabe*, MS Eng 920, f. 6	150
Figure 5.6	The first page of *The Book of Margery of Kempe*	154
Figure 5.7	The first page of the first chapter of Malory's *Morte d'Arthur*	160
Figure 5.8	The second part of the first chapter of Malory's *Morte d' Arthur*	161
Figure 5.9	Machyn, 1 May 1559	166
Figure 5.10	Machyn, 1 May 1559 transcription and translation	166
Figure 5.11	Letter from Elizabeth to Queen Mary	167
Figure 5.12	Letter 13, seemingly written by Agnes Paston, 1440	171
Figure 5.13	Caxton's rendering of Cicero's *De senectute*	172

Tables

Table 1.1	Characteristics of analytic and synthetic languages	2
Table 1.2	Cases and their main functions	6
Table 1.3	Some instances of grammaticalization	10
Table 2.1	Changes in the syntax and morphology of English	17
Table 2.2	Word order in Old English	20
Table 2.3	Some Old English (strong) noun endings	22
Table 2.4	An Old English strong verb	24
Table 2.5	An Old English weak verb	24
Table 2.6	The Old English forms of the verb *beon* 'to be'	26
Table 2.7	Late Middle English verbal inflection	26
Table 2.8	The modal paradigm for *sculan* 'be obliged to'	28
Table 2.9	Old English personal pronouns	31
Table 2.10	Late Middle English pronouns	31
Table 2.11	Demonstratives in Old English	32
Table 2.12	The *Peterborough Chronicle* for the year 1066	34
Table 2.13	Middle English dialect characteristics	40
Table 3.1	*Orosius* transcription	49
Table 3.2	A fragment from *Orosius* in Old English, word-by-word in Modern English, and in a translation	50

Table 3.3	The *-an* declension for the noun *tima*	60
Table 3.4	The definite adjective declension	60
Table 3.5	Indefinite declensions of *halig* 'holy'	63
Table 3.6	Northumbrian Glosses on the left, Mercian in the middle, and the West Saxon Gospel on the right, based on Skeat ([1881–7] 1970)	68
Table 3.7	Transcription and word-by-word gloss of *The Wife's Lament*	83
Table 3.8	Transcription and word-by-word translation of *The Wanderer*	85
Table 3.9	Two analyses of a part of (57)	88
Table 3.10	More on (57)	88
Table 4.1	The first page of the *Peterborough Chronicle* (transliteration and translation)	98
Table 4.2	*Peterborough Chronicle* for the year 1130	99
Table 4.3	*Peterborough Chronicle* for the year 1137	101
Table 4.4	Proximal demonstratives in Old English	101
Table 4.5	Transcription and translation of f. 3v and f. 4r of *Seinte Katerine*	109
Table 4.6	*The Owl and the Nightingale*, lines 1–68	115
Table 4.7	Transcription and word-by-word rendition of *The Lion*	121
Table 4.8	Transcription and translation of the first column of the Preface of Richard Rolle's *Psalter*	127
Table 4.9	Transcription and translation of the second column of the *Psalter*'s first page	128
Table 4.10	Transcription of the last entry in the *Parker Chronicle*	135
Table 4.11	*Havelok*, lines 722–811	138
Table 5.1	Transcription and word-by-word gloss of *Cleanness*, lines 1–36	144
Table 5.2	Transcription and translation of the first page of the *Astrolabe*	149
Table 5.3	Transcription and translation of the second page of the *Astrolabe*	151
Table 5.4	Transcription and translation from *The Book of Margery of Kempe*	156
Table 5.5	Transliteration and translation from Caxton's *Morte d'Arthur*	162
Table 5.6	Transcription of Elizabeth's letter	168
Table 5.7	Transcription of Agnes Paston's letter	172
Table III.1	Transcription and translation of exercise	184
Table III.2	Translation of *Havelok*	185

Series Editors' Preface

With this volume, we are delighted to introduce to the world of linguistics *Historical Linguistics*, a series of advanced textbooks on language change and comparative linguistics, where individual volumes cover key subfields within Historical Linguistics in depth. As a whole, the series will provide a comprehensive introduction to this broad and increasingly complex field.

The present volume, we believe, exemplifies the kind of content, tone and format we aim for in the series, and the volumes that are coming down the pike do as well. The series is aimed at advanced undergraduates in Linguistics and students in language departments, as well as beginning postgraduates who are looking for an entry point. Volumes in the series are serious and scholarly university textbooks, theoretically informed and substantive in content. Every volume will contain pedagogical features such as recommendations for further reading, but the tone of the volumes is discursive, explanatory and critically engaged, rather than 'activity-based'.

Authors interested in writing for the series should contact us.

Joseph Salmons (jsalmons@wisc.edu)
David Willis (dwew2@cam.ac.uk)

Preface

This book examines linguistic characteristics of English texts by studying manuscript images. I divide English into Old English, before 1100 but excluding runic inscriptions; Early Middle English, between 1100 and 1300; Late Middle English, between 1300 and 1500; and Early Modern English, after 1500. The end date of 1600 was chosen because I wanted to cover the introduction of printed text as well as some later letters. The shape of the printed letters is shown to continue the earlier scribal tradition, as does the variability in spelling. This division reflects an increase of analytic forms and a loss of synthetic ones in the twelfth and thirteenth centuries. The fourteenth century and after see a stabilization and the development of more synthetic forms due to the lexical influence of French and Latin.

The book is meant for readers who are somewhat familiar with the history of English and who want to look at the syntax and morphology using actual manuscripts. It emphasizes the original version and provides a careful, in-depth analysis of the text. The book can be used as a companion to a course book on the history of English or on its own. It focusses on morpho-syntactic analysis but also paints a certain typological picture.

The introductory chapter provides the reader with some background on case, agreement, auxiliaries, and so on. For readers less familiar with grammatical concepts, there is also a glossary of grammatical and linguistic terms at the end of the book. Chapter 2 outlines the major syntactic (and morphological) changes of the last 1,500 years. Examples have mainly been taken from the *Dictionary of Old English* texts;[1] in order not to clutter the examples, I don't give elaborate references or sources in Chapters 1 and 2 but they can be found in the DOE. A few of the example sentences and observations are taken from van Gelderen (2014).

The chapters after the introductory two each deal with texts from a particular period: Old English in Chapter 3, Early Middle English in Chapter 4, and Late Middle and Early Modern English in Chapter 5. The texts represent stages and registers in the history of English. Some are taken from early poetical material and from some prose, some are well known and some lesser known, and they are from different dialect areas when possible. In Chapter 3, I have put the easier texts first but in Chapters 4 and 5, the texts are ordered chronologically. Different registers and dialects result in very different language. In Appendix II, there is some information on all the texts.

After the two introductory chapters, I emphasize the facsimile versions that the editions are based on so that the reader becomes aware of the spelling, spacing, and punctuation conventions, the frequent lack of a distinction between main and subordinate sentences, the contractions, and the abbreviations. It is important to be able to read the originals since some of our current editions change the text, e.g. Brook and Leslie's (1963) edition of Layamon's *Brut* introduces hyphens where the original lacks them. This gives the wrong impression if one is studying reflexives or prefixes, for instance. There are other advantages to looking at manuscripts. Fischer (2007: 18) mentions this problem of editors having a 'modern' perspective. Fleischer (2009) argues that manuscripts tell us about prosody, something I haven't noticed in the texts in this book, because they were meant to be read. My goal in writing this book has been to go back to manuscripts and not to rely on editions that may, once in a while, make (unfortunate) editorial judgements. This allows the reader to makes his/her own decisions.

To make reading the manuscript images possible, I have added transcriptions, word-by-word glosses, and free translations where I thought they were needed. For the transcription, I have mainly followed Clemens and Graham (2007) except where they modernize all letters and eliminate spaces.

I have not used a lot of theory-specific terminology in the analysis sections. In Chapter 1, I explain the background to 'traditional' grammatical concepts, such as the parts of speech, grammatical functions, and complex sentences, and I briefly discuss grammaticalization. I have tried not to clutter the chapters with references to the vast literature, e.g. on English word order. There is a section at the end of each chapter with some references. These and, especially, *The Cambridge History of the English Language*, volumes 1 and 2 (Hogg 1992a; Blake 1992), and some of the recent *Handbooks of the History of English* (e.g. van Kemenade and Los 2006; Nevalainen and Traugott 2012; Kytö and Pahta 2016) should be helpful.

There are some other books that use facsimiles, in particular Freeborn (1992, updated in 1998 and 2006). His book predates the ready availability of manuscripts online. The present book, where possible, has links to and images from the manuscripts so readers can actually see the parchment and, for later periods, the paper. Freeborn is more Middle English oriented and his focus is sociolinguistic (on the development of a standard language) whereas mine is syntactic. Fischer et al. (2000) provides explanations of Old and Middle English syntax with copious example sentences but it doesn't consider excerpts of particular texts. Other helpful books that include facsimiles and transcriptions are Roberts (2005) and Wright (1960).

I would like to thank Joe Salmons and David Willis for their encouragement and to thank the latter for specific comments. Three anonymous referees provided helpful suggestions. Special thanks go to Johanna Wood for discussions on the scope, audience, and content of this book and to Naomi Dalton for highly specific comments that have improved the flow and argumentation a lot. In July 2016, I had the pleasure of teaching a summer school class on this topic in Naxos, Greece, and I thank its extremely motivated students for critical comments. I am grateful to Laura Williamson, Richard Strachan, Joannah Duncan, and Eliza Wright at Edinburgh University Press for helpful assistance.

I would also like to thank the individuals, libraries, institutions, and publishers that gave me permission to reproduce material previously published or not in the open domain. Every effort has been made to find and contact copyright holders but if any have been inadvertently overlooked, the publisher will be happy to make the necessary adjustments at the first opportunity.

Note

1. Available at <http://tapor.library.utoronto.ca/doecorpus/> (last accessed 9 May 2017).

Acknowledgments

Grateful acknowledgement is made to the following sources for permission to reproduce material previously published elsewhere. Every effort has been made to trace the copyright holders, but if any have been inadvertently overlooked, the publisher will be pleased to make the necessary arrangements at the first opportunity.

Figure 1.1 Changes in the analytic/synthetic nature of English. From Benedikt Szmrecsanyi (2016), 'An Analytic-Synthetic Spiral in the History of English', in Elly van Gelderen (ed.), *Cyclical Change Continued*, Amsterdam: John Benjamins, pp. 93–112. Reproduced with permission from John Benjamins, Amsterdam.

Figure 2.1 *Caedmon's Hymn*, from the 'Moore Bede' (Cambridge University Library, Kk. 5. 16). Reproduced with permission from the Syndics of Cambridge University Library.

Figure 2.2 Periods/points in the beginning of *Beowulf* (Cotton MS Vitellius A.XV, f. 132). Reproduced with permission from the British Library Board.

Figure 2.3 The *Peterborough Chronicle* for the year 1066 (Laud 636, 57v). Reproduced with permission from the Bodleian Library.

Figure 2.4 The beginning of Layamon's Caligula version of *Brut* (Cotton Caligula A IX, f. 3). Reproduced with permission from the British Library Board.

Figure 2.6 Old English dialects. From <http://www.uni-due.de/SHE/SHE_Old_English.htm> (last accessed 4 June 2017). Reproduced with permission from Raymond Hickey Reproduced with permission from Raymond Hickey.

Figure 2.7 Middle English dialects. From <http://www.uni-due.de/SHE/HE_DialectsMiddleEnglish.htm> (last accessed 4 June 2017). Reproduced with permission from Raymond Hickey.

Figure 3.1 Insular and Carolingian script, respectively. From <http://guindo.pntic.mec.es/jmag0042/LATIN_PALEOGRAPHY.pdf> (last accessed 4 June 2017). Reproduced with permission from Juan-José Marcos.

Figure 3.2 *Orosius*, Tollemache MS (Add MS 47967, f. 17 and 17v). Reproduced with permission from the British Library Board.

Figures 3.3–3.5 Wulfstan, first three pages (Corpus Christi College, Cambridge, 419, fos 1–3). Reproduced with permission from Cambridge University Library.

Figure 3.6 From the beginning of the Lindisfarne *Matthew*, leaf 30r (Cotton Nero D IV, f. 30). Reproduced with permission from the British Library Board.

Figure 3.7 Rushworth Glosses (MS Auctarium D.2.19). Reproduced with permission from the Bodleian Library.

Figure 3.8 West Saxon Gospels (Corpus Christi College, Cambridge, 140, f. 3r).

Figure 3.9 *The Wife's Lament* from the *Exeter Book*, f. 115r and v. Reproduced with permission from the Dean and Chapter of Exeter Cathedral.

Figure 3.11 The first lines of *The Wanderer* from the *Exeter Book*, f. 76v. Reproduced with permission from the Dean and Chapter of Exeter Cathedral.

Figure 3.13 *The Pastoral Care*, Corpus Christi College, Cambridge, 12, f. 1r.

Figure 4.1 The Gothic script. From <http://guindo.pntic.mec.es/jmag0042/LATIN_PALEOGRAPHY.pdf> (last accessed 4 June 2017). Reproduced with permission from Juan-José Marcos.

Figure 4.2 The Introduction to the *Peterborough Chronicle* (Laud Misc. 636, f. 1r). Reproduced with permission from the Bodleian Library.

Figure 4.3 *Peterborough Chronicle* for the year 1130 (Laud Misc. 636, f. 87v). Reproduced with permission from the Bodleian Library.

Figure 4.4 *Peterborough Chronicle* for the year 1137 (Laud Misc. 636, f. 89r). Reproduced with permission from the Bodleian Library.

Figure 4.5 *Seinte Katerine* (Bodley 34, f. 3v and f. 4r). Reproduced with permission from the British Library Board.

Figure 4.6. *Seinte Katerine* and transcription (Bodley 34, the last part of f. 3v and first part of f. 4r). Reproduced with permission from the British Library Board.

Figure 4.7 *The Owl and the Nightingale* (Cotton Caligula A IX, f. 233). Reproduced with permission from the British Library Board.

Figure 4.8 *The Lion* in *The Physiologus* or *Bestiary* (Arundel 292, f. 4). Reproduced with permission from the British Library Board.

Figure 4.9 Richard Rolle's *Psalter* (HM 148, f. 23). Reproduced with permission from the Huntington Library.

Figure 4.10 Last entry in the *Parker Chronicle* for the year 1070 (Corpus Christi College, Cambridge, 173, f. 31v and f. 32r).

Figure 4.11 *The Owl and the Nightingale* (Jesus College, Oxford, MS 29, f. 156r).

Figure 4.12 *Havelok*, lines 722–811 (Laud Misc. 108, f. 208r). Reproduced with permission from the Bodleian Library.

Figure 5.1 The secretary hand. From <http://genealogy.about.com/od/paleography/ig/old_handwriting/Secretary-Hand.htm> (last accessed 4 June 2017).

Figure 5.2 The italic hand. From <http://www.fountainpennetwork.com> (last accessed 4 June 2017).

Figure 5.3 *Cleanness* (Cotton Nero A X, leaf 57). Reproduced with permission from the British Library Board.

Figures 5.4 and 5.5 Chaucer's *Astrolabe*, MS Eng 920, f. 5v and f. 6. Houghton Library. Reproduced with permission from Harvard University.

Figure 5.6 The first page of *The Book of Margery of Kempe* (Add MS 61823, f. 1). Reproduced with permission from the British Library Board.

Figure 5.7 The first page of the first chapter of Malory's *Morte d'Arthur* as printed by Caxton. From *Rylands Medieval Collection*, University of Manchester.

Figure 5.8 The second part of the first chapter of Malory's *Morte d'Arthur* as printed by Caxton. From *Rylands Medieval Collection*, University of Manchester.

Figure 5.10 Machyn, 1 May 1559 transcription and translation. From Bailey et al. (n.d.).

Figure 5.11 Letter from Elizabeth to Queen Mary. From <http://www.luminarium.org/renlit/elizabib.htm> (last accessed 4 June 2017).

Figure 5.12 Letter 13, seemingly written by Agnes Paston, 1440. From <http://britishlibrary.typepad.co.uk/digitisedmanuscripts/2015/04/the-paston-letters-go-live.html> (last accessed 4 June 2017). Reproduced with permission from the British Library Board.

Figure 5.13 Caxton's rendering of Cicero's *De senectute*. Image available at <http://lcweb2.loc.gov/cgi-bin/displayPhoto.pl?path=/service/rbc/rbc0001/2009/2009rosen0562&topImages=0353r.jpg&topLinks=0353v.jpg,0353u.tif,0353a.tif,0353.tif&displayProfile=0>; transcription available at <http://quod.lib.umich.edu/e/eebo/A69111.0001.001/1:1?rgn=div1;view=fulltext> (both last accessed 9 May 2017).

Abbreviations

ACC	Accusative case
AdjP	Adjective Phrase
AdvP	Adverb Phrase
CE	Common Era
COCA	Corpus of Contemporary American English (http://corpus.byu.edu/coca/)
DAT	Dative case
DEM	Demonstrative
DOE	*Dictionary of Old English*
EETS	Early English Text Society
Extr	Extraposed
F	Feminine
GEN	Genitive case
Gr	Grammar
Lg	Language
M	Masculine
MED	*Middle English Dictionary*
N	Neuter
NOM	Nominative case
NP	Noun Phrase
OE	Old English
OED	*Oxford English Dictionary*
OV	Object-Verb
P	Preposition
PL	Plural
PP	Preposition Phrase
Pre-V	Preverbal
PRT	Particle
RC	Relative Clause
REFL	Reflexive
REL	Relative
S	Singular, or Subject

	SV	Subject-Verb
	SVO	Subject-Verb-Object
	UG	Universal Grammar
	V2/V3	Verb-second, verb-third
	VO	Verb-Object
	VP	Verb Phrase
	1	First person
	2	Second person
	3	Third person
	7	Shorthand in Latin for *et* 'and', taken over in Old and Middle English
	l	Shorthand for Latin *vel* 'or' between words
	*	Reconstructed

1

Introduction

In this book, we'll examine linguistic characteristics of several texts throughout the early history of English, using basic grammatical terminology. For each text, we will focus on issues such as the word order, the endings on nouns and verbs, the presence of auxiliaries, articles, and pronouns, the types of pronouns, and the nature of complex sentences.

To describe a language, we need to get as close to the sources as possible. For Old and Middle English, that mostly means looking at manuscripts. Examining manuscripts used to be difficult because you'd have to travel to a certain library and get permission to study the manuscript. There were (and are) facsimile editions of some texts but they were often unclear copies. Today, many of the manuscripts have been digitized and can therefore be studied using your computer without the need for travel. The reason that we can't rely on edited texts is that many of the editors up to the present, when they edit manuscripts for publication, add punctuation, hyphens, and capitals, add spacing, and insert 'missing' letters. That's why it is important to use manuscripts where possible to get close to a text.

The main parts of the book, i.e. Chapters 3, 4, and 5, provide manuscript images (sometimes from the facsimile edition and sometimes from the online copy) of a part of a text and an approximate transcription of what appears in the manuscript. Where needed, word-by-word glosses and translations are offered. The book also provides an analysis of the texts and some background on the style and dialect variety. I have selected texts from various registers and dialects to show as much variety as possible.

This introductory chapter provides background on the major changes English has undergone, the various grammatical terms that will be used, a brief discussion of language change, the sources, and resources. In the current chapter and the next one, I use sentences from edited versions that have not been checked by me against the manuscript; only occasionally are actual images shown. The reason is that the emphasis is on the big picture. Chapters 3 to 5 will focus on minute details of specific texts so there images are necessary.

1.1 The history of English in a nutshell

English has its beginnings around 450 CE, when speakers of Germanic languages settle in Britain. The account that Bede tells is of the brothers Hengist and Horsa who were invited by the Celtic-speaking King Vortigern to defend his British kingdom against invaders. The invitees turned against Vortigern and the Germanic they spoke gradually replaced the Celtic and Latin spoken there at that time. The year 450 is a relatively arbitrary date because Germanic speakers had had trade routes to Britain and had probably settled there long before 450. Moreover, the language we refer to as Old English does not change into a separate branch of Germanic right away but continues to be similar to the Germanic languages spoken outside of Britain.

Old English is a language that relies on marking its nouns, adjectives, and verbs but that has relatively free word order. Such a language is called synthetic. Over time, however, English becomes a language that relies more on prepositions, auxiliaries, and articles, also known as grammatical words, and on word order than on case markings on nouns and agreement on verbs. This kind of language is called analytic. Table 1.1 summarizes differences between synthetic and analytic languages. The change from synthetic to analytic might have been caused by the contact with speakers of Celtic, Scandinavian, and other languages or be due to language-internal factors or both.

By 1100, the date we adopt here as the start of Middle English, many case endings have disappeared and the use of grammatical words is on the increase. This development continues between 1100 and 1500, and the English at the end of the Middle English period resembles present-day English in many respects. During the Middle English period, French and Latin words come into the language and cause changes in the sound system (expanded use of [v] and [dʒ]) and the lexicon (many derivational affixes such as *-ity* and *-ify* are introduced). Generally, we won't discuss the changes to the sounds or to the lexicon. Figure 1.1 is taken from from Szmrecsanyi (2016: 102) and provides a visualization of the changes,

TABLE 1.1. Characteristics of analytic and synthetic languages

analytic	synthetic
use of prepositions, e.g. *the leg of the table*	use of endings, e.g. *the table's leg*
use of word order to indicate subject, e.g. **The man** saw his friend	use of case to indicate subject, e.g. **De-r Mann** sah sein-en Freund (German) [the-NOM man saw his-ACC friend]
auxiliaries mark aspect, e.g. *am* going marks progressive aspect	verbs are marked for tense and aspect, e.g. *ge-* on the verb marks perfective
no markings on the verb to indicate subject but frequent pronouns, e.g. **They** leave tomorrow	verb is marked for subject, and pronoun is optional e.g. *þriowa me onsæc-est* (Old English) [thrice me deny-2S] 'You will deny me three times'

based on written texts. Szmrecsanyi's figure shows that twelfth-century texts are most synthetic but that there is a major change in the thirteenth century to less synthetic and then to more analytic in the fourteenth.

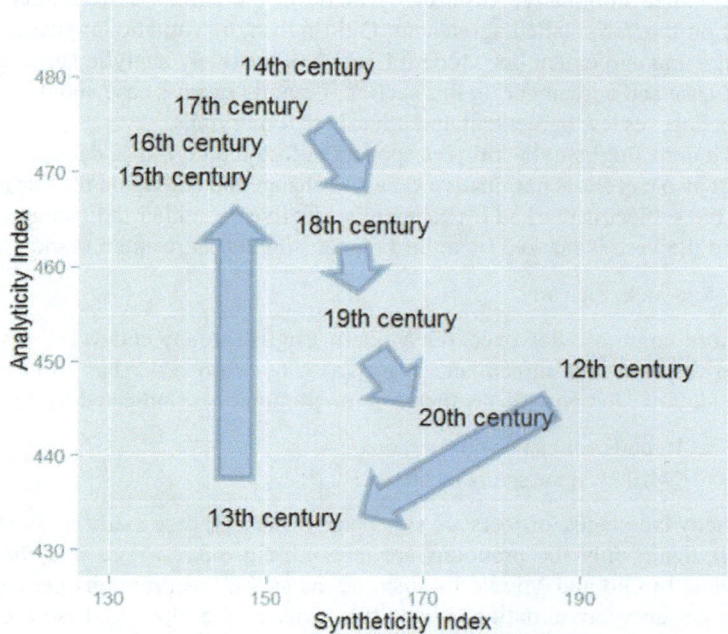

FIGURE 1.1. Changes in the analytic/synthetic nature of English (from Benedikt Szmrecsanyi (2016), 'An Analytic-Synthetic Spiral in the History of English', in Elly van Gelderen (ed.), *Cyclical Change Continued*, Amsterdam: John Benjamins, pp. 93–112. Reproduced with permission from John Benjamins, Amsterdam.)

The period after 1500 is another transition period with some changes in grammar and sounds. The major change is perhaps the adoption of tens of thousands of Latin, Greek, and newly invented words. Because of their complex morphology, these loans increase the syntheticity, as shown in Figure 1.1. This phenomenon also causes the appearance of dictionaries of hard words and gives rise to concerns about the purity of the language. The result is a set of prescriptive rules for spelling, pronunciation, and grammar that are still adhered to today.

The period after 1700 – one we won't discuss in this book – is best characterized by the spread of English around the world: the increased use of English in different parts of the world leads to variation while globalization encourages stabilization. Politically, we could argue that Australian, Nigerian, and Indian English are separate languages though most people would argue that these varieties are all English despite differences in the phonology, grammar, and lexicon. All Englishes display the analytic character that English has been moving towards: an abundance of grammatical words (auxiliaries and prepositions) and reliance on word order.

1.2 Functions and case

Synthetic languages indicate the function of subject either by a marking on the subject, called nominative case, or by marking the person and number of the subject on the verb, called agreement. Old English, a synthetic language, marks both case and agreement but Modern English, a relatively analytic language, has limited case and agreement. In this section, I mainly discuss case and then, in the next section, review agreement and other verbal markings.

In Modern English, the **subject** appears before the verb in a declarative sentence. It also can show nominative **case** and change the ending on the verb. Thus, in (1), the subject is marked by being a nominative *she* rather than an accusative *her*, and the verb is marked by a third person singular agreement marker *-s*.

(1) **She** walks regularly.

It is more common, however, for Modern English nouns and verbs not to be marked for case and agreement, as in (2a). The word order has to be strictly observed, however, and (2b) is therefore ungrammatical (indicated by *).

(2) a. **Rabbits eat** mallow in the spring.
    b. *Mallow in the spring rabbits eat.

In many languages, **objects** are signaled by a special case marking. In Modern English, again only the pronouns are marked, e.g. *him*, *me*, *us* and *them*, not the nouns. In Old and Middle English, nouns as well as pronouns get case and objects get accusative, dative, or genitive case. In the glosses, these are ACC, DAT, and GEN, respectively. The nominative will be abbreviated as NOM. The Early Middle English sentence in (3) has a subject *Willelm cyng* that happens not to show its marking for nominative, an indirect object *Rodberde eorle*, marked dative, and a direct object *þone earldom*, marked accusative. (If the ending cannot clearly be separated, I use a period between the word and the grammatical abbreviation; if it is clear, I use a hyphen.)

(3) *Willelm cyng   geaf   Rodberd-e   eorl-e   þone earldom*
     Willelm king.NOM   gave   Rodberd-DAT   earl-DAT   that.ACC earldom
     on   Norðhymbra   land
     in   Northhumbrian   land
     (*Peterborough Chronicle* for the year 1068)

The *þ* and *ð* are called thorn and eth, respectively, and both represent the voiceless interdental fricative. Other Old English letters are wynn and ash, *p* and *æ*. More on this in Chapter 3.

A very important function is that of **adverbial**, which provides background on where, when, why, and how the event or state described by the verb takes place. In (1), *regularly* tells you how often the walking takes place and, in (2), *in the spring* tells you about the time of the eating. In (3), however, *on Norðhymbra land* modifies the noun *þone earldom* and is therefore not an adverbial. In (2a), we could have added a place (*in Arizona*) or a reason (*because they are hungry*). All of the following constituents are adverbials: Preposition Phrases such as *in Arizona*, adverbs such as *regularly*, and clauses such as *because they are hungry*.

So, note that adverbials are a function but that adverbs are a word class; they overlap but are not identical. In Modern English, many adverbs end in -*ly* and, in Old English, many adverbs end in -*e* or in -*lice*.

In the next chapter, there will be some tables on how to recognize the endings of the cases that appear in (3). For the moment, just make sure you know that subjects have nominative, that direct objects most often show accusative case, and that indirect objects have dative. (3) would be translated as (4) in Modern English, with the ending -*e* on *Rodberde* replaced by the preposition *to*.

(4) King Willelm gave (to) Earl Rodberd the earldom in Northhumbria.

In Old English, the main functions of the **nominative (NOM)** case are subject, such as *se cyning* in (5); and subject predicate, such as *se fæder* in (5).

(5) **Se cyning** for ofer sæ
    the.NOM king.NOM went over sea
    'the king went across the sea.' (*Peterborough Chronicle* for the year 1076)

(6) þæt is **se fæder**
    that is the.NOM father
    'that is the father.' (*Homilies*, by Aelfric)

Wulfstan's *Homilies* in Chapter 3 will show a number of subject predicates. The latter appear after copula verbs, e.g. forms of *be* and *become*, which that text has many of.

The main function of the **genitive (GEN)** case is to express possession: the -*es* ending on *engles* in (7) shows that what is meant is 'fingers of the angel'. This case is mostly replaced by *of* in Modern English.

(7) mid **engl-es** fingrum awritene
    with angel-GEN fingers written
    'written by the fingers of an angel.' (*Homilies*, by Wulfstan)

The genitive case is also used to indicate objects after certain verbs, where only part of the object is involved, as in (8); to indicate measure or number, as in (9); to indicate an adverbial use of a noun, such as *dæges* 'by day'; and to mark the object of a few prepositions. The latter is not common so I haven't given an example.

(8) Ic gyrnde þara fixa
    I desired those.GEN fish.GEN
    'I wanted some of that fish.' (*Mary of Egypt*)

(9) 7 þær forwearþ cxx **scip-a** æt Swanawic
    and there perished 120 scips-GEN at Swanwick
    'and 120 ships perished at Swanwick.' (*Parker Chronicle* for the year 877)

The **dative (DAT)** case is used for the object of many prepositions, as in (10); the indirect object, such as *Rodberd* in (3); the regular object with certain verbs, as in (11); and to express means or manner, as in (12), or time, as in *hwilum* 'at times'.

TABLE 1.2. Cases and their main functions

	function	example
nominative	subject; subject predicate	*They* see the book; *þæt is **se fæder*** [that is the father]
genitive	possession; object	the roof *of* the house; I ate *of* the apple
dative	object of a preposition; indirect object	*mit mir* (German) [with me.DAT]; Give *me* some apples
accusative	(direct) object	The woman saw *them*

(10) Her   on   **þys-um**   **gear-e**   for   se   micla   here
     Now   in   this-DAT   year-DAT   went   the   great   army
     'in this year, the great army went.' (*Peterborough Chronicle* for the year 892)

(11) ðæt   heafod   sceal   wisian   **þæm**   **fot-um**
     the   head   shall   guide   the.DAT   feet-DAT
     'the head shall guide the feet.' (*Pastoral Care* 131.22)

(12) **sweord-e**   ne meahte   on   ðam   aglæcean   wunde   gewyrcean
     sword-DAT   not might   on   that   creature   wounds   make
     'with a sword he could not inflict wounds on that creature.' (*Beowulf* 2904–5)

The **accusative** (**ACC**) is often used as object, such as *þone earldom* in (3); as object of a preposition, such as *geond* 'through' in (13), when the preposition indicates movement; and adverbially.

(13) geond   þa   wud-as   and   þa   feld-as
     through   the.ACC   woods-ACC   and   the.ACC   fields-ACC
     'through the woods and the fields.' (*Homilies*, by Aelfric)

A summary of the cases and their main functions is given in Table 1.2. The subject predicate is marked by nominative case in Old English but mostly by accusative case in later English, so I have given the Old English.

In addition to marking nouns and pronouns for the function they have, verbs can also be marked for which noun or pronoun is the subject, as we saw in (1). We'll look at that more in the next section as well as at the marking for tense, mood, and aspect.

1.3 Verbal inflection and clause structure

Like nouns, verbs can also have endings. On verbs, these endings indicate which noun is the subject of the sentence, i.e. they show **agreement**, and the tense, mood, and aspect of the event or state. In this section, I will provide some background to the terminology using Modern English examples. The next chapter will provide the endings for the verbs in earlier English. I end this section by looking at clause structure because that is determined by verbs.

Some agreement remains marked in Modern English, as (14) shows.

(14) They leave/She leaves.   third person plural/singular agreement

In addition to verbal agreement, verbs can mark a situation as real or not (i.e. mood), as past or present (i.e. tense), and as ongoing or finished (i.e. aspect). **Mood** can be divided into indicative, imperative, subjunctive, and interrogative mood. A declarative mood signals that the speaker wants to express a statement whereas the subjunctive signals he or she is expressing a wish, possibility, or opinion. Interrogatives ask for information and imperatives give a command.

Modern English declaratives show no special inflection or word order but imperatives leave out the subject, as (15) shows. Interrogatives switch the auxiliary, as in (16), and subjunctives are indicated mainly through modal auxiliaries, as in (17). Using auxiliaries is analytic as opposed to using endings on verbs, as we'll see happens in Old English.

(15) Don't do that! imperative
(16) **Will** you go? interrogative
(17) It **might** rain. modal marking unreal situation

Modern English marks present and past **tense** mainly through endings on verbs, as (18) shows. **Aspect** in Modern English is marked with auxiliaries such as *have* and *be*, as in (19) and (20).

(18) She walks/she walk**ed**. present and past tense
(19) She **had** gone by five. perfective aspect
(20) She **is** swimming. progressive aspect

Auxiliaries, through their name, suggest a helping function. They add grammatical information and therefore have to occur together with a lexical verb, e.g. *walk* and *swim*, the latter conveying the meaning of the actual event or state.

Beside auxiliary and lexical verb, other terms we'll use are those of main verb and finite verb. The **main verb** is the verb in the main clause, e.g. *noticed* in (21). The clause in brackets functions as the object of the main verb and is therefore the subordinate or embedded but not the main clause. Both *noticed* and *left* in (21) are **finite verbs**. Finite verbs agree with their subjects and show tense.

(21) They never noticed [that I left].

In addition to finite verbs, there are non-finite verbs. In Modern English, some examples of those verbs from the *Corpus of Contemporary American English* (COCA) are given in bold in (22) to (24). The clauses that go with the non-finite verbs are in brackets.

(22) She wants [them to **know** these facts]. Infinitive
(23) Police think this man, [**arrested** last night], allegedly stole money.
    Past participle
(24) [By **leaving** early], I would be free of interference, phone calls, ...
    Present participle

Non-finite verbs need not agree with a subject, as in (22), or even have a subject, as in (23) and (24). Auxiliaries can also be non-finite, as in (25), where the first auxiliary (*has*) is finite but the other two auxiliaries (*been* and *being*) and the lexical verb (*used*) are non-finite. From a prescriptive point of view, (25) with its perfect passive progressive, is often regarded as unacceptable but such examples do occur!

(25) The house has **been being used** as a rental property (from an advertisement).

A complete sentence should have at least a finite verb in it but can contain many other (subordinated) clauses with non-finite verbs.

Styles vary as to whether a **hypotactic** arrangement of clauses, using subordinating conjunctions, as in (21) to (24), or a **paratactic** one is used, as in (26), an alternative for (23).

(26) Police think this man stole money; they arrested him last night.

Modern English formal styles tend towards (23) rather than towards (26). As we'll see, a number of older texts are quite paratactic and use coordination or just a break.

This section has provided some background on agreement, tense, mood, and aspect markings on the verb. Some of this is still synthetic in Modern English (*-s* and *-ed*) but a lot is analytic (*might, had, is*). In the next section, I introduce grammaticalization which accounts for the creation of analytic forms.

1.4   Change: how and why

In this section, we will discuss a model, formulated by Klima (1965) and adapted by Andersen (1973) and Lightfoot (1979), accounting for language change in terms of language acquisition. Since the late 1950s, Noam Chomsky (e.g. 1957) has articulated theories of language acquisition that rely on **Universal Grammar** (UG), an innate language faculty that when 'stimulated by appropriate and continuing experience, ... creates a grammar that creates sentences with formal and semantic properties' (Chomsky 1975: 36). Our innate language faculty, or Universal Grammar, enables us to create a set of rules, or grammar, by being exposed to (generally rather chaotic) language.

Chomsky (1986) sees Universal Grammar as the solution to what he calls Plato's Problem: how do children acquire their language(s) so fast given that the input is so poor? The set of rules we acquire for our native language(s) enables us to produce sentences we have never heard before. These sentences could also be infinitely long (if we had the time and energy). Language acquisition, in this framework, is not imitation but interplay between Universal Grammar and the exposure to a particular language. We know that acquisition is not just imitation since children create, e.g., *drawed* as the past tense of *draw*, and we know that input is essential from the fact that children who were neglected by their parents never acquired a regular language (see Curtiss 1977 on Genie). The need for exposure to a particular language explains why, even though we all start out with the same Universal Grammar, we acquire slightly different grammars. It also explains why we acquire grammars slightly different from those of our parents.

The Minimalist Program (Chomsky 1995, 2015) has shifted the emphasis from Universal Grammar to innate factors that are not specific to the language faculty. One of the reasons for Chomsky to deemphasize Universal Grammar is the evolutionary time it had to develop. If language arose in humans between 100,000 and 150,000 years ago, Universal Grammar would not have had much time to develop. The factors not specific to language are therefore preferred and listed as (27).

(27) Principles not specific to FL [the Faculty of Language]. Some of the third factor principles have the flavor of the constraints that enter into all facets of growth and evolution. ... Among these are principles of efficient computation. (Chomsky 2007: 3)

Figure 1.2 represents the current model.

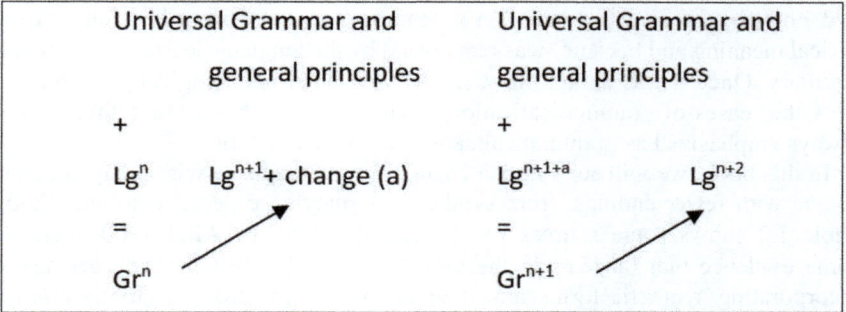

FIGURE 1.2. Universal Grammar and the acquisition of grammars

In this model, a child starts to construct a grammar (Gr^n) on the basis of the language he or she hears (Lg^n) with guidance from Universal Grammar and other innate cognitive abilities. The resulting grammar (Gr^n) will produce sentences that might be slightly different from those in the input (Lg^n). The language the child produces (Lg^{n+1}) undergoes changes during his or her lifetime: words get added and constructions are adopted for external reasons, e.g. fashion, wanting to be creative, or contact with other languages. This modified output serves as the input for a new generation building its grammar (Gr^{n+1}) from scratch, based on the Lg^{n+1} that has undergone change. This Gr^{n+1} will produce yet another output, Lg^{n+2}. This output is then of course modified when the child goes to school and learns certain (prescriptive) rules that are not really part of the child's grammar, e.g. to use *whom*.

Languages use categories of words. The main lexical categories are Noun (e.g. *table*), Verb (e.g. *see*), Adjective (e.g. *yellow*), Adverb (e.g. *quickly*), and Preposition (e.g. *to*). These categories are called **lexical** because they carry meaning (they have synonyms and antonyms). There are also **grammatical** categories: Determiner (e.g. *the*, *a*, and *those*), Auxiliary (e.g. *might*), Coordinator (e.g. *and*), and Complementizer (e.g. *because*). These categories are called *grammatical* since they determine the syntactic relationships in a sentence. Prepositions and adverbs do a little of both. The distinction between lexical and grammatical categories is important because the change from Old to Modern English involves an increase in the number of grammatical categories, i.e. a rise in analyticity, as mentioned in section 1.1. Such an increase in grammatical categories is a process also referred to as grammaticalization.

TABLE 1.3. Some instances of grammaticalization

Negative phrase *na wiht* 'no creature' > *not/n't*
Demonstrative > definite article
Verbs *have, be, will, do* > auxiliaries
Preposition *for* and *till* > complementizer
Preposition *to* > future/unreal marker
Preposition *like* > complementizer and discourse marker

Grammaticalization involves a lexical item losing its semantic and phonological features and increasing its grammatical function. For instance, in Old English, *willan* was a main verb meaning 'to want', but it lost some of its lexical meaning and became (was reanalyzed by the language learner as) a modal auxiliary. Once it was an auxiliary, it also weakened phonologically, becoming *'ll*. Other cases of grammaticalization discussed in this book (even though not always emphasized as grammaticalization) are listed in Table 1.3.

In this book, we will see English change from a language with many endings to one with fewer endings, from synthetic to analytic, especially around 1200. Table 1.3 shows some sources for the analytic markers. After 1500, there is some evidence that (at least in the verbal system) English speakers are again incorporating synthetic forms into their grammars. In (28), the auxiliary *have* has become an affix, in (29) the negative *not* has become an affix, and, in the colloquial (30), the first person pronoun *I*, right next to the auxiliary, serves as an agreement marker on the verb (*me* is the subject pronoun).

(28) *it xuld a be seyd*
'it should have been said' (Paston Letters, #131, for the year 1449, Margaret Paston)
(29) **Don't** speak so loud. (From the OED, 1672)
(30) **Me, I** try and calculate without having Social Security in my retirement goal. (From the COCA, 2010)

This change where pronouns start marking the agreement on the verb and a new subject pronoun appears is known as a linguistic cycle (see van Gelderen 2011). It is not unexpected: languages go from synthetic to analytic and to synthetic again, as shown in Figure 1.1. If the pronoun *I* in (30) becomes the agreement on the verb, there is an increase in synthetic marking. A cycle, known as the negative cycle, accounts for (31) where the weakening of the negative *n't* may cause an additional negative.

(31) Oh' I did**n't** read **no** letters. (song lyric)

In the case of English, the change towards synthetic seems to involve only the verbal system. The case endings on nominals that we saw in section 1.2 are not reappearing, however.

A very obvious reason for change is external contact, as happened when the speakers of Old English interacted with Celtic, Scandinavian, Latin, and later (Norman) French speakers. Of the texts we'll discuss, there may be Latin influence in *Orosius*, because it was translated, Scandinavian influence in the

Peterborough Chronicle, because of the region in which it was produced, and French influence in Chaucer's *Astrolable*, because of his knowledge of that language. A major reason the entire language changes is also replacement of the lexical inventory, pronouns, and sounds. As the various languages come into contact with English, this changes the latter, sometimes resulting in regional varieties. We'll discuss these more in section 2.6 of the next chapter.

1.5 Sources and resources

In this section, I very briefly discuss the kinds of texts we have left, the extent of literacy, and then the resources to study Old and Middle English.

The earliest remnants of Old English are in the form of runic letters on stones and wood. A proper discussion of these would need a book by itself so I am not considering these texts. They show one aspect of medieval literacy, a flourishing writing system which was replaced by the Latin script in the sixth century. Because wood disintegrates, we don't know how extensive the use of runic writing was. The runic letters are clues in the riddles so knowledge of runes was not obscure. During the Old English period, like today, oral communication is crucial in stories, sermons, poetry, and debates, and closely tied to written communication. The people who could read Old English, and especially compose in it, were fewer than in later periods. The reflection of orality on the text is undeniable in the poetry and chronicles that we'll see in the chapters below.

Early Old English texts were produced on papyrus which, like wood, doesn't survive well. Later texts were produced on vellum or parchment, made from calf's hide. The parchment would be ruled and the scribe would use a quill pen, made from a feather, and the ink was made of gall balls or other acidic substances that burn a little into the vellum. Paper doesn't appear until the middle of the fifteenth century. Manuscripts were often copied from other ones (e.g. the first part of the *Peterborough Chronicle*), sometimes with a scribe's regional and other idiosyncrasies showing. Some poetic texts must have been copied from memorized oral texts and this transmission must have had an influence on the actual forms.

Turning to the resources we have, Bosworth and Toller (1898) and Clark Hall (1894) continue to be the go-to dictionaries. They can be used to check the translation of an Old English word, to find the gender of a noun, and to check the typical verb endings. Quirk and Wrenn (1955) is good as a basic grammar. Many of these resources can be found online.[1]

The *Oxford English Dictionary* (OED), the *Dictionary of Old English* (DOE) Webcorpus, and the *Middle English Dictionary*[2] (MED) are also excellent resources. The OED will give you many other examples of a word; use 'advanced search' for Old and Middle English words. The DOE is not freely available; it is particularly helpful if you want to check where an Old English quote comes from and the proper way to cite it. The MED enables the user, for instance, to browse Middle English texts. The *Linguistic Atlas of Late Mediaeval English*[3] has maps displaying linguistic features of areas and linguistic profiles of texts.

1.6 Conclusion

In this chapter, I have provided an introduction to the broad changes that English has undergone: a change from synthetic to analytic and possibly to more synthetic again. I have also provided some background to terms such as case marking, functions, verbal agreement, tense, mood, aspect, main and subordinate clauses, finite and non-finite verbs, and lexical and auxiliary verbs. This information will be relevant to understanding more about older English. The question of what sets change in motion is one that many people have different answers for. The one I have given is that each generation constructs a new grammar (using UG and general cognitive principles) and that changes are due to how children analyze the input.

Exercises

A Explain in your own words what accusative case is and give an example of a sentence that contains it.

B In the text below, bold (or circle) the subjects and underline the verb that shows agreement.

> The National Weather Service has issued an excessive heat warning for Tuesday and Wednesday. Much of south-central and southwestern Arizona will see hotter temperatures over the next two days.
>
> The area in Arizona covered by the warning stretches from Yuma and other communities along the Colorado River eastward into the Phoenix area and the Pinal County communities of Casa Grande, Coolidge and Florence. Officials say the temperature is expected to climb to between 112 and 115 degrees on both days. The warning is in effect from 11 a.m. until 8 p.m. both days.
>
> Residents who work or play outdoors face a greater risk of heat-related illness. The Weather Service is advising people to drink more water than usual, wear a hat outside and take rest breaks in air-conditioned places.
>
> (Adapted from the *East Valley Tribune*, 4 August 2015)

C Identify hypotactic or paratactic sets of clauses in the text above.

D Explain in your own words what synthetic and analytic mean and how you can use these terms to describe language change.

E Jamaican is an English-based creole. How would you characterize its grammar, based on the below sentence?

(1) *Yu   dash   we   mi   gud   bran   nyuu   sipaz   we   mi*
     2S   dash   away   1S   good   brand new   slippers REL   1S
    jos   bai   laas   wiik?
    just buy   last   week

'You threw away my perfectly new slippers which I just bought last week?'
(Farquharson 2013: 89)

Further reading

We have discussed a number of issues in this first chapter but language change is perhaps the most prominent one. Aitchison (2012) provides a lively introduction to language change in general and takes a linguist's stand on the question of whether change is good or bad in arguing it is neither. Lightfoot (2006) is more technical and focusses on the emergence of language in children. Hogg and Denison's (2006) chapter offers more introduction to the history of English. Van Gelderen's (2010) grammar provides more background on categories (nouns, verbs, etc.) as well as on functions (subjects, objects, etc.) and clause structure (main or subordinate). Kelly (1990) discusses medieval English orality and literacy. The Getty Museum has an informative video on book making at <http://www.getty.edu/art/exhibitions/making/> (last accessed 9 May 2017).

Aitchison, Jean (2012), *Language Change: Progress or Decay?*, Cambridge: Cambridge University Press.
Hogg, Richard and David Denison (2006), 'Overview', in Richard Hogg and David Denison (eds), *A History of the English Language*, Cambridge: Cambridge University Press, pp. 1–42.
Kelly, Susan (1990), 'Anglo-Saxon Lay Society and the Written Word', in Rosamond McKitterick (ed.), *The Uses of Literacy in Early Medieval Europe*, Cambridge: Cambridge University Press, pp. 36–62.
Lightfoot, David (2006), *How New Languages Emerge*, Cambridge: Cambridge University Press.
van Gelderen, Elly (2010), *An Introduction to the Grammar of English,*. Amsterdam: John Benjamins.

Notes

1. For example, *Bosworth-Toller Anglo-Saxon Dictionary*, available at <http://www.bosworthtoller.com> and John R. Clark Hall (1916), *A Concise Anglo-Saxon Dictionary*, 2nd edn, available at <http://www.ling.upenn.edu/~kurisuto/germanic/oe_clarkhall_about.html> (both last accessed 9 May 2017).
2. Available at <http://quod.lib.umich.edu/m/med/> (last accessed 9 May 2017).
3. Available at <http://www.lel.ed.ac.uk/ihd/elalme/elalme.html> (last accessed 9 May 2017).

2

The Syntax of Old, Middle, and Early Modern English

The previous chapter supplied a short introduction to the history of English, some background to case, agreement, tense, mood, and aspect, and an explanation of the terms synthetic and analytic. The changes in English were characterized as a swinging back and forth between more synthetic or analytic stages. In the current chapter, I will look at specific characteristics of the syntax that can be linked to those changes, for instance, in word order and the use of grammatical words. I also provide tables with endings for the case on nouns and pronouns and endings on verbs of the English in its most synthetic stage.

In section 2.1, I take a broad view of the changes by looking at a few lines from Early Old English, Late Old/Early Middle English, Late Middle English, and Early Modern English. The evidence from these texts justifies the division used in Chapters 3, 4, and 5. In sections 2.2 and 2.3, we look at word order and markings on nouns and verbs and, in section 2.4, at the pronominal system. In section 2.5, we examine complex sentences in more detail. Here, I show that it is necessary to examine the manuscript because many sentence boundaries are not actually marked and it is hard to see where one sentence ends and the other starts. Section 2.6 on dialect variation follows, illustrating the effect of external influences. Section 2.7 provides a conclusion. In the later chapters, we return to the points made on word order and inflection in greater detail. Some of the examples used in this chapter will reappear in the next chapters, partly to consolidate the information.

2.1 Major changes in the syntax of English

As mentioned, Old English is synthetic in its copious use of nominal and verbal endings. As a result, the word order in Old English can be freer than that of later English. Compare the first lines of the Old English (Northumbrian) version of *Caedmon's Hymn* with its translation into a Modern English word-by-word gloss underneath and then its free translation.

(1)   *Nu*   *scylun*   *hergan*   *hefaenricaes*   *uard metudæs*   *maecti*   *end*
      Now   shall   praise   heavenkingdom's   guardian Lord's   might   and

Syntax of Old, Middle, and Early Modern English

his modgidanc	*uerc*	*uuldurfadur*	*sue*	*he*	*uundra*	*gehuaes*
his thought	work	wonderfather	as	he	wonders'	each's

eci	*dryctin*	*or*	*astelidæ*
eternal	lord	beginning	established

'now we must honor the guardian of heaven, the Lord's power and his purpose, the work of the father of glory, as he, the eternal Lord, established the beginning of each wonder.'

The original, part of Bede's Latin *Historia ecclesiastica*, is reproduced as Figure 2.1. As you can see, very few spaces and periods appear.

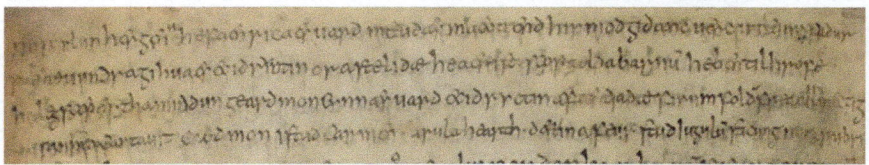

FIGURE 2.1. *Caedmon's Hymn*, from the 'Moore Bede' (Cambridge University Library, Kk. 5. 16. Reproduced with permission from the Syndics of Cambridge University Library)

Apart from the fact that many of the words are different (something we won't focus on), the Modern English translation has the grammatical words 'we', 'the', and 'of' that the original doesn't have, which illustrates the change to an analytic language from a synthetic one. For instance, in Old English, the verbal ending *-un* indicates a plural subject and that may make the presence of the subject pronoun optional. There are more case endings such as the possessive *'s* that can be recognized in the final *s* of *hefaenricaes* 'of the heavenly kingdom' and *metudæs* 'of the Lord'. The change from synthetic to analytic can be seen by comparing the Old English in (1) with its translation in Modern English. The total number of words in the Old English is twenty and that in the free translation is thirty-two. The text in (1) lacks articles and prepositions, has fewer auxiliaries, but makes up for that with the endings on nouns and verbs.

The word order in the first line of (1) is not so far removed from the current one: there is an adverb *nu*, two verbs, and an object. The nouns in line 2 add more to the object of line 1. The word order in lines 3 and 4 is much harder to understand. Both *uundra* and *gehuaes* are genitives so they depend on another noun, namely *or* 'beginning'. Even though this noun *or* is not next to *uundra* and *gehuaes*, they can still go together and render 'the beginning of all wonders'. The verb *astelidæ* 'established' is at the end of the fourth line right after its object *or* 'beginning'.

The version of *Caedmon's Hymn* in (1) may be from the seventh century CE. We'll now turn to the beginning of the entry for the year 1066 of the *Peterborough Chronicle*, i.e. a text of several hundred years later than *Caedmon's Hymn*, and see substantial changes.

(2)	*On*	*þyssum geare*	*man*	*halgode*	*þet*	*mynster*	*æt*	*westmynstre*
	In	this year	one	hallowed	that	minster	at	Westminster

> on   cyldamæsse   dæg .   7   se   cyng   eadward   forðferde   on
> on   Childermas   day   and that king   Eadward   died   on
> twelfts   mæsse   æfen ...
> Twelfth   mass   eve ...
> 'in this year man, the minster at Westminster was consecrated on Childermas
> day and King Eadward died on Twelfth mass evening.'

In (2), the word order is as it would be in Modern English, namely adverbial and subject and verb, and the number of words used is fairly similar; the only difference is the addition of the demonstrative *se* before *king Eadward* and we might use a passive 'was hallowed' rather than the indefinite pronoun *man* 'one'. Some readers will know the archaic English verb *to hallow*, that is still recognizable in the fifth word but is now replaced by the Latinate *to consecrate*. There are still more case endings on pronouns and nouns than in Modern English, e.g. *þyssum* and *geare* have dative case. However, because of the increased use of grammatical words, the text that (2) appears in is seen as marking the change from Old to Early Middle English.

The next leap we take is 300 years later to the beginning of *Sir Gawain and the Green Knight* in (3). *Gawain* abounds in alliteration, a poetic device that 'rhymes' by using the same initial sound, which the free translation of this late fourteenth-century text reflects.

> (3)   SIÞEN   þe   sege   and   þe   assaut   watz   sesed   at   Troye,
>   Since   the siege   and   the   assault   were   ceased   at   Troy
>   Þe   borȝ   brittened   and   brent   to   brondeȝ   and   askez,
>   the battlements   broken   and   burnt   to   brands   and   ashes
>   Þe   tulk   þat   þe   trammes   of   tresoun   þer   wroȝt
>   the man   that the   plots   of   treason   there made/framed
>   Watz   tried   for   his   tricherie,   þe   trewest   on   erþe:
>   was   tried   for   his   treachery,   the   worst   on   earth
>   'as soon as the siege and assault had ceased at Troy, the burg broken and burnt
>   to brands and ashes, the traitor who trammels of treason there wrought was tried
>   for his treachery, the foulest on earth.' (Adapted from Kline 2007)

The word order of the Middle English in (3) is fairly similar to present-day English, especially in the main clause: the subject *þe sege and þe assaut* 'the siege and the assault' precedes the auxiliary *watz* 'was' and the verb *sesed* 'ceased', which in turn precede the adverbial *at Troye* in the first line. In the second line, *brent* 'burnt' precedes *to brondeȝ and askez* 'to brands and ashes', and *tried* precedes *for his tricherie* in line 4. In contrast, in the relative clause in line 3 the verb *wroȝt* 'made' follows the object *þe trammes of tresoun* 'the plots of treason', a remnant of the older order. The use of case is not obvious and the use of the article 'the' frequent. There is also a preposition *of* in *þe trammes of tresoun* where Old English might have had a possessive *-es*. This makes the syntax of (3) relatively 'modern'.

The last example we'll look at is a stage of the language 200 years later, namely Richard Mulcaster's *Elementarie* of 1582. I have not given a translation because the main differences between it and present-day English lie in the spelling and the style.

> (4)   THere be two causes, which moue me to the penning of this Elementarie,
>   whereof the one is mine own promis, the other is the argument it self. The

Syntax of Old, Middle, and Early Modern English

argument it self persuades me to the penning thereof, bycause it is so fit for the training vp of childern, as nothing can be fitter: and the stream of discourse in my former book, which I name Positions, did carie me on to promis it, and binds me to perform it.

The word order is similar to that of Modern English as is the use of articles and pronouns and the paucity of case on the nouns and inflection on the verbs. Interesting aspects of this text are the use of *be* (rather than the later 'are'), the use of *mine* (instead of 'my'), the separation of *it* and *self*, and various spellings that betray earlier English, such as *bycause* and *childern*. We'll come back to some of these features and others.

The short excerpts we've considered lack negation but major changes in negatives occur throughout the history of English. In the oldest texts, there is a single negative *no* or *ne*, which later becomes contracted with verbs such as *is* into *nis*. A second negative, in the form of e.g. *na wiht* 'no creature', starts to occur which develops into Early Modern English *not*. I'll point the negatives out where relevant. The next sections will study the phenomena just mentioned in more depth. We start with word order.

2.2 Word order

As we have seen in section 1, the word order in Old English can be fairly free and I now give more specific details on restrictions in word order. In section 2.2.1, I first focus on the position of the Old English verb and its relationship to the subject and then, in section 2.2.2, on the position of the other elements. In section 2.2.3, I show how this order changes after Old English. As a preview to the rest of the chapter, the main changes we'll discuss are summarized in Table 2.1. The main trend is from OV to VO and from V2 to SV.

TABLE 2.1. Changes in the syntax and morphology of English

OE	late OE	early ME	late ME	early ModE
Free word order but often V2 and OV		OV > VO	SV; some V2	loss of V2
Case endings on nouns and pronouns		...loss of case on nouns...>		
Inflection on V for subject and tense		...less inflection...>		
No articles, only demonstratives		articles ...>		
Some omission of subject pronoun		pronoun is obligatory...>		
Limited use of auxiliaries and prepositions	more 'to' and 'of'		many auxiliaries...>	
Negation before the V	reinforcement with second negative		negative after the auxiliary...>	

2.2.1 The subject and the verb

In the main, independent clause, there is a tendency for the finite verb to occur in the second (V2) or third position, and for the non-finite verb to be at the end. In the subordinate, dependent clause, verbs tend to be final (V-last, i.e. OV). I use 'tend' since these word orders are variable. The subject in Old and Middle English is not necessarily in the first position when the finite verb is in second position.

In (5), I have underlined the finite verb and have bolded the subject.

(5) Ðes   ilces   geares   <u>com</u>   se   **abbot   heanri**   of   **angeli**
    this   same   year   came the abbot   Henry   of   Anglia
    æfter æsterne to   burch.
    after Easter to   Peterborough
    'in the same year, Abbot Henry came to Peterborough after Easter.'

In (5), an adverbial *Ðes ilces geares* starts the sentence and the finite verb *com* is in second position. Note that 'second position' doesn't mean the second word in the sentence because the three words in the adverbial count as one unit. The V2-order here means that the subject follows the verb. Many main clauses start with 'and' but this conjunction doesn't count in calculating second or third position.

The first position may be quite long, as (6) shows, where I have put brackets around the first element, which in this case is the subject.

(6) *[se helend þa witende þohtas heora]* <u>cweþ</u>   to heom
    the healer then knowing thoughts their   said   to them ...
    æghwilc rice   gedeled wið   him   seolfum   awoested   bið ...
    each   kingdom divided against it   self   destroyed will.be
    'the Lord, knowing their thoughts, said to them every kingdom divided against itself will be destroyed ...' (*Matthew* 12.25, Rushworth Glosses)

Thus, (6) is another instance of a V2 sentence but with the (long) subject in initial position preceding the finite verb *cweþ* in second position.

If a main clause has more than one verb, the finite verb will be in second position (V2) and the non-finite verbs will be last. This is also often the case in a coordinate sentence, as (7) is, where the non-finite *gewyrcean* occurs last but where the finite verb *sceal* is in V2.

(7) Swa <u>sceal</u> geong guma gode **gewyrcean**
    So   shall   young man   good perform
    'such should a young man accomplish.' (*Beowulf* 18–19)

In subordinate clauses, all verbs (finite and non-finite) typically occur at the end, as shown in in the embedded clause of (6): *awoested* and *bið* are in final position. See also (8) and (9), where I have underlined these finite verbs in final position.

(8) þæt hio Beowulf-e ...   ... medoful   <u>ætbær</u>
    that she Beowulf-DAT   ... meadcup   at.bore
    'that she brought the meadcup to Beowulf.' (*Beowulf* 623–4)

(9) Ecglafes bearn þe   æt fotum   sæt
    Ecglaf's child who   at feet   sat
    'the child of Eglaf, who sat at his feet.' (*Beowulf* 499–500)

In short, Old English is typically classified as V2, with the finite verb in second position in the main clause, and as OV, with the other verbs in final position. Sentences (5) to (9) show this very well. If there is only one verb in the main clause, it will be in second position, as in (5) and (6); if the clause is subordinate, the verb(s) will be in final position, as in (8) and (9). If there are two verbs in the main clause, the finite one will be in second and the non-finite one in final position, and (7) shows this.

The position of the subject is relatively free. In (5), it follows and in (6), it precedes the verb. If the subject is a pronoun, it will more likely precede the verb even if that 'pushes' the verb into a third position. The question of word order in the coordinated clause, such as (7), is hard to determine because it is sometimes difficult to see where a clause ends and begins. If a period precedes the symbol for 'and' and if it has its own subject, does that mean it is an independent clause? Scholars of Old English are divided on whether the word order is predominantly V2 or V-final in these clauses.

2.2.2 The position of other elements

Having looked at where verbs and subjects are in the Old English sentence, let's look at the position of the object relative to the verb in the above sentences. In most cases, the object will follow the verb in second position and precede the verb in final position. In (5), there is no object; in (6), the indirect object *to heom* and the (long) direct object indeed occur after the verb in second position. In (7), the object *medoful* occurs before the final verb, and in (8), there is no object but the adverbial *æt fotum* precedes the verb. In (7), *þæt lond* is the object and it occurs before the non-finite verb(s). In short, the object occurs after the finite main clause verb and before the non-finite verb in the main clause but before any verb in the subordinate clause.

The order of pronouns can vary; object pronouns often occur before the subject and verb, as (10) shows.

(10) oð   **him** se   mæsta dæl   wearð   underþieded.
     until him   that most   part   became   subjugated.
     'until most of it became subjugated to him.' (*Orosius*, chapter 2)

Another frequently occurring phenomenon is what has been called extraposition, a process where a prepositional or other phrase appears to the right of the verb that we would otherwise expect in V-final position, as in (11), where I have marked the extraposed material.

(11) 7   he Uesoges   Egypta   cyning wæs   siþþan mid   firde
     and   he Vezoges   Egypt's   king   was   after   with army
     farende [on Sciþþie   on   ða   norðdælas]
     going   to   Scythia   in   those   northern.parts
     'and Vezoges, Egypt's king, went afterwards with his army into Scythia into the North.'
     (*Orosius*, see (2) chapter 3)

TABLE 2.2. Word order in Old English

main clause	finite verb = V2 non-finite verb(s) = V-final
	subject position is variable though often before or after the finite verb
	object position is variable but often after the finite verb and before the non-finite verb
subordinate	all verbs = V-final
	subject and object before V
pronouns	relatively early
questions	*wh*-element and the verb are fronted

A last point on word order involves questions. The lexical verb in (12) is placed first, where Modern English uses a 'dummy' *do*. If there is an auxiliary, as in (13), this auxiliary moves.

(12) **gehyrest** þu   eadwacer
     hear   you   Eadwacer
     'do you hear, Eadwacer?' (*Exeter Book, Wulf and Eadwacer* 11)

(13) Hwæt **sceal** ic winnan cwæð   he
     'what shall   I   gain   spoke he?' (*Junius, Genesis* 278)

A summary of the word order possibilities appears in Table 2.2; again note that these rules are not absolute.

2.2.3   After Old English

The examples of word order in (5) to (11) were selected from Old English texts and some were taken from texts we'll come back to in Chapter 3. OV sentences (start to) disappear around 1200 and V2 before 1600. As usual, texts are quite varied, though, and a lot of differences can be observed. I will take some examples from Middle and Early Modern now to show the changes to an SVO, i.e. a non-V2 and non-OV order.

Excerpt (14) is from *Ayenbite of Inwyt*, from the middle part of the fourteenth century.

(14) Efterward   <u>comþ</u>   **slacnesse** þet   comþ   of   þe   defaute of
     After   comes   slackness   REL   comes   from   the fault   of
     herte   and   of   kueade   wone.   þat   bint   zuo
     courage   and   of   evil   habits. that   binds   so
     þane   man   þet   onneaþe   **he**   **him**   yefþ   to   done   wel
     the   man   who   hardly   he   him   gives   to   do   well
     'afterwards, slackness comes which arises from the fault of courage and of evil habits that bind the man who hardly troubles himself to do well.'

The first line has the finite verb *comþ* in second position as it follows the adverbial *efterward* and precedes the subject *slacnesse*. There are no verbs in clause-final positions, typical in a post-1200 text. Pronouns still precede the verb, as is obvious from the position of *he* and *him* in the second line. This too is predictable in a fourteenth-century text. However, this text also has morphological characteristics that are archaic for this time period, such as the use of an accusative masculine demonstrative *þane* and the infinitival ending *-ne* on *done*.

Excerpt (15) from Ascham's *The Scholemaster* is later, namely from 1570.

> (15) After **the childe** <u>hath</u> learned perfitlie the eight partes of speach, let him then learne the right ioyning togither of substantiues with adiectiues, the nowne with the verbe, the relatiue with the antecedent. And in learninge farther hys Syntaxis, by mine aduice, **he** <u>shall</u> not vse the common order in common scholes, for making of latines: wherby, **the childe** commonlie <u>learneth</u>, first, an euill choice of wordes, (and **right choice of wordes**, [...], <u>is</u> the foundation of eloquence) than, a wrong placing of wordes: and lastlie, an ill framing of the sentence, with a peruerse iudgement, both of wordes and sentences. **These faultes**, taking once roote in yougthe, <u>be</u> neuer, or hardlie, pluckt away in age. Moreouer, **there** <u>is</u> no one thing, **that** <u>hath</u> more, either dulled the wittes, or taken awaye the will of children from learning, then the care **they** <u>haue</u>, to satisfie their masters, in making of latines.

In (15), I have bolded the subjects and they all occur before their finite verbs, which are underlined. This shows that V2 is not present in this text but that it now has an SV-order. There are no instances of V-final word order either.

One last point about changes in word order concerns verb-movement in questions that we have seen in (12) and (13) above. In Old, Middle, and Early Modern English questions, all finite verbs move to initial position, as (12) shows. After 1600, the movement of a lexical verb increasingly becomes restricted and only the auxiliary verb moves. If there is no auxiliary, a 'do' is used. Note the older usage in (16) and the later usage with a dummy 'do' in (17) by the same author.

> (16) What <u>cares</u> these roarers for the name of King ... (Shakespeare, *Tempest* I, i, 17)
>
> (17) <u>Do</u> you not hear him? (Shakespeare, *Tempest* I, i, 13)

Having provided some background on the word order of the various stages of English, let's turn to the morphology, i.e. the endings on nouns inform us about their function in the sentence and the inflection on verbs tells us what subjects they agree with and their tense and aspect of the sentence.

2.3 Case on nouns and pronouns and agreement and tense/aspect/mood on the verb

As mentioned, Old English is a synthetic language with lots of case (nominative, genitive, dative, and accusative on the noun), agreement (with the subject on the verb), and tense, aspect, and mood endings that mark the verb for present/past, perfective, and indicative/subjunctive. We'll look at the inflection on nouns and the role of prepositions in section 2.3.1 and at the inflection on verbs and the role of auxiliaries in section 2.3.2.

2.3.1 Nouns

The first lines of *Beowulf* in (18) show many endings, both nominal and verbal, and they are illustrated by means of hyphens.

(18) hwæt   we   garden-a   in   geardag-um   þeodcyning-a
     indeed we   spear.danes-GEN in   yore.days-DAT   kings-GEN
     þrym   gefrun-on hu   ða   æþeling-as   ellen freme-don
     glory   hear-PST   how   those nobles-NOM   courage do-PST
     'indeed, we have heard of the courageous deeds of the Danes (and) their kings in earlier times,
     how the noble ones accomplished courageous deeds'.

The main verb *gefrunon* is at the end of the first line and its *-on* ending marks it as an indicative plural past; the *-um* on *geardagum* marks it a plural dative noun that goes with the preposition *in*; and the two genitive nouns ending in *-a* mark that they go with *þrym*, as possessors. The *-as* on the noun *æþelingas* in the second line of (16) marks a nominative or accusative plural. There is one demonstrative *ða* in the second line that is marked for nominative or accusative.

Note that the word order in the two clauses in (18) is V-final, i.e. different from what the rules in Table 2.2 predict. The V-last word order is expected in the subordinate second clause but not in the first one. I am not sure what the reason is.

In Table 2.3, I have provided some of the endings on different kinds of nouns; the ending differs not only depending on what case it is but also what class of noun it is (traditionally rendered as M(asculine), F(eminine), and N(euter)).

One needs to check an Old English dictionary to check if a noun is masculine, feminine, or neuter. For instance, *æþeling* in (18) is masculine so its *-as* ending tells you it is plural nominative or accusative. In section 3.3.2, I'll add another class, that of weak nouns, and also provide some endings for adjectives.

In the first few decades of the twelfth century (e.g. in the *Peterborough Chronicle*), there is evidence that case marking is changing: demonstratives are no longer marked with their usual endings and the genitive object is no longer marked, as argued by Allen (1995: 177) for (19). Here, the accusative object *ðone riht hand* would have been genitive in Old English.

(19) benam ælc   **ðone**   riht   hand
     took   every that.ACC   right hand
     'deprived each of their right hands.' (*Peterborough Chronicle* for the year 1125)

TABLE 2.3. Some Old English (strong) noun endings

		stan (M) 'stone'	word (N) 'word'	lufu (F) 'love'	sunu (M) 'son'
singular	NOM	stan	word	lufu	sunu
	GEN	stanes	words	lufe	suna
	DAT	stane	worde	lufe	suna
	ACC	stan	word	lufe	sunu
plural	NOM	stanas	word	lufa	suna
	GEN	stana	worda	luf(en)a	suna
	DAT	stanum	wordum	lufum	sunum
	ACC	stanas	word	lufa	suna

Other changes in case are taking place. For instance, (20) and (21) provide more archaic case endings in (a), from the Caligula version of Layamon's *Brut*, and less archaic ones in (b), from the Otho version.

(20) a. 7   to Corinee **hine**   sende
        and to Corineus 3S.ACC   sent
        'and sent him to Corineus.' (Layamon, Caligula 1209)
   b. *and to Corineus **him** sende.* (Layamon, Otho 1209)
(21) a. 7   **hine**   fæire   on-feng
        and 3S.ACC   fairly received
        'and received him heartily.' (Layamon, Caligula 2442)
   b. *and onderfeng **him** deore.* (Layamon, Otho 2442)

Apart from the replacement of the special accusative *hine* by the more general *him*, note also some modification of the name *Corineus* in (20a) but an invariant in (20b).

One of the consequences of the loss of case marking after Old English is an increase in prepositions, especially *of*, which is used frequently where earlier a genitive is used; and *to* and *for* are used where an earlier dative ending marks the indirect object. Prepositions that mark location and direction and so on are used throughout the history of English although many differences occur. The loss of case on demonstratives and pronouns is discussed in more detail in section 2.4. We'll look at markings on verbs next.

2.3.2 Verbs

Old English verbs have endings marking the person and number of the subject (agreement) and the tense, aspect, and mood. After Old English, these endings decrease and auxiliaries are introduced to mark mood and aspect. Agreement with the subject and present and past tense continue to be indicated on the verb in much reduced form.

As we'll see, Old English verbs differentiate for indicative, subjunctive, and imperative moods, present and past tense, and for the various subjects. Old English also makes a distinction between strong and weak verbs, mainly relevant for the past tense, a distinction that persists until Modern English. The strong paradigm appears in Table 2.4 and the weak in Table 2.5. Strong verbs show a change in stem vowel between the present indicative and the past; weak verbs do not but have a -*d*/-*t* to mark the past. Note that third person -*þ* and -*ð* endings are used interchangeably.

Examples of agreement on the verb with second person subject *Þu* are given in (22) for the present tense.

(22) *Þu   to   dæge þissum adem-**est**   me fram duguðe and*
     2S   to   day   this   deprive-2S   me from good   and
     *adrif-**est** from earde minum.*
     drive-2S   from earth mine
     'you deprive me from good and drive me from my home.' (*Junius, Genesis* 1031–3)

TABLE 2.4. An Old English strong verb

			indicative	subjunctive	imperative
present	1S	ic	drife	drife	
	2S	þu	drifest	drife	drif
	3S	he/heo/hit	drif(e)ð	drife	
	PL	we/ge/hi	drifað	drifen	drifað
past	1S	ic	draf	drife	
	2S	þu	drife	drife	
	3S	he/heo/hit	draf	drife	
	PL	we/ge/hi	drifon	drifen	
participles	drifende, (ge)drifen				

TABLE 2.5. An Old English weak verb

			indicative	subjunctive	imperative
Present	1S	ic	fremme	fremme	
	2S	Þu	frem(e)st	fremme	freme
	3S	he/heo/hit	frem(e)þ	fremme	
	PL	we/ge/hi	fremmaþ	fremmen	fremmaþ
Past	1S	ic	fremede	fremede	
	2S	Þu	fremedest	fremede	
	3S	he/heo/hit	fremede	fremede	
	PL	we/ge/hi	fremedon	fremeden	
Participles	fremende, (ge)fremed				

Old English has impersonal verbs that are always inflected for third person. An example is given in (23) where the finite verb *Þinceð* remains the same regardless of the nouns in the sentence. This changes in Middle English and a dummy *it* appears, as in (24).

(23) *Þinceð   him   to   lytel*
   seem.3S   him   too   little
   '(his possessions) seem too little to him.' (*Beowulf* 1748)

(24) *as **it** thynketh me To maken vertu of necessitee.*
   'as it appears to make virtue of necessity.' (Chaucer, *Canterbury Tales, The Knight's Tale* 2177)

This dummy subject is typical for analytic stages.

Different moods can be used in Old English for expressing real, non-real, or future events. The indicative in (22) suggests a real situation, whereas the subjunctive in (25) is used for uncertain or future events.

(25) *Swa   sceal   geong   guma   gode gewyrcean ...*
   So   shall   young   man   good perform ...
   *þæt   hine   on   ylde   eft   gewunig-**en**   wilgesiþas*
   that him   in   old   again stand.by-SUBJ   companions

þonne wig   cum-*e*   leode   gelæst-*en*
then   war   come-SUBJ   people   help-SUBJ
'such should a young man accomplish with good deeds ..., so that later in life
his companions may stand by him and, when war should come, (the) people
may help him.' (*Beowulf* 20–4)

The subjunctive mood in (25) appears on the plurals *gewunigen* 'will stand by' and *gelæsten* 'will help' and the singular *cume* 'should come' to mark them as hypothetical. Modern English uses modals to mark the uncertainty.

There is, in Old English, a present and past progressive aspect with a present participle, namely that in (26). Most scholars, however, consider this present participle not the direct precursor of the present day use of that *-ing* participle. For instance, Jespersen (1931: 165) points out that this form is much more frequent in translations from Latin, which (26) is.

(26) Đa   **wæs**   se Hælend   **utadrifende**   sume   deofolseocnysse
     Then was   the savior driving.out   a   devil.sickness
     'he was driving out devils.'   (*Luke* 11.14, West Saxon Gospels, Corpus)

The past participle is frequently marked by a *ge-* prefix, as in (27), which disappears quite early in the North and Northeast but lingers as *-i* in the South. There are other prefixes that indicate an action is finished, as in (8). Many of these are replaced by particles, such as *ut* in (28), where the earlier prefix *a-* is still visible as well.

(27) *Headda abbot heafde ær   **gewriton**   hu   Wulfhere ...*
     Headda abbot had   before   written   how   Wulfhere
     'Headda the abbot had written earlier how Wulfhere ...' (*Peterborough Chronicle* for the year 963, Interpolation)
(28) *þanan heora   nan   ne   mæg   syððan   **ut**   **aberstan***
     thence of.them none   not   may   afterwards out   escape
     'none of them may escape from there afterwards.' (*Homilies*, Dominica VI post Pentecosten 166, Pope 1967–8)

The verb 'to be' is a fascinating mixture of forms, as Table 2.6 shows. The *s*-forms may go back to an old demonstrative *sa and the *be*-forms to the reconstructed Indo-European *bheu 'grow'. The *wes(ende)* goes back to *wes 'remain, dwell' and the passive *weorðan*, that we'll see in Chapter 3, goes back to *wert 'turn'.

In Old English, the *am, art, is*, and *sind(on)* forms are used in the present when the reference is to the current situation, and forms of *beo* are used when the reference is future or generic, as in (29). This situation persists quite long, as we saw in sixteenth-century (4), the beginning of which is repeated here in (30).

(29) *Saga   hwæt   ic   hatte,   oþþe   hwa   mec   rære,*
     Say   what   I   am.called,   or   who   me.ACC   rear.SUBJ
     þonne   ic   restan   ne   mot   oþþe   hwa   mec   stæðþe,
     then   I   rest   not   may   or   who   me   stays
     *þonne   ic   stille   **beom***
     then   I   still   be.1S

TABLE 2.6. The Old English forms of the verb *beon* 'to be'

		indicative	subjunctive	imperative
present	ic	eom	sie/beo	
	þu	eart	sie/beo	wes/beo
	he/heo/hit	is	sie/beo	
	PL	sint/sindon	sien/beon	wesaþ/beoþ
past	ic	wæs	S wære	
	þu	wære		
	he/heo/hit	wæs		
	we/ge/hi	wæron	PL wæren	
future	ic	beom		
	þu	bist		
	he/o	biþ		
	we/ge/hi	beoþ		
participles		wesende, beonde, gebeon		

'say what I am called or who raises me up when I may not rest or who restrains me when I am silent.' (*Exeter Book, Riddle 3* 72–4)

(30) THere **be** two causes, ...

Tables 2.4 to 2.6 provide some details on the shape of the verb in Old English. In Middle and Early Modern English, these endings gradually change. The change starts in the North, like most loss in endings, and a Middle English paradigm is given in Table 2.7.

Unlike Old English, Modern English makes abundant use of auxiliaries, as (31) shows, where a modal, perfect, progressive, and passive auxiliary occur before the lexical verb *put*.

(31) While he **may have been being** put under undue pressure, ...[1]

Old English doesn't have these sequences and some people argue the auxiliaries are less auxiliary-like. In (32), an Old English fragment from *The Wanderer* which we'll see more of in Chapter 3, I have bolded the possible auxiliaries.

(32) Oft   him   anhaga   are gebideð   metudes   miltse   þeahþe
     Often   him   solitary   kindness comes God's   mildness   though

TABLE 2.7. Late Middle English verbal inflection

		indicative	subjunctive	imperative
present	1S	ic find(e)	S find(e)	
	2S	thou findes(t)		find
	3S	he/heo/hit findeþ/findes		
	PL	we, ye(e), thei findeþ/en	find(en)	findeþ/es
past	S	found(e)	founde	
	PL	found(en)	founde(n)	
participles		findende, (y)founden		

he	mod	cearig	geond		lagu lade	longe	**sceolde**	hreran
he	heart	troubled	through		sea ways	long	should	stir
mid	hondum	hrim	cealde	sæ	wadan	wræc	lastas	wyrd
with	hands	frost	cold	sea	travel	exile	tracks	fate
bið	ful	ared.		Swa	cwæð	eard	stapa	earfeþa	gemyndig
is	fully	determined		so	says	earth	walker	hardship	mindful
wraþa	wæl		sleahta		wine mæga		hryre.	Oft	ic **sceolde**
hostile	foreigner		slaughters		loyal kinsmen		fall	Often	I should
ana		uhtna		gehwylce	mine ceare	cwiþan	nisnu		cwicra
alone		morning		each	my cares	say	not.is.now		alive
nan	þe	ic him	modsefan minne		**durre**	sweotule	asecgan
none	REL	I him	thoughts mine		dare	clearly	tell

'Often the solitary dweller waits for favor, the mercy of the creator, although he, troubled in heart, has for a long time, across the sea-ways, had to stir with his hands the ice-cold sea, travel the paths of an exile; fate is fully determined. Thus spoke the wanderer, mindful of troubles, of cruel battles, of the fall of kinsmen. Often, alone at each dawn, I have had to lament my sorrow; now there is nobody alive to whom I dare openly reveal my thoughts.' (Translation based on various online and print sources, mainly Hogg 1992b: 22–3)

As mentioned in Chapter 1, an auxiliary is a verbal element used for tense, mood, or aspect that has to accompany a lexical verb. The auxiliaries in (32) all go with lexical verbs, i.e. *sceolde* with *hreran*, *bið* with *ared*, *sceolde* with *cwiþan*, and *durre* with *asecgan*. Apart from *bið*, these are all modal auxiliaries, in fact **root modals**. These root modals express how the world ought to be and differ from epistemic modals where the speaker evaluates the event or state described by the verb. An example of an **epistemic modal** would be the Modern English *might* in (33).

(33) It **might** snow there in July!

Reasons for arguing that modals in Old English are still lexical verbs are the following. Some modals can occur on their own, as in (34), there are few epistemic modals, and sequences of auxiliaries, as in (35), don't start till late Middle English.

(34) *He on mode wearð forht on ferhðe; no þy ær*
He on mind became afraid on mind; not through.that before
fram meahte.
from might
'fear came to his mind; nowhere had he power (to move).' (*Beowulf* 753–4)

(35) *If I so ofte myghte have ywedded bee.*
'because I was allowed to be wedded so often.' (Chaucer, *Canterbury Tales*, *The Wife of Bath Prologue*, 7)

Modals in Old English are sometimes referred to as preterite-present. This means that, in the present, their forms are those of the past (also known as preterite). A paradigm of the modal *sculan*, the precursor of 'should' in Modern English, is given in Table 2.8. If we compare this paradigm with those in Tables 2.4 and 2.5,

TABLE 2.8. The modal paradigm for *sculan* 'be obliged to'

		indicative		subjunctive	
present	1	ic	sceal	S	scyle
	2	þu	scealt		
	3	he/heo/hit	sceal		
	PL	sculon		PL	scylen
past	1	ic	sceolde	S	sceolde
	2	þu	sceoldest		
	3	he/heo/hit	sceolde		
	4	we/ge/hi	sceoldon	PL	sceolden

the present tense endings for the first and third persons are absent just like the past endings of the earlier tables.

The paradigms in Tables 2.4 to 2.6 show participle forms, and we have seen some of these. The present participle ends in *-ende*, as shown in (7); and the past participle has a *ge-* prefix, as in (27), and *-en* or *-ed* (or some variant thereof) suffix. The *ge-* is still detectable in the *y-* of *ywedded* in (35). The infinitival ending is not listed but is *-an* in (32) or *-en(ne)* when there is an infinitival *to*, as in (36), more typical of later Old English.

(36) On   hwilcum godum   tihst   þu   us   **to gelyfenne.**
     In   which   gods   urge   2S   us   to believe
     'in which gods do you urge us to believe?' (*Aelfric Lives*, from Los 2005: 53)

In conclusion to sections 2.2 and 2.3, word order in Old English is relatively free for nouns and somewhat more fixed for verbs (e.g. V-final and V2) but endings on nouns help make clear the grammatical function they have. Endings on verbs show what the subject is and also help indicate the mood, tense, and aspect. During the Middle English period, V-final and V2 are lost in favor of a more rigid SVO order, and nouns and verbs lose endings. By 1600, a difference between auxiliary and lexical verbs emerges, namely that only the former undergoes movement to the front in questions.

2.4 Demonstratives, pronouns, and articles

In this section, I first explain how demonstrative, personal, and relative pronouns are used and then turn to their paradigms, how these simplify, and when articles come into being.

2.4.1 Pronominals in Old and Middle English

Old English, as we have seen, lacks articles but has personal pronouns and demonstratives. Some examples of personal pronouns are given in (37) and (38) in bold.

(37) Wes   **þu**   **us**   larena   god
     Be   thou   us   teaching   good
     'give us good counsel.' (*Beowulf* 269)

(38) *Nalæs* **hi** **hine** *læssan lacum teodan*
No.less they him less gifts prepared
'they made him no fewer gifts.' (*Beowulf* 43)

Note that the third person has overlapping forms like *hi* and *hie* for the nominative and accusative plural and for the accusative feminine singular; *him* for the dative plural and the masculine and neuter singular. Personal pronouns of this *h*-variety are also used reflexively, as shown in (39).

(39) **him** *bebeorgan ne con*
REFL hide not can
'(he) could not hide himself.' (*Beowulf* 1746)

Subject pronouns are less obligatory in Old English, as (39) shows, than they are in Middle and Modern English. Other examples of left out subjects are given in (40); see the boldings in the translation.

(40) *Gegrette ða gumena gehwylcne* ... *Nolde ic sweord beran*
Greeted then men every not-wanted I sword bear
wæpen to wyrme gif ic wiste hu wið ðam aglæcean
weapon to dragon if I knew how against that monster
elles meahte
otherwise might
'**he** greeted then the men ... I would bear no sword, weapon against the dragon, if I knew what else **I** could do against the monster.' (*Beowulf* 2518–20)

Demonstratives can also be used for personal reference, as the first *se* in (41) shows, which may happen to shift the topic of the sentence, and as relative pronouns, as the second *se* in the same sentence shows.

(41) *Huelc* **se** *beon sceal* **se** *ðærto cuman ne sceal.*
Which.kind DEM be shall DEM thereto come not shall
'what kind shall he be who is not to come?' (Alfred, *Pastoral Care* 11)

Old English relative clauses are introduced in three different ways. There is a demonstrative on its own, as seen in (41), or a demonstrative reinforced with a *þe* or *ðe* or *þat* particle, as in (42), or the particle on its own, as in (43).

(42) *Ece is se æþeling* **se** **þe** *him þæt ead gefeð.*
Eternal is that noble.one DEM REL him that bliss gives
'eternal is that noble one who gives him that bliss.' (*Exeter Book, The Phoenix* 319)

(43) *and sugged feole þinges* ... **þat** *næuere nes iwurðen*
and say many things REL never not.was happened
'and say many things that never happened.' (Layamon, Caligula 11472–3)

This system changes to one where either the particle *þe* or *þat* appears or nothing does. Only later in Middle English is the relative *wh-* pronoun introduced, as in (44).

(44) *þe grace of God,* **who** *preserue зow.*
'the grace of God, who keeps you.' (*Paston Letters* 395, Davis 1971: 636)

Demonstratives often appear before nouns, as in (45), but this is less frequent in early Old English. The shift towards many pre-nominal demonstratives signals a turn towards analyticity.

(45) wið **ðam** aglæcean
'against that monster.' (*Beowulf* 2519)

In short, Old English demonstratives can be used to shift to a new topic and are used as relative pronouns whereas Old English personal pronouns often refer to a close antecedent and can be used reflexively. Subject pronouns can also be left out. Around 1200, this situation changes drastically: (1) demonstratives are no longer used as personal pronouns and less so for relatives; (2) two new personal forms appear, namely the feminine *she* and the plural *they*; and (3) more and more, a special reflexive with *self* is used.

Another major change occurs around 1200, namely the use of definite articles. In Old English, demonstratives appear before a noun to indicate definiteness, as in (45) and (46). These demonstratives differ depending on their case and number; for instance, ðam in (45) is dative singular and ða in (46) is plural nominative or accusative. By Middle English, the demonstrative is phonetically reduced to the article þe, as in (47), not marked for gender or case.

(46) hu   **ða**   æþelingas   ellen   fremedon
     how   those   nobles   courage   did
     'how those nobles performed heroic acts.' (*Beowulf* 3)

(47) &   gaddresst   swa   **þe**   clene corn   All   fra   **þe** chaff togeddre
     and   gather.2S   so   the   clean wheat   all   from   the chaff together
     'and so you gather the clear wheat from the chaff.' (*Ormulum* 1484–5, Holt edition)

In Chapters 3 and 4, I'll point out this use of articles where relevant.

2.4.2 Some paradigms and change

I'll now provide the personal and demonstrative paradigms and then point out some of the changes involving them in more detail. The Old English personal pronouns are illustrated in Table 2.9.

Most notable, from a contemporary point of view, is the use of special accusatives and the dual: the accusative second person singular ðec appears in (48), the accusative first person singular mec in (49), and two duals in (50). The dual is used when only two persons are involved.

(48) þæt   **ðec**   dryhtguma   deaþ   oferswiþ-eþ
     that   2S.ACC   mighty.ruler   death   overpower-3S
     'that death overpowers you, mighty ruler.' (*Beowulf* 1768)

(49) hwilum   **mec**   ahebbað ...   hyrste   mine   ond þeos hea lyft
     sometimes   1S.ACC   lifts.up ... ornaments   mine   and this high air
     'sometimes these ornaments of mine and the high air lift me up.' (*Exeter Book, Riddle* 7)

(50) **Wit**   þæt   gecwædon   cnihtwesende
     We   that   said   boys.being

TABLE 2.9. Old English personal pronouns

		singular	dual	plural
first	NOM	ic	wit	we
	GEN	min	uncer	ure
	DAT	me	unc	us
	ACC	me, mec	unc, uncit, uncet	us, usic
second	NOM	þu	git	ge
	GEN	þin	incer	eower
	DAT	þe	inc	eow
	ACC	þe, þec	inc, incit	eow, eowic
third	NOM	he/heo/hit	–	hi, hie, heo
(M/F/N)	GEN	his/hire/his	–	hira, hiera
	DAT	him/hire/him	–	him
	ACC	hine/hi(e)/hit	–	hi, hie

ond	*gebeotedon*	*wæron*	*begen*	*þa*		*git*
and	vowed	were	both	then		still
on	*geogoðfeore*	*þæt*	**wit**	*on*	*garsecg*	*ut*
in	youth	that	we	on	ocean	out
aldrum	*neðdon,*	*ond*	*þæt*	*geæfndon*		*swa.*
lives	ventured	and	that	carried.out		so

'the two of us agreed, being boys, and promised that we would risk our lives out on the ocean and that we did.' (*Beowulf* 535–8)

Second person pronouns have a singular, as in (48), and a plural. In Middle English, these are used as familiar and polite forms, respectively, before the familiar *thou* and *thee* disappear.

In late Old English prose, the accusative first and second person forms disappear and the dative is used for both accusative and dative instead. The duals also disappear. By the Middle English, the pronouns are mostly as in Table 2.10 with a few distinct third person accusatives still appearing in early Middle English.

Immediately obvious from Table 2.10 is that there are fewer forms in Middle English than in the Old English in Table 2.9. The dual has disappeared as have

TABLE 2.10. Late Middle English pronouns

		singular	plural
first	NOM	ic	we
	GEN	min	ure/our
	DAT/ACC	me	us
second	NOM	thou	ye(e)
	GEN	thi(n)	your
	DAT/ACC	thee	you
third	NOM	she/he/it	they
	GEN	her/his/it	their
	DAT/ACC	her/him/it	them

32   *Analyzing Syntax through Texts*

TABLE 2.11. Demonstratives in Old English

	masculine	feminine	neuter	plural
NOM	se	seo	þæt	þa
GEN	þæs	þære	þæs	þara
DAT	þæm	þære	þæm	þæm
ACC	þone	þa	þæt	þa

the special accusative, such as *mec, þec, hine, usic*, and *eowic*. The loss of these case forms is in accordance with the trend towards less synthetic marking.

New in Middle English are special forms for feminine and plural third person, namely *she* and *they*. Around 1600 another shift occurs among the second person pronouns and *you* will emerge as the only form for singular and plural nominative and accusative cases. Not listed in the table are the reflexives that start to be marked in this period. Only by late Old English does the third person become reinforced by an adjectival *self* and first and second person do so only later.

The Old English demonstrative paradigm is given in Table 2.11; it shows a lot of case and gender distinctions. In Modern English, there are only three forms left from this paradigm, namely *the (se), that (þæt)*, and *those (þa)*.

Indefinite articles, such as *a* and *an*, do not occur either in Old English. The OED gives the first instances as (51). Note a missing *a* before *tune* 'town' in (51a).

(51) a. *Wel þu myhtes faren al **a** dæis fare, sculdest thu neure finden man in tune sittende.*
  'well might you all travel a day's journey, you would never find a man sitting in a town.' (*Peterborough Chronicle* for the year 1137)
  b. *He spedde litel & be gode rihte, for he was **an** yuel man*
  'he prospered little and by good right because he was an evil man.'
  (*Peterborough Chronicle* for the year 1140)

Summarizing sections 2.3 and 2.4, the change between Old and Modern English can be characterized by an increase in the use of grammatical words, such as demonstratives, articles, auxiliaries, and prepositions, and a loss of endings on nouns, pronouns, and verbs. In Chapter 1, this change was phrased in terms of grammaticalization and a shift from synthetic to analytic.

One grammatical word that hasn't been discussed is the conjunction and we'll look next at how clauses are connected to each other in the various stages.

2.5 Clause boundaries: punctuation, word order, and conjunctions

In Modern English writing, we rely on periods and semi-colons to see where sentences end. In Old English, the clausal boundaries are not so clearly marked by punctuation and that makes it hard to see if a clause is subordinate, dependent or a main, independent clause. Word order sometimes helps in Old English because the main clause has V2 and the dependent clause has V-last, but this is not decisive. To make matters more complex, conjunctions are sometimes lacking to indicate structural dependence of one clause on another and the structures are more paratactic to begin with. In this section, I provide some background to these issues of punctuation, word order, and conjunctions.

The Beowulf manuscript is said to have 700 points, according to Orchard (2001), that appear every so often but that are not indicative of each sentence boundary. See Figure 2.2.

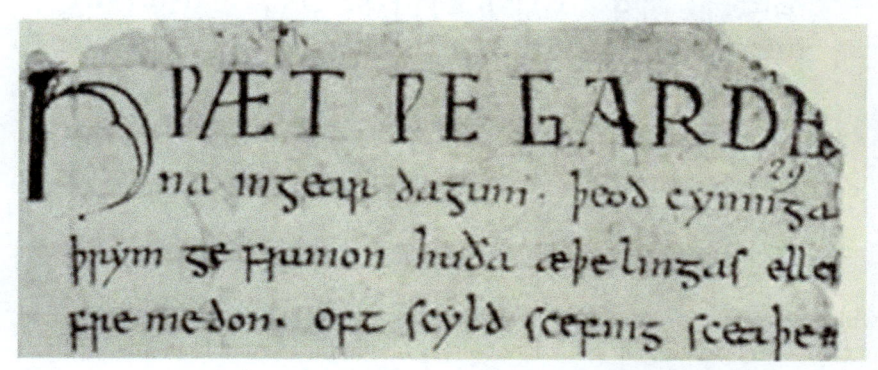

FIGURE 2.2. Periods/points in the beginning of *Beowulf* (Cotton MS Vitellius A.XV, f. 132. Reproduced with permission from the British Library Board)

The first point in the middle of the second line doesn't indicate a clause boundary but the second one in the fourth line does. So, it is safe to say that periods do help.

The passage is transcribed in (52) with some of the special characters modernized, e.g. the *s*, *r*, and *f*; a word-by-word gloss appears to the right. Note how difficult it is to decide where to put the spaces.

(52) HÞÆT ÞE   GARDE   indeed we spearda
     na   inȝear daȝum . þeod cynniȝa   nes inyore days people kings
     þrym ȝe frunon huða æþelinȝas   glory heard how those nobles
     ellen   courage
     fre medon . Oft   scyld   scefinȝ   did Often Scyld Scefing
     sceaþe   shadow

'indeed, we have heard of the courageous deeds of the Danes (and) their kings in earlier times, how the noble ones accomplished courageous deeds. Often, Scyld Scefing ...'

As I have mentioned in section 2.2, word order is often indicative of clausal independence or dependence but it is not completely reliable. The first sentence in Figure 2.2 is an example of a V-final order yet the clause is independent. Later on, there is a conjunction *hu* to show that the clause that follows is part of the previous one.

In addition to sporadic points or periods, there is – in late Old and Early Middle English – the frequent use of a shorthand symbol 7 for a coordinating 'and', as the late Old English text in Figure 2.3 shows. This text is transcribed

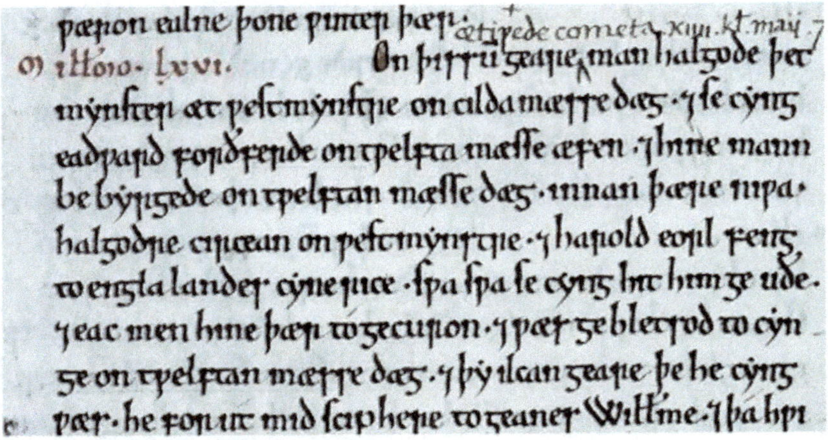
wæron ealne þone winter þær. ætiwede cometa xiiii kl. maii 7
m. lxvi. On þyssu[m] ȝeare man halȝode þet
mynster æt westmynstre on cilda mæsse dæȝ. 7 se cynȝ
eadward forðferde on twelfta mæsse æfen. 7 hine mann
be byrȝede on twelftan mæsse dæȝ. innan þære niwa
halȝodre circean on westmyntre. 7 harold eorl fenȝ
to enȝlalandes cyne rice. swa swa se cynȝ hit him ȝe uðe.
7 eac men hine þær to ȝecuron. 7 wæs ȝebletsod to cyn
ȝe on twelftan mæsse dæȝ. 7 þa ylcan ȝeare þe he cynȝ
wæs. he for ut mid sciphere toȝeanes Willme. 7 þa hwi

FIGURE 2.3. The *Peterborough Chronicle* for the year 1066 (Laud 636, 57v. Reproduced with permission from the Bodleian Library)

with a word-by-word gloss in Table 2.12 and translated in (53), with the inserted phrase left out. The first 7-like symbol appears in the second line after a period and the second in line 3, again after a period. The third one in line 4 doesn't mark a sentence-boundary, however.

(53) In this year the monastery at Westminster was hallowed on Childermas day (28 December). And King Eadward died on Twelfth-mass eve (5 January) and he was buried on Twelfth-mass day, in the newly hallowed church at Westminster. And Earl Harold succeeded to the Kingdom of England, as the king had granted it to him and men had also chosen him thereto and (he) was blessed as king on

TABLE 2.12. The *Peterborough Chronicle* for the year 1066

On þyssũ ȝeare man halȝode þet		In this year man hallowed that
mynster æt westmynstre on cilda mæsse dæȝ . 7se cynȝ	2	monastery at Westminter on Childermas day. And the king
eadward forðferde on twelfta mæsse æfen. 7hine mann		Eadward died on Twelfth-mass eve and him man
be byrȝede on twelftan mæsse dæȝ . innan þære niwa	4	buried on Twelfth-mass day, in that newly
halȝodre circean on westmyntre. 7 harold eorl fenȝ		hallowed church at Westminster. And Harold earl
to enȝlalandes cyne rice. swa swa se cynȝ hit him ȝe uðe.	6	succeeded to England's kingdom as the king it him granted
7 eac men hine þær to ȝecuron. 7 wæs ȝebletsod to cyn		and also men him thereto chosen and (he) was blessed to
ȝe on twelftan mæsse dæȝ. 7 þa ylcan ȝeare þe he cynȝ	8	king on Twelfth-mass day. And the same year that he king
wæs. he for ut mid sciphere toȝeanes Willme. 7 þa hwi		was. he went out with ships against William. ...

Twelfth-mass day. And in the same year that he was king he went out with a naval force against William ... (Thorpe 1861: 169)

This passage is typical of a paratactic style because most clauses are strung together by means of 'and', not by means of a subordinating conjunction. And again periods and word order do not always signal the same about clause status. For instance, in lines eight and nine of Figure 2.3, repeated as (54), the first clause is dependent if we go by the V-final word order of *wæs* and the presence of a conjunction *þe* but not if we go by the punctuation which has the clause stop after *wæs*. I have translated it as if it is a subordinate clause.

(54) 7 þa ylcan geare **þe** he cyng **wæs**. he for ut mid sciphere
and the same year that he king was. he sailed out with ships
togeanes Willelme.
against William
'And in the same year that he was king, he sailed out against William.'

In Middle English, we still can't determine the exact clausal boundaries from the punctuation. In the Layamon manuscript of *Brut*, shown in Figure 2.4 and transcribed in (55), we see some punctuation, a colon and a period. Also included are a few special markings that the scribe used, e.g. the superscripted *s* in *we*[s] 'was' and the mark above the last letter in *drihtē* (though very hard to see) to mark a nasal. The style is paratactic and few conjunctions appear, and the word order is consistent with that, namely mostly V2. A typical translation into Modern English would be (56) with more dependent clauses than the original.

FIGURE 2.4. The beginning of Layamon's Caligula version of *Brut* (Cotton Caligula A IX, f. 3. Reproduced with permission from the British Library Board)

(55) *An preost wes on*   A priest was among
  leoden: laʒamon   people Layamon
  wes ihoten. He we[s]   was named. He was
  leouenaðes sone.   Liefnoth's son.
  liðe him beo drihtē   Let God have mercy on him.
  he wonede at ernleʒe: at aðelen   He lived at Areley, at a lovely
  are chirechen. vppen seuarne sta church up Severn's bank.
  þe; sel þar him þuhte. On fest   Blissful he thought it. Close ...

(56) 'a priest, who was named Layamon, was living among the people. He was Liefnoth's son – God have mercy on him. He lived in Arely, at a lovely church on the banks of the Severn close (to Redstone).'

At what point does the punctuation become a reliable marker for sentence boundaries? Letters from the late Middle English/Early Modern period show little punctuation, as will be shown in Chapter 5, and periods will only indicate sentence-boundaries after 1600. As Denholm-Young (1964: 78) puts it, 'the use of capitals and punctuation was largely haphazard in the manuscripts of Elizabethan authors' and of course before.

For instance, the compositor of Shakespeare's printed text uses many subordinate clauses with a variety of punctuation. Hamlet's soliloquy from the First Folio of one of the copies in the Folger Library, reproduced as Figure 2.5, is challenging because it is hard to understand which clause depends on which and the punctuation doesn't help. There are semi-colons where a modern reader might like more guidance as to how to interpret the relationship between the clauses so connected. As far as the punctuation tells us, the first sentence ends in line 8 with a question mark. Other sentences are also quite long and complex.

In the previous four examples of earlier texts, we have seen how punctuation, word order, and conjunctions help decipher clausal boundaries. I'll say a

```
Enter Hamlet.

Ham. To be, or not to be, that is the Question:
Whether 'tis Nobler in the minde to suffer
The Slings and Arrowes of outragious Fortune,
Or to take Armes against a Sea of troubles,
And by opposing end them: to dye, to sleepe
No more; and by a sleepe, to say we end
The Heart-ake, and the thousand Naturall shockes
That Flesh is heyre too? 'Tis a consummation
Deuoutly to be wish'd. To dye to sleepe,
To sleepe, perchance to Dreame; I, there's the rub,
For in that sleepe of death, what dreames may come,
When we haue shuffel'd off this mortall coile,
Must giue vs pawse. There's the respect
That makes Calamity of so long life:
For who would beare the Whips and Scornes of time,
The Oppressors wrong, the poore mans Contumely,
The pangs of dispriz'd Loue, the Lawes delay,
The insolence of Office, and the Spurnes
That patient merit of the vnworthy takes,
When he himselfe might his Quietus make
With a bare Bodkin? Who would these Fardles beare
To grunt and sweat vnder a weary life,
But that the dread of something after death,
The vndiscouered Countrey, from whose Borne
No Traueller returnes, Puzels the will,
And makes vs rather beare those illes we haue,
Then flye to others that we know not of.
Thus Conscience does make Cowards of vs all,
And thus the Natiue hew of Resolution
Is sicklied o're, with the pale cast of Thought,
And enterprizes of great pith and moment,
With this regard their Currants turne away,
And loose the name of Action. Soft you now,
The faire Ophelia? Nimph, in thy Orizons
Be all my sinnes remembred.
```

FIGURE 2.5. Hamlet's Soliloquy by Shakespeare (III, i), from the First Folio, Folger Library 68

little more about conjunctions. They are mostly specialized to indicate a type of subordinate clause, e.g. *that* for declarative complements and *after*, *before*, and *since* for adverbial clauses. In Old English, this is not so clear, as (57) shows, taken from the West Saxon Gospels discussed at length in Chapter 3. In this sentence, the two clauses are related through the repetition of *þa* but this adverb doesn't indicate main/subordinate status. In this case, the word order in the first clause indicates that it is subordinate because the finite verb *wæs* has not moved to a V2 position.

(57) [*Eornustlice*   **þa**   *se*   *Hælend*   *acenned*   <u>*wæs*</u> *on Iudeiscre Bethleem*
     Indeed   then   DEM   savior   born   was in Judah's Bethleem
     on þæs   *cyninges*   *dagum*   *Herode]*   **þa**   <u>*comon*</u>   *þa*
     in DEM   kings   days   Herod's   then   came   DEM
     tungolwitegan   *fram*   *eastdæle*   *to*   *Hierusalem.*
     astrologers   from   east   to   Jerusalem
     'when Jesus was born in the village of Bethlehem in Judea during the days of Herod, wise men from the East came to Jerusalem.'

Conjunctions are also important in our characterization of the language. We have characterized Old English as a synthetic language with lots of endings and few function words, whereas Modern English has lost endings but has gained a good number of articles and auxiliaries. How do conjunctions fit in this picture? Conjunctions are divided into coordinating and subordinating conjunctions, often called coordinators and complementizers, respectively. I will use the terms interchangeably. Although conjunctions are function words, it cannot be said that synthetic languages lack them but rather that certain registers or styles make more use of certain conjunction types. Thus, mentioned above, the first sentence of *Beowulf* (52) has an embedded object, *huða æþelingas ellen fremedon*, which is introduced by the word *hu* 'how'. *Beowulf* has many such embeddings, as well as relative clauses and adverbial clauses. The much later *Peterborough Chronicle* abounds in coordinate structures, i.e. has a paratactic character, as we have seen in Figure 2.3.

In section 2.5, we have looked at the sentence from the outside, so to speak, i.e. what delineates it. We have considered punctuation, word order, and conjunctions since they help but are not decisive in earlier English. As for what conjunctions tell us about analytic or synthetic stages of a language, the answer is 'maybe not so much'. It may depend on stylistic considerations.

2.6 Dialectal variation in the time period

In this section, I discuss the dialect situation in Old and Middle English. Regional varieties persist of course until the present. Some of this variety depends on the origin of the settlers and some on the languages they come in contact with.

Old English can be divided into several varieties, usually Northumbrian, Mercian, West Saxon, and Kentish. Their location is given in Figure 2.6.

In Old English there is not very much evidence of dialect distinctions in the writings we have. In section 2.1, we looked at one part of *Caedmon's Hymn*, provided here again as (58a). A (later) West Saxon version is given in (58b).

FIGURE 2.6. Old English dialects (from <http://www.uni-due.de/SHE/SHE_Old_English.htm>, last accessed 4 June 2017. Reproduced with permission from Raymond Hickey)

(58) a. **Northumbrian** b. **West Saxon**

Northumbrian		West Saxon
Nu scylun hergan hefaenricaes uard	1	Nu we sculan herian heofonrices weard
Now shall praise heavenkingdom's guardian		
metudæs maecti end his modgidanc	2	metodes mihte and his modeþonc
Lord's might and his thought		
uerc uuldurfadur sue he uundra gehuaes	3	weorc wuldorfæder swa he wundra gehwæs
work wonderfather as he wonders' each's		
eci dryctin or astelidæ	4	ece dryhten ord onstealde
eternal lord beginning established		

There are phonological and scribal differences connected with the dialect differences, e.g. palatalization of the Northumbrian velar stops *g* and *c* into a West Saxon glide or fricative in *herian* (line 1), *mihte* (line 2), and *dryhten* (line 4); the use of *u(u)* in *uerc* and *uundra* as compared with a *w* in *weorc* and *wundra* (line 3); the use of *eo* in *weorc* in West Saxon; and the non-use of the thorn in the earlier, northern version's *modgidanc* (line 2).

Syntactic and morphological dialect differences typical for the South involve a less strict V2, negative contraction, the loss of the special accusatives *mec* and *þec*, and the more frequent use of *þe* relatives. We shall see some of these exemplified in Chapter 3. In (58), the only syntactic differences are V2 in (58a) and V3 in (58b) and the absence of the pronoun *we* (line 1) in (58a). The relevance of left out pronouns for dialects is debated, however.

One issue related to the discussion of Old English dialects is that there are only a few texts from the different areas that can be compared. Even the different

Syntax of Old, Middle, and Early Modern English 39

versions of *Caedmon's Hymn* are from different time periods. The texts that remain are also different in style: we have a lot of interlinear glosses from the North and much prose from the South. There are also texts, such as *Beowulf*, where we know very little about the author, date, and place of composition.

In Middle English, dialectal differences are more obvious since we have more texts available from the different areas. The differences are also obvious because a Middle English standard had not arisen yet so that pronunciation differences are often clear from the spelling of words. In this section, we will examine a few of the features that characterize the different areas. Figure 2.7 offers a simplified picture of where the northern, southern, and Midlands areas are situated.

FIGURE 2.7. Middle English dialects (from <http://www.uni-due.de/SHE/HE_DialectsMiddleEnglish.htm>, last accessed 4 June 2017. Reproduced with permission from Raymond Hickey)

The sound changes happening in Old and Middle English do not have the same impact in all areas and therefore serve as dialect indicators. For instance, palatalization of the velar stops [k] and [g] to [tʃ] and [j] is a southern phenomenon as is the voicing of initial fricatives in words such as *vather* 'father' and the change of long *a* to *o* in *hom* 'home'. On the other hand, the fronting of the fricative [ʃ] to [s], as in *sal* 'shall', is typically northern. More sound change seems to occur in non-northern areas. Changes in the morphology are typically northern, e.g. the endings on the finite and non-finite forms are lost early. An exception is the loss of special accusative pronouns, e.g. *mec* and *þec*, that is faster in southern areas.

The main characteristics of Middle English dialects are provided in Table 2.13, where the East and West Midlands are combined. The East Midlands varieties pattern more with northern ones and the West Midlands dialects more with the southern types. Not all texts display all these characteristics.

We'll now apply the features listed in Table 2.13 to Middle English texts. The text in (59) is taken from the northern (Cotton) version of *Cursor Mundi* and dates from 1300.

TABLE 2.13. Middle English dialect characteristics

	North	Midlands	South
Sound and spelling			
palatalization of velars	no change: [k]; [g], e.g. *frankis, egg*	mixed: [k]; [g] or [tʃ]; [j]	change to: [tʃ]; [j], e.g. *French, eye*
long [a] > [ɔ]	[a], e.g. *ham*	mainly [ɔ]	[ɔ], e.g. *hom*
short *on-an*	*on*, e.g. *mon*	*on* and *an*	*an*, e.g. *man*
voicing of initial fricatives	[f]; [s], e.g. *father, sea*	[f]; [s]	[v]; [z], e.g. *vather, zea*
hw-/qu- spelling	*qu-*, e.g. *quere* 'where'	*hw-*	*hw-*, e.g. *hwere* 'where'
fronting of [ʃ] to [s]	[s], e.g. *sal* 'shall, Inglis'	[s] or [ʃ]	[ʃ], e.g. *shal, English*
Morphology and syntax			
third plural pronoun	change to: *they/them*	mixed: *they/hem*	no change: *hi/hem*
feminine third NOM S	*she*	*she/heo*	*heo*
verbal present tense	*-(e)s*	mixed	like Old English
present participle	*-ande*	*-ende*	*-ing/inde*
past participle	no prefix	*y-/i-*	*y-/i-*
word order	V-second (V2)	V2 and V3	V2 and V3
infinitive marker	occasionally *at*	*to* only	*to* only
preposition *till*	yes	only later	only later

(59) þis ilk bok is es translate
    In to Inglis tong to rede   2
    For the loue of Inglis lede
    Inglis lede of Ingland   4
    For the commun at understand
    Frankis rimes here I redd   6
    Comunlik in ilka sted
    Mast es it wroght for frankis man   8
    Quat is for him na frankis can?
    Of Ingland the nacion   10
    Es Inglis man þar in commun
    þe speche þat man wit mast may spede   12
    Mast þarwit to speke war nede
    Selden was for ani chance   14
    Praised Inglis tong in france
    Giue we ilkan þare langage   16
    Me think we do þam non outrage
    To laud and Inglis man i spell   18
    þat understandes þat i tell.

Inglis, Frankis, comunlik, ilkan 'each', and *mast* 'most' are characteristic of a northern text because of the [s] rather than [ʃ], [k] rather than [tʃ], and [a] rather than [ɔ]. The spelling of *quat* 'what' confirms that it is a northern text. The morphological features provide further evidence: *þam* 'them', not *hem*, and a verbal ending on *understandes* in the last line are both northern. The use of the infinitival *at* is likewise typical of a northern text. Word order is more strictly V2 in northern texts and that is followed in e.g. line 8, which might be 'most it is wroght' in the South. An exception to this, however, is line 6 where the verb occurs in third position.

In (60) and (61), two characteristic lines for other dialects are provided. In (60), the voiced initial fricative in *vingre* 'fingers' indicates southern origin as do the palatalized *-ʒ-* and *y-* in *almiʒti* and *yaf*, and the *i-* prefix on the participle *iwrite*. In (61), there is a mix of northern and southern characteristics, typical of the Midlands. For instance, the spelling of *micth, kirke,* and *ricth* indicates a northern origin because of a lack of palatalization but the use of *hem* shows southern affinities.

(60) *Almiʒti god yaf ten hestes ine þe laʒe of iewes þet Moyses*
 'almighty God gave ten commandments in the law of (the) Jews that Moses
 onderuing ine þe helle of Synay ine tuo tables of ston
 received in the hell of Sinai on two tables of stone
 þet were iwrite mid godes vingre.
 that were written with God's fingers.' (*Ayenbite of Inwyt*, Preface 1–2)

(61) *He lovede God with al his micth, And Holy Kirke, and soth ant ricth.*
 'he loved God with all his might, and holy church, and truth and justice.
 Ricthwise men he lovede alle, And overal made hem for to calle.
 Just men he loved all and everywhere summoned them.' (*Havelok* 35–8)

Sentence (60) is taken from Dan Michel's *Ayenbite of Inwyt* ('Remorse of Conscience'), which is from Kent, i.e. a southern area, from 1340, and (61) is from *Havelok*, a Northeast Midlands text from the end of the thirteenth century.

The lines in (62) are from the beginning of an early Middle English work that we have seen before. The pronouns and participles in this excerpt tell us it is linguistically more southern: the use of the third person plural *heo* and the participle *ihoten*, with its prefix *i-*.

(62) *þet he wolde of Engle; þa æðelæn tellen. wat heo ihoten weoren;*
 'that he wanted of (the) English, the noble (things) tell, what they were called
 & wonene heo comen. þa Englene londe; ærest ahten.
 and whence they came. (who) the English land first owned
 æfter þan flode; þe from Drihtene com.
 after the flood that came from the Lord.' (Layamon, Caligula 7–10)

In this section, I have given several phonological, morphological, and syntactic characteristics of certain dialect areas. This will enable us to identify the dialects of the texts we examine in later chapters.

2.7 Conclusion

In this chapter, some of the major changes taking place throughout the history of English have been introduced. I have noted a rigidification of word order, the loss of inflection, and changes in pronouns, auxiliaries, and conjunctions. English has its beginnings around 450 CE, when speakers of Germanic languages settle in Britain. This date is quite arbitrary because the language does not change right away. Over time, however, the speakers of Old English acquire a more analytic language. This change may have been caused by the contact with speakers of Scandinavian and other languages or due to language-internal factors or both. Around 1100, many case endings have disappeared and the use of grammatical words is on the increase. This development continues between 1100 and 1500, and the English at the end of the Middle English period resembles present-day English in many respects. English keeps changing, as we'll see in the period after Middle English.

Exercises

A By now, we have talked about the following terms: analytic/synthetic, word order, V2, V-final, personal and demonstrative pronouns, relative and reflexive pronouns, auxiliaries, clause boundaries, and conjunctions. Pick two terms and discuss them with examples.

B Look at the text below from Bede (Miller 1890: 186–70), whose punctuation and capitals I have kept, and try to provide a more idiomatic translation.

Đa   æt nehstan se cyning,   se   ðe Seaxna   gereorde an cuðe,
Then   at last   that king,   DEM   PRT Saxon   language only knew
wæs aðroten his   elreordre spræce: aspon þa
was tired   his (=the bishop's)   foreign speech   invited then
in Westseaxe
into Wessex
oðerne biscop, se   ðe   his   gereorde   cuðe:
other   bishop DEM   PRT   his (=the king's) language knew
se   wæs   Wine   haten &   se   wæs   in   Gallia rice   gehalgod
DEM   was   wine   called and DEM   was   in   Gaul kingdom   consecrated
Ond he   þa   todælde   in   twa   biscopscire   Westseaxna   mægðe
And he (=the king) then divided into two   bishoprics   Wessex   people
ond   þæm   Wine   gesealde   biscopseðl   in   Wintaceastre.
and   DEM   Wine   gave   bishopseat   in   Winchester

C Identify the verbs in the above text; which are auxiliary verbs and which are lexical? What rules do they follow: V2 or V-final, and are these as you'd predict?

D List any personal, demonstrative, relative, and reflexive pronoun you recognize in the text.

E Which are the conjunctions; are they coordinating or subordinating?

F Discuss the use and morphological shape of the following:

se in line 1,
aspon in line 2,
se in line 3,
gehalgod in line 4, and
þæm in line 6.

G Discuss if the text in B is paratactic, hypotactic, or both.

Further reading

The 1980s saw a lot of work on the word order of Old English and how it differed from V2/OV languages such as Dutch and German, e.g. starting with Canale (1978), and many others followed, such as Bean (1983), van Kemenade (1987), and Pintzuk (1991). Recently, Bech (2001), Los (2012), Taylor and Pintzuk (2015), and Komen et al. (2014) have updated our knowledge on how information structure is relevant to the position of subject, object, and verb. Kroch and Taylor (1997) first noted the dialectal differences in word order. Almost every aspect of morphology and syntax has been examined in great detail, aspect, modals, articles. If, for instance, you wanted to read more about the *-ende* and *-ing*, read Mossé (1938: 99), Mustanoja ([1960] 2016): 594), and Scheffer (1975). Moore and Marckwardt (1951: 25–31) lists a good set of phonological and morphological dialect differences.

Excellent further reading on the syntax of earlier English would be Bech (2001), Fischer and van der Wurff (2006), Traugott (1992), and Fischer (1992).

Bean, Marian (1983), *The Development of Word Order Patterns in Old English*, London: Croom Helm.
Bech, Kristin (2001), *Word Order Patterns in Old and Middle English: A Syntactic and Pragmatic Study*, PhD thesis, Universitetet i Bergen, <https://bora.uib.no/handle/1956/3850> (last accessed 9 May 2017).
Canale, Michael (1978), *Word Order Change in Old English*, PhD dissertation, McGill University.
Fischer, Olga (1992), 'Syntax', in Norman Blake (ed.), *The Cambridge History of the English Language, Volume II: 1066–1476*, Cambridge: Cambridge University Press, pp. 207–408.
Fischer, Olga and Wim van der Wurff (2006), 'Syntax', in Richard Hogg and David Denison (eds), *A History of the English Language*, Cambridge: Cambridge University Press, pp. 109–98.
Komen, Erwin, Rosanne Hebing, Ans van Kemenade and Bettelou Los (2014), 'Quantifying Information Structure Change in English', in Kristin Bech and Kristine Gunn Eide (eds), *Information Structure and Syntactic Change in Germanic and Romance Languages*, Amsterdam: John Benjamins, pp. 81–110.
Kroch, Anthony and Anne Taylor (1997), 'Verb Movement in Old and Middle English: Dialect Variation and Language Contact', in Ans van Kemenade and Nigel Vincent (eds), *Parameters of Morphosyntactic Change*, Cambridge:

Cambridge University Press, pp. 297–325.

Los, Bettelou (2012), 'The Loss of Verb-Second and the Switch from Bounded to Unbounded Systems', in Anneli Meurman-Solin, Maria Jose Lopez-Couso and Bettelou Los (eds), *Information Structure and Syntactic Change in the History of English*, Oxford: Oxford University Press, pp. 21–46.

Moore, Samuel and Albert Marckwardt (1951), *Historical Outlines of English Sounds and Inflections*, Ann Arbor: George Wahr.

Mossé, Fernand (1938), *Histoire de la forme périphrastique être + participe présent en germanique*, Paris: Klincksieck.

Mustanoja, Tauno [1960] (2016), *A Middle English Syntax*, Amsterdam: John Benjamins.

Pintzuk, Susan (1991), *Phrase Structures in Competition: Variation and Change in Old English Word Order*, PhD dissertation, University of Pennsylvania.

Scheffer, Johannes (1975), *The Progressive in English*, Amsterdam: North Holland.

Taylor, Ann and Susan Pintzuk (2015), 'Verb Order, Object Position, and Information Status in Old English', in Theresa Biberauer and George Walkden (eds), *Syntax over Time: Lexical, Morphological, and Information-Structural Interactions*, Oxford: Oxford University Press, pp. 318–35.

Traugott, Elizabeth (1992), 'Syntax', in Richard M. Hogg (ed.), *The Cambridge History of the English Language, Volume 1: The Beginnings to 1066*, Cambridge: Cambridge University Press, pp. 168–289.

van Kemenade, Ans (1987), *Syntactic Case and Morphological Case in the History of English*, Dordrecht: Foris.

Note

1. JasonFruit, *Hacker News*, available at <https://news.ycombinator.com/item?id=5057574> (last accessed 9 May 2017).

3

Old English before 1100

In this chapter, we'll analyze several Old English texts, organized in terms of complexity, not chronologically. Some of the texts have been used as examples in earlier chapters. For each text, a facsimile of the manuscript, a transcription of that text, and a translation are given in the first subsection. After that, a sentence-by-sentence analysis follows in the second subsection with comments on the issues discussed in Chapter 2, namely word order, nominal and verbal endings, pronouns, and clause combining. The third subsection provides a general characterization of the stage that the text is in and its dialect, if it is possible to determine that.

In section 3.1, we'll start with some notes on the scripts used by the scribes and on the transcription method. Then, in section 3.2, a part from a West Saxon prose text in a narrative style, *Orosius*, is analyzed. In section 3.3, we'll analyze a part of Aelfric's *Homilies*, again in West Saxon. In section 3.4, we discuss two glosses and a version of the New Testament book of Matthew from three different dialect areas, namely the Northumbrian, Mercian, and West Saxon ones. In section 3.5, parts of two early poetic texts, namely *The Wanderer* and *The Wife's Lament*, are analyzed. Section 3.6 is a brief conclusion.

3.1 The script

Old English scribes use a script that had been developed by Irish monks, called the insular script. It was adapted from the script used to write Latin, the uncial script, and incorporates some (Germanic) runic letters, an indication that runic literacy was possibly common. The uncial script can be written in what we might refer to as capitals, called majuscule, or with lower case letters, referred to as minuscule. The uncial script is used for the Latin produced in England. For instance, the Latin that is the base of the English gloss in Figure 3.6 is written in the (half-)uncial script. Later developments from the insular minuscule are the Anglo-Saxon minuscule, the Carolingian minuscule, and the Gothic scripts, and many forms in between. Gothic scripts become important in the Middle English period so I discuss them in Chapter 4.

The capital letters of the insular script used for Old English are relatively easy to recognize; the lower case letters are as in Figure 3.1 to which should be added the ash *æ*; the Carolingian letters appear below it. The thorn and eth are replaced by *th* and the wynn by *w* in the latter, and *v* and *z* are added. The actual texts display amazing variation. We will see that the Lindisfarne glosser often has an open *a*, resembling a *u*, although the general hand is insular.

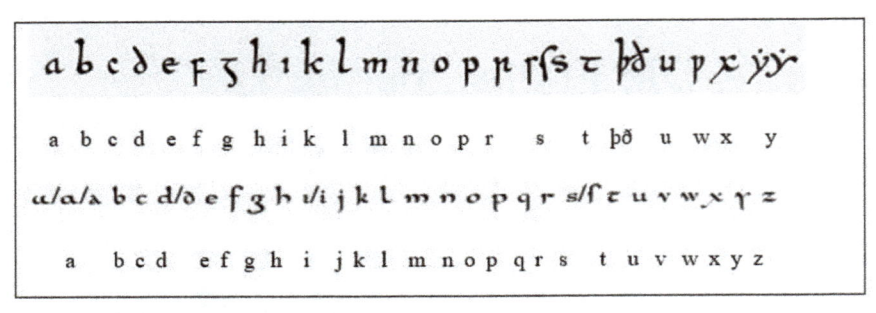

FIGURE 3.1. Insular and Carolingian script, respectively (from <http://guindo.pntic.mec.es/jmag0042/LATIN_PALEOGRAPHY.pdf>, last accessed 4 June 2017. Reproduced with permission from Juan-José Marcos)

The insular hand is exemplified in *Beowulf* and the texts of this chapter. It shows a 5-like *g*, an *f* that lies low, an *r* with a long tail (which is very similar to the *s*), lacks dots on the *i*, and has a closed *a*, among other characteristics. See the snip taken from Figure 2.2.

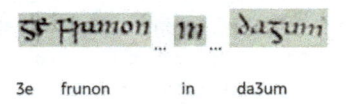

3e   frunon   in   da3um

The *-unon* and *-um* show letters made up of vertical strokes, called minims, which make certain sequences of *m*, *i*, *u*, and *n* hard to read, especially before the use of a dotted *i*.

Typical for the Carolingian hand, which is used for Latin manuscripts, is the emphasis on legibility and less variation in the shapes of letters. Its *g* is rounder at the top, its *f* is higher on the line, the *r* is without a tail, the *i* may be dotted, and the *a* may have a hook at the top. The next snip, taken from the tenth-century *Ramsey Psalter*, illustrates some differences from the insular script. Note the *a* and *r* in *misericordia* and *mea* and the *r*, *f*, and *g* in *refugium*. These are all typical for the Carolingian script.

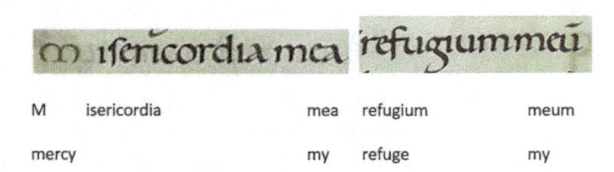

M	isericordia		mea	refugium		meum
mercy			my	refuge		my

(from <http://medievalwriting.50megs.com/scripts/examples/carol1.htm>, last accessed 9 May 2017)

The Carolingian hand originates on the continent with Charlemagne, and is used for Latin manuscripts in the time of Alfred and has some influence on English as well. The manuscripts discussed in this chapter can all be said to use the insular or Anglo-Saxon minuscule with some influence from the Carolingian script. Capitalization, abbreviation, and punctuation differ in interesting ways among texts as well. These characteristics will be pointed out when looking at the specific texts.

In transcribing the manuscripts, I have kept the special letters æ, Þ, ð, 3, and p, but modernized the r, s, and f. Occasionally, the difference between 3 and g is interesting, as in the early and later versions of the *Peterborough Chronicle*. I have kept the 7 'and' and abbreviated conjunctions because the vowels could be pronounced differently in different varieties. The frequent dot above the y is not shown.

3.2 Historical prose narrative: *Orosius*

Orosius was a theologian who wrote a history of world events in Latin in the fifth century and this history was translated into English freely and elaborated upon, possibly by King Alfred, in the late ninth century. Its syntax may therefore be influenced by Latin. The Old English *Orosius* is known to us from two manuscripts, the older of which is known as the Tollemache or Lauderdale Orosius and is used here (see Figure 3.2); the other is referred to as Cotton Tiberius B 1. The language is West Saxon and it was most likely produced in Winchester in the early tenth century, and so it was copied later than King Alfred's time. The text is written using the Anglo-Saxon minuscule, a slightly adapted insular minuscule.

3.2.1 The text

The manuscript is housed in the British Library and is also available as a facsimile edition in Campbell (1953). In the transcription of Table 3.1, I have changed some letters to their modern variants, e.g. the symbols for s and r. Spacing between words is hard to determine accurately but I have left a space when it was clear, e.g. between 3e and *timbred* in line 1. The thorn with a slash through it stands for the conjunction *þæt* and there are other shorthand symbols, for instance a line over a vowel signals a nasal that follows. The 7-like symbol stands for both for the conjunction *and*, e.g. in lines 2, 4, and 5, and for the prefix *ond* in *ondwyrdon* and *ondwyrde* in lines 9 and 12.

In Table 3.2, I give the Old English version from Bately (1980: 28–31; ix), word-by-word glosses, and a translation into Modern English. Bately's edition is the one usually used in scholarly work and I use it in section 3.2.2 because it makes the text easier to parse. The numbers correspond to the sentences in the analysis part.

3.2.2 Analysis

The analysis goes sentence by sentence. As I said above, I have used Bately's spacing and rendering of some letters to make it easier to read. Whenever interesting, however, I point out the differences between Bately and the manuscript.

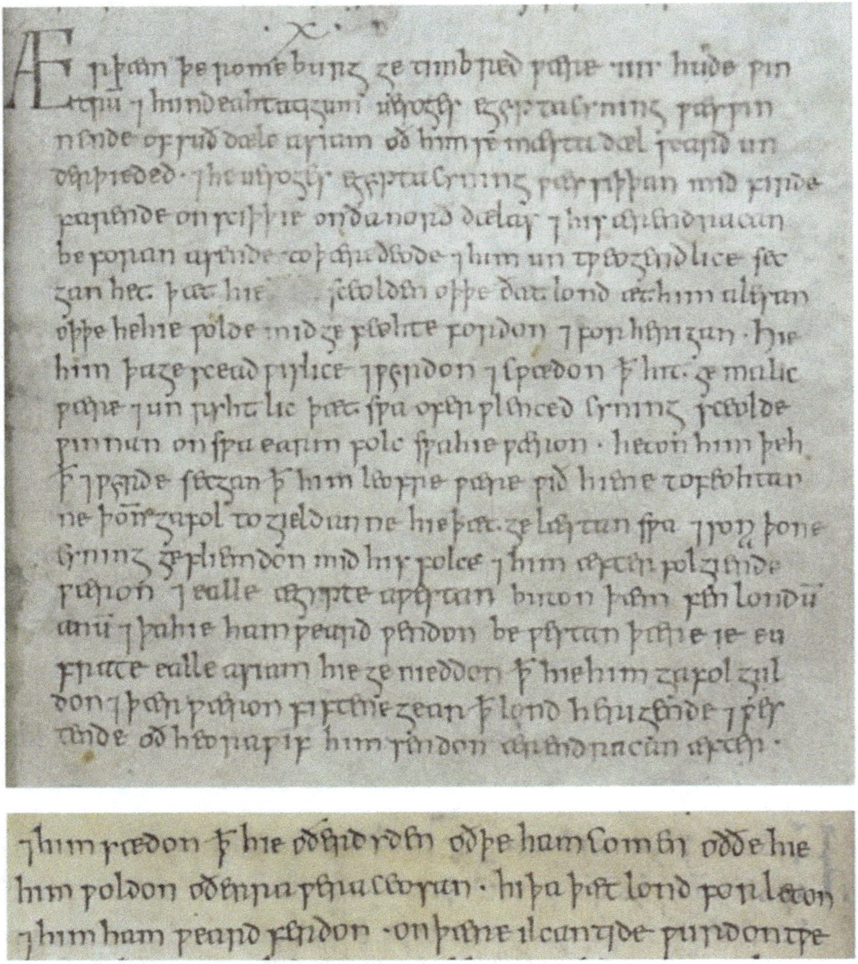

FIGURE 3.2. *Orosius*, Tollemache MS (Add MS 47967, f. 17 and 17v. Reproduced with permission from the British Library Board)

Because it is the first text, I will emphasize word order rather than morphology, which is more challenging perhaps. Remember that plural third person pronouns are very similar to singular ones. Thus, *him* can be dative plural 'them' or singular 'him'; *hie* is nominative or accusative plural 'they' or feminine. The periods used in the manuscript are quite helpful in indicating clausal boundaries.

The first sentence starts with a complicated adverbial clause, then the main clause, and then another adverbial clause. I have put brackets around the subordinate clauses, and have bolded the subject and underlined the finite verb of the main clause.

(1) [[Ær þæm þe Romeburg getimbred wære] iiii hunde wintrum 7 hundeahtatigum] **Uesoges Egypta cyning** <u>wæs</u> winnende of suðdæle Asiam, [oð him se mæsta dæl wearð underþieded].

TABLE 3.1. *Orosius* transcription

Ærþæm þe romeburʒ ʒe timbred pære iiii hunde pin	
trū 7 hundeahtatiʒum uesoʒes eʒyptacyninʒ pæspin	
nende of suð dæle asiam oð him se mæsta dæl pearð un	3
derþieded. 7 he uesoʒes eʒyptacyninʒ pæs siþþan mid firde	
farende on sciþþie on ða norð dælas 7 his ærendracan	
beforan asende to þære ðeode 7 him un tpeoʒendlice sec	6
ʒan het þæt hie — sceolden oþþe ðæt lond æt him alesan	
oþþe hehie polde mid ʒe feohte fordon 7 forheriʒan. Hie	
him þaʒesceadpislice 7pyrdon 7 cpædon ᵬ hit ʒe malic	9
pære 7 un ryhtlic þæt spa oferplenced cyninʒ sceolde	
pinnan on spa earm folc spahie pæron. heton him þeh	
ᵬ 7pyrde secʒan ᵬ him leofre pære pið hiene to feohtan	12
ne þoñ ʒafol to ʒieldanne hie þæt ʒelæstan spa 7 sona þone	
cyninʒ ʒefliemdon mid his folce 7 him æfterfolʒiende	
pæron 7 ealle æʒypte apestan buton þæm fenlondū	15
anū 7 þahie hampeard pendon be pestan þære ie eu	
frate ealle asiam hie ʒe nieddon ᵬ hiehim ʒafol ʒul	
don 7 þær pæron fiftene ʒear ᵬ lond heriʒende 7 pes	18
tende oð heora pif him sendon ærendracan æfter.	
7him sædon ᵬ hie oðerdyden oðþe ham comen oðða hie	
him poldon oðerra pera ceosan. hi þa þæt lond forleton	21
7him ham peard ferdon.	

'four hundred and eighty years before Rome was built, Vesoges, Egypt's king, was fighting in the southern part of Asia, until he had subjugated most of it.'

The first line is introduced by the complex complementizer *ær þæm þe* 'before that that' which can be translated as 'before' in Modern English. It consists of a Preposition Phrase *ær þæm* followed by the complementizer *þe*. After this complementizer, the subject *Romeburg*, a past participle *getimbred* 'built', and auxiliary *wære* 'was' follow before the specification of how long the event of the next clause takes place before the building of Rome, namely 480 years. The form of *wære* is subjunctive (see Table 2.6) because the building of Rome is still in the future. The structure of this initial adverbial shows a formula used to indicate that another part of the story starts and reappears often in *Orosius*. Its structure is very complex. I think that *iiii hunde wintrum 7 hundeahtatigum ær þæm* is the main phrase which has a clause added to the *ær þæm*. The PP including the clause is then preposed because *iiii hunde wintrum 7 hundeahtatigum* is a focused element.

The second part of the sentence (line 2) is the main clause and, in it, we learn that *Uesoges*, Egypt's king, was at war in the southern part of Asia, *suðdæle Asiam*. Note that *winnende* makes speakers of Modern English think of 'winning' but in Old English *winnan* is more like 'to labor, to fight'. The word order in this main clause (line 2) has the finite verb in second position and the non-finite verb *winnende* immediately following. PP extraposition, as mentioned in Chapter 2

TABLE 3.2. A fragment from *Orosius* in Old English, word-by-word in Modern English, and in a translation

(1) Ær þæm þe Romeburg getimbred wære iiii hunde wintrum 7 hundeahtatigum, Uesoges, Egypta cyning, wæs winnende of suðdæle Asiam, oð him se mæsta dæl wearð underþieded.	(1) Before that Rome city built was four hundred winters and eighty, Vesoges, Egypt's king, was conquering of south part Asia, till him the most part became subjugated.	(1) 480 years before Rome was built Vesoges, Egypt's king, was fighting in the southern part of Asia, until he had subjugated most of it.
(2) 7 he Uesoges, Egypta cyning, wæs siþþan mid firde farende on Sciþþie on ða norðdælas, 7 his ærendracan beforan asende to þære ðeode, 7 him untweogendlice secgan het þæt hie [oðer] sceolden, oþþe ðæt lond æt him alesan, oþþe he hie wolde mid gefeohte fordon 7 forherigan.	(2) And he Vesoges, Egypt's king, was then with army going to Scythia in the north parts, and his messengers before sent to that people, and them undoubtingly say commanded that they either should, or that land for him pick or he them wanted with fighting destroy and ravage.	(2) And Vesoges, Egypt's king, then went with his army to the northern parts of Scythia, and sent his messengers before him to the people, and commanded them to say in no uncertain terms that they either should pay him for that land or that he would destroy them through war.
(3) Hie him þa gesceadwislice ondwyrdon, 7 cwædon þæt hit gemalic wære 7 unryhtlic þæt swa oferwlenced cyning sceolde winnan on swa earm folc swa hie wæron.	(3) They him then wisely answered and said that it was greedy and unjust that such rich king should wage war on such poor people as they were.	(3) They then wisely answered him and said that it was greedy and unjust that such a rich king should wage war on such a poor people as they were.
(4) Heton him þeh þæt ondwyrde secgan, þæt him leofre wære wið hiene to feohtanne þonne gafol to gieldanne.	(4) (They) told them though that answer give, that them better was against him (the king) to fight than taxes to yield.	(4) They told the messengers to answer the king that they would rather fight to pay taxes.
(5) Hie þæt gelæstan swa, 7 sona þone cyning gefliemdon mid his folce, 7 him æfterfolgiende wæron, 7 ealle ægypte awestan buton þæm fenlondum anum.	(5) They that did so, soon that king drove away with his people, and him chasing were, and all Egypt waste lay except the fenlands only.	(5) They that did and soon drove the king away with his people, and they were chasing him and destroyed all of Egypt except the fenlands only.
(6) 7 þa hie hamweard wendon be westan þære ie Eufrate, ealle Asiam hie genieddon þæt hie him gafol guldon, 7 þær wæron fiftene gear þæt lond herigende 7 westende, oð heora wif him sendon ærendracan æfter, 7 him sædon þæt hie oðer dyden, oþþe ham comen oððe hie him woldon oðerra wera ceosan.	(6) And then they homewards turned by West (of) the river Euphrates, all Asia they forced that they them taxes yielded, and (they) there were 15 years that land harassing and wasting, until their wives them sent messengers after, and them told that they either did, either home come or they them would other men choose.	(6) And then they turned homewards at the West of the river the Euphrates, and forced all of Asia to pay them taxes and they were there for 15 years harassing and wasting that land, until their wives sent messengers after them, and told the men that they either come home or that the women would choose other men.
(7) Hi þa þæt lond forleton, 7 him hamweard ferdon.	(7) They then the land left, and them home took.	(7) The men then left the land and took themselves home.

(section 2.2.2), accounts for this word order in that *of suðdæle Asiam* is placed to the right of the verbs.

Then (line 3), we encounter another adverbial, introduced by the complementizer *oð*, meaning 'until', telling us at which point Vesoges stopped the war, namely when the largest part, *se mæste dæl*, of southern Asia became subjugated, *underþieded*, to him. The verbs are all in final position, typical of a subordinate clause. The subject is *se mæsta dæl* 'the most part' and it follows the object pronoun *him* 'to him' because pronouns often occur before other heavier phrases.

The three lexical verbs in (1), *getimbred*, *winnende*, and *underþieded*, are participles accompanied by what we now call passive and progressive auxiliaries. As mentioned in Chapter 2, there is some debate as to how much lexical flavor these verbs still have. The two passive auxiliaries, *wære* and *wearð*, are often seen as counterparts to stative 'be' and active 'become'. Note the order of the participle and the auxiliary: in the main clause, *wæs winnende* has the order with the auxiliary first but, in subordinate clauses, either order is possible. It is interesting that, in the manuscript, *wæs* is contracted with *win* of *winnende*, a sign of grammaticalization perhaps. See the snip!

ꝑᵹꞃꞇᵻꞃ

The sentence in (2) is again complex and consists of six subparts. The main clause appears in line 1 and has coordinated clauses in lines 2 and 3 and then a complex embedded object in the last lines. Again, I have indicated the subject of the main clause in bold, the finite verb of the main clause through underlining, and the subordinate clause in brackets; the italicized Preposition Phrases (i.e. PPs) are extraposed.

(2)   7 **he Uesoges, Egypta cyning**, <u>wæs</u> siþþan mid firde farende *on Scippie on ða norðdælas*, 7 his ærendracan beforan asende *to þære ðeode*,
7 him untweogendlice secgan het
[þæt hie (oðer) sceolden,
oþþe ðæt lond æt him alesan,
oþþe he hie wolde mid gefeohte fordon 7 forherigan].
'and Vesoges, Egypt's king, then went with his army to the northern parts of Scythia, and sent his messengers before him to the people, and commanded them to say in no uncertain terms that they either should pay him for that land or that he would destroy them through war.'

The sentence starts with the coordinator 'and', represented by the shorthand symbol 7 that introduces the main clause. There is a personal pronoun *he* together with the name *Uesoges* and then the apposition *Egypta cyning* 'Egypt's king', written as one word, which repeats information from the previous sentence. This group is the subject of the first part of the sentence that describes how afterwards, *siþþan*, Vesoges went to the northern parts, *ða norðdælas*, to the Scythians with an army, *mid firde*.

The Modern English simple past 'went' is rendered by means of a past progressive *wæs ... farende*. Its meaning may be more of a durative, i.e. 'continued to go'. Note that this clause has the finite verb *wæs* in the second position but that the other verb *farende* is not in clause-final position. This clause (again) shows extraposition of two PPs. The sentence continues in line 2 after another coordinator to say that Vesoges sent his messengers, *his ærendracan ... asende*, to the people, *to þære ðeode*, beforehand, *beforan*. The word order would be V-final if the PP *to þære ðeode* had not been extraposed. Vesoges is not mentioned explicitly in this clause nor is he mentioned in the third clause in line 3 where he commands the messengers to say, *him ... secgan het*, '*þæt hie [oðer] sceolden, oþþe ðæt lond æt him alesan, oþþe he hie wolde mid gefeohte fordon 7 forherigan*'.

The object of *secgan* is given in the last three lines which tells the people that they, *hie*, either must pay, *sceolden alesan*, him for the land or that he will destroy, *wolde fordon*, and ravage them, *hie ... forherigan*, through battle, *mid gefeohte*. Something has been scratched out in the manuscript, as I show here, which Bately supplies as *oðer*.

This sentence has numerous verbal prefixes, e.g. *a-sende*, *a-lesan*, *for-don*, and *for-herigan*. These add a sense of perfectivity to the meaning and, in the case of *for-*, may transitivize the verb. Note that the three last clauses are verb-final as usual in embedded clauses. The exact meanings of *sceolden* and *wolde* are debated as well: how modal are these auxiliaries really?

The third full sentence starts with the main clause followed by a clausal object in the next three lines. This clausal object has a dummy subject *hit* that stands in for the clause in lines 3 and 4 and the line 4 modifies *folc*.

(3) **Hie** him þa gesceadwislice <u>ondwyrdon, 7 cwædon</u>
 [þæt *hit* gemalic wære 7 unryhtlic
 [þæt swa oferwlenced cyning sceolde winnan *on swa earm folc*
 [*swa hie wæron*]]].
'they then wisely answered him and said that it was greedy and unjust that such a rich king should wage war on such a poor people as they were.'

The main clause starts with the plural pronominal subject *hie* 'they', which refers back to the people that Vesoges had sent a message to. These people then answered, *þa ondwyrdon*, him in a wise manner, *gesceadwislice*, and said, *cwædon*, that it was greedy, *gemalic*, and unjust, *unryhtlic*, that a king so wealthy should wage war (again the verb *winnan*) on so poor a people, *earm folc*, as, *swa*, they were. The three final clauses in lines 2 to 4 are the object of the compound verb *ondwyrdon 7 cwædon* in line 1. The subjunctive *wære* is used in line 2 because the event is not yet realized.

The finite verb of the main clause, *ondwyrdon*, is sentence-medial and the reason for this may be the presence of the coordinated verb *cwædon*. The two would be too heavy in second position and having *ondwyrdon* by itself in second position might lose the emphasis that the two have together. There is extraposition of the PP *on swa earm folc swa hie wæron* after the verb *winnan*.

I have put some brackets in the next full sentence. The points in the manuscript are again helpful.

(4) Heton [him þeh þæt ondwyrde secgan,
    [þæt him leofre wære
    [wið hiene to feohtanne]
    [þonne gafol to gieldanne]]].
    'they told the messengers to answer the king that they would rather fight than to pay taxes.'

As I see it, (4) starts with the main clause and then an embedded clause that itself consists of three other clauses. The first line lacks a subject but it is obvious from the plural *-on* on *heton* 'told' that it is the people who told *him*, i.e. the messengers, to tell (literally *secgan* 'to say') the answer that it was better, *leofre*, for them to fight against *hine*, i.e. the king, than to pay taxes, *gieldanne gafol* . The *þeh* in the first clause can be translated as 'though' or 'however'.

The word order in line 1 is predictable because *heton* is the finite verb and *secgan* the subordinate verb. The three subordinate clauses in lines 2 to 4 are V-final, again as expected. Note that the infinitives in lines 3 and 4 are preceded by *to* and therefore have a *-ne* ending, as compared with the bare infinitive in line 1. Bare infinitives tend to follow modals and verbs of 'command'; *to*-infinitives often express purpose or goal. Here they are subjects to the predicate *leofre wære*.

The next sentence starts with a clause and three finite coordinated clauses follow that all have the same subject as the first clause. I have italicized the extraposed phrases.

(5) **Hie** þæt gelæstan swa,
    7 sona þone cyning gefliemdon *mid his folce*,
    7 him æfterfolgiende wæron,
    7 ealle ægypte awestan *buton þæm fenlondum anum*.
    'they that did and soon drove the king away with his people, and they were chasing him and destroyed all of Egypt except the fenlands only.'

This sentence, unlike (4), has an overt pronoun *hie* 'they' that is the subject of the verb *gelæstan* 'carry out'. The *-an* ending (ᴀɴ) is an infinitival ending but it is likely to be an 'error' for a past tense *-on*, in which case it translates as 'they so carried that out'. The finite verb is not in V2 position because the object *þæt* is a pronoun and can precede the verb.

The next three clauses are coordinated ones and provide us with a follow-up. They say, with an unexpressed subject but a finite verb in the past tense in line 2, that they soon put to flight, *gefliemdon*, the king and his people and that they were pursuing, *æfterfolgiende wæron*, him and laid to waste, *awestan*, all of Egypt except only, *buton ... anum*, for the fenlands. From the accusative demonstrative *þone* before *cyning* in the second clause, it is clear that the king is not the subject but the object of the verb 'put to flight'. The word order of these three coordinate clauses is neither V2 nor V-final but more complex. It could be V-final with

PP-extraposition in line 2 and V-final in line 3. Line 4 shows an infinitival *-an*, and with that, it means 'in order to lay to waste all of Egypt except for the fenlands'.

Sentence (6) consists of three independent sentences.

(6) 7 þa **hie** hamweard <u>wendon</u> be westan þære ie Eufrate,
ealle Asiam **hie** <u>genieddon</u>
[þæt hie him gafol guldon],
7 þær <u>wæron</u> fiftene gear þæt lond herigende 7 westende,
[oð heora wif him sendon ærendracan æfter],
7 him sædon þæt hie oðer dyden, [oðþe ham comen
oððe hie him woldon oðerra wera ceosan].

'and then they turned homewards at the West of the river the Euphrates, and forced all of Asia to pay them taxes and they were there for fifteen years harassing and wasting that land, until their wives sent messengers after them, and told the men that they either come home or that the women would choose other men.'

The first line stands on its own; the next two lines do too; and the last four lines include two coordinated clauses. Again, the main clause subjects, finite verbs, and all extraposed phrases are marked.

The verb *wendon* is used in its older meaning of 'returned' rather than as 'went', as in Modern English. 'They' return homewards, *hamweard*, by the west of the river, *be westan þære ie*, the Euphrates. Lines 2 and 3 in (6) are independent of the one preceding them and say that *hie genieddon* 'they forced' all of Asia to pay them taxes. In Modern English, we would use an infinitival clause in line 3 but, in Old English, this is rendered as *þæt hie him gafol guldon* (literally 'that they them taxes paid').

A coordinated clause follows in line 4 that translates as '(they) were there fifteen years harassing and wasting the land'. This is a sentence with the finite verb *wæron* in V2 position and the non-finite verbs *herigende 7 westende* in V-final position. In line 5, we find out that this stay lasted *oð* 'until' – we see the same *oð* as in (1) but reinforced with *þe* – their wives sent, *heora wif... sendon*, messengers, *ærendracan*, after them. The word order in line 5 is atypical for a speaker of Modern English because the pronoun *him* 'them' going with *æfter* is dislocated from it. The verb *sendon* is in V3 position because the pronominal object needs to precede it.

The clause in line 6 is coordinated to the previous ones with the wives as unexpressed subject. The wives told them in lines 6 and 7 that there were two choices: either (for the men) to come home or for the wives to choose, *ceosan*, other *wera* 'men'. The structure of the disjunction in lines 6 and 7 is quite complex. The verb *dyden* has *oðer*, meaning one of the two, as its object but this object is then explained more by an *oðþe ... oððe* 'either ... either' clause.

The word order in the last sentence of this excerpt is unusual in that it is a main clause which has the object *þæt lond* precede the finite verb *forleton*.

(7) **Hi** þa þæt lond <u>forleton</u>,
7 him hamweard ferdon.
'the men then left the land and took themselves home.'

Old English before 1100

The verb *ferdon* in the coordinated clause is the past plural of a verb that means 'go' but it has a reflexive pronoun *him* – sometimes referred to as ethic(al) dative – that may indicate that the action was finished (perfective aspect). It too has a V-final word order. Structurally, the passage is a coordinated clause and translates as 'they then left that land and got themselves home'.

3.2.3 Stage of the language and dialect

In the above, a few linguistic characteristics were pointed out that are relevant to understanding the meaning and syntax of the fragment of *Orosius*. Let's now add a summary of the stage the language is in. The word order and inflections in this text show it to be solidly synthetic, the style is quite complex, and the dialect West Saxon. There is, however, a dummy subject it, *hit*, in (3), and lots of auxiliaries, both signs of analyticity.

As for the word order, main clauses often have their verbs in the 'middle' due to the extraposition of PPs; the second line in (1) and the first line of (2) are good examples of this. Subordinate clauses also may have their verbs in the 'middle', and the third line of (3) is a good example. Hence, the V2 and V-final claimed for Old English are not always visible in this text. Pronouns occur in fairly initial position, as e.g. line 3 of (10) and lines 3 and 6 of (2) show, which is typical for Old English.

The case system retains all distinctions of the system outlined in Chapter 2 although I haven't commented on the morphology a lot. There is a dative *-e* and accusative plural *-as* in (2). The accusative third person accusative (*hine* and *hiene*) and dative (*him*) still differ in (4). Demonstratives are not used here to refer to persons but appear before nouns and are marked with case, e.g. the accusative demonstrative pronoun *þone* before *cyning* in (5). There are no articles yet.

The endings on verbs show past tense plural, e.g. *ondwyrdon*, *cwædon* and *wæron* in (3); present participle endings, e.g. *herigende 7 westende* in (6); infinitival endings on *secgan*, *forlesan*, and *forherigan* in (2) – and on *fordon*. Auxiliaries are relatively frequent. I counted ten, including the modals *sceolden*, *wolde*, *sceolde*, and *woldon*. The remaining six auxiliaries include two passives (*wære* and *wearð* in (1)) and four progressives (*wæs* in (1) and (2) and *wæron* in (5) and (6)). There are three copula verbs, all subjunctive or past *w*-forms (*wære* in (3) and (4) and *wæron* in (3)). As mentioned, aspectual prefixes on verbs are frequent, e.g. *a-* and *for-*; this is typical for Old English. Note that the *ge-* participial prefix is often separate from the verb, as in line 1. One sees this in many manuscripts, e.g. the *Peterborough Chronicle*.

The structure of the sentences is quite complex, i.e. not paratactic; the minimum complexity is two clauses in (7) and, depending on the analysis, the maximum is nine in (6), and varies in conjunctions and clause type. The periods in this part of the manuscript initially follow full sentences, i.e. ones with at least one finite clause, in lines 4, 8, 11, but then cease until they reappear in lines 19 and 21.

As for the dialect, Bately (1980: xxxix) types it as early West Saxon with some possible northern influences. The occurrence of *lond* (line 8) and *ond-* (line 11) might indicate northern influence; *earm* (line 13) and *eall(e)* (lines 18 and 20) show it to be West Saxon rather than non-West Saxon *arm/erm* and *all(e)*. The main clause word order doesn't provide V3 sequences that are more likely in the South than the North but many clauses are subordinate so there aren't many instances to check this with. There are no negatives to use for an analysis and pronouns are solidly Old English, namely the singular *he*, *his*, *him*, and *hiene* and the plural *hi(e)* and *heora*.

3.3 Sermon: Wulfstan on the Antichrist

Wulfstan was a bishop of London and of Worcester and later archbishop of York who wrote homilies, i.e. sermons, and law codes in English and in Latin. In this section, we'll look at a text by Wulfstan called 'Of the times of the Anti Christ'. The language is late West Saxon with some northern influence, especially on the vocabulary, and the text contains some code switching between English and Latin.

3.3.1 The text

The first three pages of the Corpus Christi College, Cambridge manuscript 419 appear in Figures 3.3 to 3.5. Napier (1883) provides an edited version of Homily 42.[1] The manuscript is small and it is really hard to see the periods and the abbreviations so the transcription of Figures 3.3 to 3.5 may not be completely accurate. As before, the transcription is given with some modernized letters, a word-by-word translation, and a regularized translation.

3.3.2 Analysis

The homily starts with an address, *leofan men* 'dear men', which is a nominative plural form, as we'll see below.

The first sentence includes three clauses. The punctuation is certainly less sparse than in *Orosius* as there are three periods in this one sentence. The periods mark clauses or phrases, not just sentences.

(8) us is mycel þearf. [þ we wære beon. þæs egeslican timan [þe towerd is]].
     'we need to be aware of the awful time that is approaching.'

The first clause involves an impersonal construction which, in Modern English, would be rendered as 'we have need' with a nominative 'we' instead of dative 'us' in 'us is much need'. In Chapter 2, an impersonal verb was defined as one that always has third person singular inflection, and 'is' does. The second clause is the subject of *is mycel þearf*. The need is further explained in 'that we should be aware of the terrible time that is before us' which includes the third clause as relative.

The word order in the first main clause is V2, but the order in the second (subordinate) clause is more complex. There, the verb *beon* occurs after the subject *we* and adjective *wære* but the complement of the adjective *wære*, namely *þæs egeslican timan þe towerd is*, occurs after the adjective. The relative clause *þe towerd is* V-final.

	De temporibus anti cristi	Of times Anti Christ	Of the times of the Antichrist
	LEOFAN MEN:	Dear men:	Dear men:
	us is micel þearf . þ pe þære beon . þæs eʒeslican timan þe topæred is:	us is much need that we aware be . the awful time that approaching is:	We need to be aware of the awful time that is approaching. Very soon now, the time of the Antichrist will arrive which we think and know consciously about. It is the most awful time that ever will have been since the creation of the world.
	Nu bið spyðe raðe ante cristes tima . þæsðe þe pe nan maʒan.7 eac ʒeorne pitan. 7þ bið se eʒeslicesta þe æfre ʒepearð syððan þeos porold ærost ʒescea -ed pæs.	Now be very soon anti christ's time . which we thi- -nk may.and also willingly know. and that is the most.awful that ever became since this world first creat- -ed was.	
	Beþam eʒerlican timan . matheus se ʒod spellere. soðlice þus cpæð. In diebus illis erit tribulatio talis qualis non fuit abinitio mundi nec postea erit þt is on enʒlisc . þspylc	About.that awful time . Matthew that pro- -phet . truly says thus. In days those shall.be tribulation such that not was from.beginning world nor after will.be that is in English . that.such	About that awful time, the prophet Matthew says "For then shall be great tribulation, such as was not since the beginning of the world to this time, no, nor ever shall be" (=KJV, Matt 24.21). In English, this means

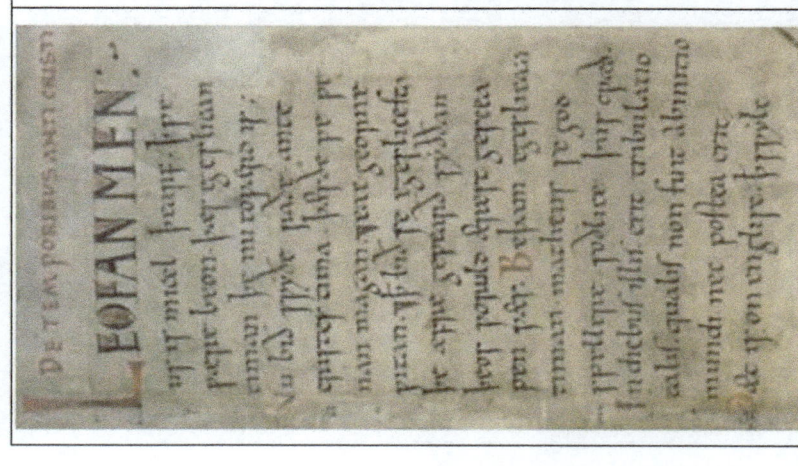

FIGURE 3.3. Wulfstan, first page (Corpus Christi College, Cambridge, 419, f. 1. Reproduced with permission from Cambridge University Library)

yrmð . 7 earfoðnesse . bið þōn on þorulde . sþylce næfre ær næs ne eft ne 3eþeorþeð. Hebið sylf deo	misery . and hardshipness be then on world . such never before not.was not after nor will.become. He is self de-	Misery and hardship will be on the world such as never has been seen or will be seen.
fol. 7þeh menniscman 3eboren. Crist is soð 3od 7 soð man. 7 ante crist bið soðlice deofol.7 man. Se sylfa deofol þe on helle is seþyrð on þā earmscea þenan men ante criste	-vil . and though of.men born. Christ is true god and true man. and anti christ be truly devil and man. The same devil that in hell is he becomes on the wretched-created men anti christ.	He is himself the devil though born of humans. Christ is a true god and man and the antichrist is a true devil and man. The same devil who is in hell becomes the antichrist to wretched men and is truly either devil or man.
7 bið soðlice æ3ðer 3edeo fol 3eman. Nu ma3e þe eoþ eac sec3an . beþæs deofles an3inne. hu he 3eboren bið 7 afedd. spa spa þe on	and is truly either or de--vil or man. Now may we you also say. through that devil's beginning. how he born was and raised. so so we in	Now we may tell you about the devil's origins, how he was born and raised as we have found it in the holy book and which the holy men who came before us often reminds us about
hal3u bocu funden hab bað . 7 us hali3e men þe beforan us þæron oft	holy book found ha--ve and us holy men that before us were often	

FIGURE 3.4. Wulfstan, second page (Corpus Christi College, Cambridge, 419, f. 2. Reproduced with permission from Cambridge University Library)

rædlice on heora ʒepritu mynʒiað.7 sæʒað þæt ante crist sceal beon acenned	wisely in their writings remind . and say that anti christ shall be known	in their writings, (the holy men) wisely remind us and say that the Antichrist shall come from the clan of Dan.
of iudeiscus cynne: 7 of danes mæʒðe. spa spa seo piteʒunʒ sæʒð. *fiat dan coluber in uia: ceras tes insemita.* þæt issy dan	from jewish people and of dan's clan. as as that prophesy says [shall.be dan serpent in way: snake in path] that is. be dan	As the prophesy says, [...] that is in English 'A snake shall be on the road and an adder on the path'. That is then to be understood that the venomous will be on the road
snaca on peʒe. 7 næddre on pæðe. þæt is þon spa to under standenne. þæt spa spa seo atter beren d e nædre liʒeð on ðam	snake on road and adder on path that is then so to understand that as as the poison bear -ing down lies on that	and will want to bite the traveler with its poisonous teeth
peʒe.7 pyle þa peʒ faren dan mid hire ættriʒū toðū slitan.	road . and wants that traveler with its poisonous teeth bite.	

FIGURE 3.5. Wulfstan, third page (Corpus Christi College, Cambridge, 419, f. 3. Reproduced with permission from Cambridge University Library)

TABLE 3.3. The -*an* declension for the noun *tima*

	singular	plural
NOM	se tima	þa timan
GEN	þæs timan	þara timena
DAT	þæm timan	þæm timum
ACC	þone timan	þa timan

All three verbs are copulas but the choice of the second verb *beon* indicates something special. It may be a future or modal meaning, i.e. we should be aware, where the shape of the first and third verbs shows more immediate relevance. The case on the determiner *þæs* is genitive, since we should be 'aware of' something.

The endings on the adjective *egeslican* and the noun *timan* are ones we haven't discussed before. These words should be marked for genitive singular (after *wære*). The noun *tima* has M(asculine) gender but Table 2.3 doesn't mention the *-n* ending. Nouns of this kind have a special paradigm, the *-an* declension – sometimes called the weak declension – with the forms given in Table 3.3. Knowing this, *timan* indeed has the appropriate ending for a genitive singular.

Adjectival endings haven't been discussed either in Chapter 2. They can be weak (definite) or strong (indefinite) with the weak ones in pre- or post-nominal position or on their own, as in (9), and the strong ones in either pre- or post-nominal position, as in (10). The situation is quite complex in Old English, as e.g. Mitchell (1985: 51–80) shows.

(9) *Ic þæm* **godan** *sceal for his modþræce madmas beodan.*
    I that good shall for his daring precious-things give
    'I'll give treasures to the good one for his daring acts.' (*Beowulf* 384–5)

(10) *þæt wæs* **god** *cyning*
     'that was a good king.' (*Beowulf* 11)

The adjective we are looking at (*egeslican*) appears after a demonstrative and is therefore definite. The entire set for adjectives agreeing with masculine nouns is given in Table 3.4 and again the ending is as predicted for a singular genitive. The neuter and feminine differ only slightly.

The next sentence consists of one main and a subordinate relative clause with a compound verb.

TABLE 3.4. The definite adjective declension

	singular	plural
NOM	egeslica	egeslican
GEN	egeslican	egeslicra
DAT	egeslican	egeslicum
ACC	egeslican	egeslican

Old English before 1100

(11) Nu bið swyðe raðe **ante cristes tima**. [þæsðe we wenan magan . 7 eac georne witan].
'very soon now, the time of the Antichrist will be, which we may think and know consciously about.'

The first finite verb *bið* is in V2 position and the choice of *bið* rather than *is* indicates a future reference. The relative clause that follows has a main verb followed by a modal and then a coordinated clause with the verb *witan* in final position.

This time, *tima* is a subject and the nominative indeed lacks an *-n* ending, according to Table 3.4. *Christes* has a genitive ending. There is nothing striking about the verbal endings, except for *magan*, which has an infinitival *-an* (magan) rather than the present plural *-on* typical for these verbs (see Campbell 1959: 345–6 and Table 2.8). The relative pronoun is a genitive demonstrative *þæs* followed by the complementizer *ðe*, a possible sequence in Old English.

The third sentence includes three clauses, a main clause, a relative, and an adverbial.

(12) 7 þ bið se egeslicesta [þe æfre gewearð [syððan þeos woruld ærost gesceapen wæs]].
'and it is the most awful (time) that has ever been since the world was created.'

The verb in the main clause is the copula *bið* and it sits in V2 position (not counting the 7) followed by a V-final relative clause and an adverbial which is also V-final and is headed by the conjunction *syððan*. The relative pronoun, as in (8), is a simple particle *þe*.

There are appropriately case marked demonstratives, e.g. the nominatives *se* and *þeos*. These demonstratives are possibly more frequent here than they are in early Old English. The adjective *egeslicesta* has a superlative ending *-est* and the ending *-a* is appropriate for a nominative; see Table 3.4. This word (and its demonstrative) have nominative case because they are subject predicates.

Leaving the Latin quote out, we encounter a main clause with the verb *cwæð* in a relatively late position. The verb may be late because the emphasis is on the quote that follows it.

(13) Beþam egerlican timan. **matheus se god spellere**. soðlice þus cwæð.
'about that awful time, the prophet Matthew truly says the following.'

Again there are two demonstratives that precede nouns, *þam* and *se*, appropriately marked for dative and nominative, respectively. The adjectives *egerlican* and *god* and the noun *timan* are appropriately marked for dative singular (of the definite declension), nominative singular (which we'll learn more about below), and dative singular, respectively.

The sentence after the quote explains what the Latin says.

(14) þt is on englisc [þ swylc yrmð. 7 earfoðnesse bið þōn on worulde. [swylce næfre ær næs [ne eft ne geweorþeð]]].
'that means in English that such misery and hardship will be on the world as has never before been seen or will be seen.'

It starts with the verb *is* in second position. Three more clauses follow each headed by a copula verb, the future *bið*, the negative *næs* 'not was', and the verb *geweorþeð* 'become'. These subordinate clauses are not strictly V-final as would be usual. Note the multiple negatives for which I provide the manuscript image.

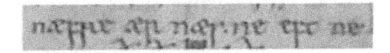

The next sentence consists of two clauses.

(15) **He** bið sylf deofol. [7 þeh menniscman geboren].
'he is himself the devil although born of humans.'

The main clause has the verb *bið* in V2 position whereas the subordinate the verb has *geboren* last, all as expected. Note the emphatic *sylf*, which can occur without a pronoun attached to it in Old English.

Then follow some clauses with more copula verbs in V2 position.

(16) **Crist** is soð god 7 soð man. 7 **ante crist** bið soðlice deofol . 7 man. **Se sylfa deofol [þe on helle is]** se wyrð on þã earmsceapenan men ante criste 7 bið soðlice ægðer gedeofol ge man.
'Christ is a real god and real man and the Antichrist is truly devil and man. The same devil who is in hell becomes the Antichrist to wretched men and is truly either devil or man.'

Christ and the Antichrist are juxtaposed by the choice of the unmarked *is* versus the *bið*, which has the meaning 'not yet realized'. The subject of the third clause, *se sylfa deofol þe on helle is*, contains a relative clause introduced by the relative *þe* with its verb *is* in final position. This subject is repeated before the copula *wyrð* 'becomes' by the demonstrative *se*. A coordinate clause follows without a subject. Its copula is followed by an adverb *soðlice* 'truly' and a disjunctive *ægðer gedeofol ge man* 'either devil or man'.

Let's examine some of the endings. Because we are dealing with copulas, both the subject and subject predicate are in the nominative, so that accounts for the numerous instances of *Crist, man, god*, and *deofol* without an ending. There are two demonstratives and two adjectives. These have the appropriate endings, knowing what we've seen in Tables 2.10 and 3.4. *Se sylfa deofol* is a subject so *se* is the expected nominative and the *-n* less adjectival form of *sylfa* is expected too. The PP *on þã earmsceapenan men* has a nasal indicated above the vowel and *þam* is an expected dative; the adjective *earmsceapenan* occurs after a demonstrative so follows the endings of Table 3.4 for the dative and, of course, *men* is the appropriate plural in Old English, as it still is in Modern English.

Next comes a sentence headed by an adverb *nu* followed by the verb *mage* and then the subject pronoun *we*, making the main clause V2 with a PP *beþæs deofles an ginne* and object clause both of which are extraposed.

(17) Nu mage **we** eow eac secgan. *beþæs deofles an ginne*. [hu he geboren bið 7 afedd. [swa swa we on halgu bocu funden habbað]].
'now we may tell you about the devil's origins, how he was born and raised as we have found it in the holy book.'

In the first part, the subjunctive form of the modal *mage* goes with the verb *secgan* in final position. *Mage* has a plural subject and is reduced from *magen* because it occurs before the subject. The pronoun *eow* is a dative or accusative, appropriate as object. The extraposed PP contains a genitive 'of the devil's'.

The second clause tells us what is said, namely how the devil was born and raised, and contains an adverbial with its verbs *funden* and *habbað* in final position. Most verbs have the markings that are usual in Old English, the infinitival *-an*, the prefixes *ge-* and *a-* on *geboren* and *afedd*, and the present plural *-að*. The *ge-* prefix will start to disappear in Middle English so it is interesting that we already see that happening here: the participle *funden* lacks the *ge-*.

The PP *on halgu bocu* has nasals marked on the *u*-endings, which makes them dative plurals. I reproduce the image here.

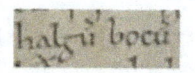

I have not yet provided the paradigm for the indefinite declension of the adjective, but Table 3.5 does that for *halig*. You can see the *halgum* is right for Old English. Irrespective of the gender of the noun, the ending is always the same in the plural. In this case, *boc* is feminine.

In (18), there is a main clause containing two other clauses, a relative clause *þe beforan us wæron*, and an object clause *þæt ante crist sceal beon acenned of iudeiscsu cynne: 7 of danes mægðe*.

(18) 7 us **halige men** [þe beforan us wæron] oft rædlice on heora gewritu myngiað .7 sægað [þæt ante crist sceal beon acenned *of iudeiscus cynne: 7 of danes mægðe*].

'and the holy men who came before us often remind us in their writings and say that the Antichrist shall be known from Jewish people and of Dan's clan.'

The verbs that go with the main clause, *myngiað* 'remind' and *sægað* 'say', appear at the end and this is possibly connected to being coordinated and too complex to be in V2 position. What the holy men remind us of is contained in the last clause where the verbs appear in the middle, i.e. where the preposition phrases appear on the right.

The first three verbs are plural, namely a past plural *wæron* and two present plural verbs ending in *-að*. The clause after that has a modal and a passive, namely *sceal beon acenned* 'shall be recognized'. The first word of this entire sentence is the object *us* with the subject *halige men þe beforan us wæron* 'holy men that came before us' following. *Men* is masculine so *halig* has

TABLE 3.5. Indefinite declensions of *halig* 'holy'

	Smasc	Pmasc	Sfem	Pfem	SNeuter	Pneuter
NOM	halig	halge	halgu	halga	halig	halgu
GEN	halges	haligra	haligre	haligra	halges	haligra
DAT	halgum	halgum	haligre	halgum	halgum	halgum
ACC	haligne	halge	halge	halge	halig	halgu

retained its second syllable in appearing as *halige* rather than as *halge* (compare Table 3.5).

Sentence (19) may be subordinate to the previous sentence. It consists of an object clause with a relative clause that itself has another (coordinated) object clause.

> (19) swa swa **seo witegung** sægð ... þæt is [sy dan snaca on wege. 7 næddre on pæðe. [þæt is þon swa to under standenne. [þæt swa swa seo atterberende nædre ligeð on ðam wege .7 wyle þa wegfarendan mid hire ættrigū toðū slitan]]].
> 'as the prophesy says ... which is in English "a snake shall be on the road and an adder on the path". That is to be understood that the venomous will be on the road and will want to bite the traveler with its poisonous teeth.'

It introduces a warning in Latin (from the Old Testament book of Genesis) about snakes on the road and rephrases that in English by means of a subjunctive *sy* 'will be'. Probably for emphasis, it is yet again rephrased using the verb *is* and an infinitive *to understanne* 'to understand' that we need to be cautious about the venomous snake. The tense on the verb *ligeð* 'lies' is present which emphasizes the real possibility of such a scenario of who wants to bite us.

The word order is as expected: the first clause has a subject and a verb and the lengthy object follows. The object is translated by a verb-initial clause and a main clause with the verb *is* in second position and the verb *to understanne* appearing last. The last clause is the object of the verb 'understand' and is a coordination of two clauses with varied word order: *ligeð* 'lies' is after the adverb but before the locational PP and *wyle* 'will' seems to be in V2 with *slitan* 'bite' in last position.

The inflections on the verbs and the case marking on the nouns are as expected. The subject *witegung* is feminine and therefore the demonstrative preceding it is *seo*. There are dative singular -*e* endings on *wege* and *pæðe* and presumably dative plural -*um* endings on *ættrigum* and *toðum*.

3.3.3 Stage of the language

As mentioned, Wulfstan's *Homilies* are relatively late West Saxon. The verbal and nominal endings are intact, as *egeslican* and *timan* show in (8). The word order is more often strictly V2 and V-last than in *Orosius*. When auxiliaries and verbs are placed at the end of a (subordinate) sentence, the auxiliary is last, as in (12) and (17), typical of a verb-final stage. There are many copula verbs and auxiliaries, such as *magan* in (11), *mage* in (17), and *sceol* in (18), that have a modal meaning. The negative concord evident in (14) presents a southern feature.

The demonstrative forms are clearly inflected and there are no indications of articles. There are no special accusatives, such as *hine* or *mec*, and this suggests southern origin. Relative markers are frequent, the simple *þe* in (8), (12), (16), and (18) and the demonstrative followed by *þe* in (11). The simple relative markers are expected in this West Saxon dialect and for a text from later Old English.

Although I don't focus on phonological characteristics, these are also southern, e.g. the singular *man* in (15) and (16), not *mon*, and the *ea* in *earm* in (16). There is no evidence of palatalization, e.g. *mycel* appears in (8) and not *muchel* or *michel(e)*, as appear in some Old English texts.

Although the frequent use of periods may suggest a paratactic style, this is not the case. There are frequent, clearly marked subordinate clauses, e.g. in (8) with two distinct markers of subordination, the slashed thorn for the object and the relative marker *þe*.

3.4 The Old English Gospels

In this section, we'll examine three versions of the same text to discover some differences between the (earlier) Old English from Northumbria, the Old English from Mercia, and the (later) West Saxon Old English of Wessex. Although the dates and the format (glosses versus translation) are quite different, we encounter some interesting dialect features.

The Northumbrian Glosses date from around 950 CE, the Mercian Glosses from the latter half of the same century, and the Wessex original text dates from around 1000. Glosses provide the Old English translation above the Latin words that the reader was perhaps no longer familiar with. Skeat ([1881–7] 1970) provides a good edition, which I will use below.

In section 3.4.1, I present the texts and a translation, and in 3.4.2, an analysis of the texts. Then in section 3.4.3, I discuss the dialectal differences.

3.4.1 The texts

The Northumbrian interlinear glosses were most likely done by a priest named Aldred but there has been a long and lively debate as to what his source was and what accounts for the linguistic and scribal variation (see Cole 2014: ch. 2).

The Latin original and the glosses above the Latin words are shown in Figure 3.6. A transcription of the Latin is given in (20) and a translation of the Latin appears in (21). Start on the third line of Figure 3.6, which is the beginning of the second book of Matthew. After all three texts have been presented as facsimiles, Table 3.6 will give a transcription of the English of all three. For the analysis of the glosses, I will show images of the text so that the glosses are easier to read.

(20) The Latin; left-hand column:
Cum ergo natus esset iesus in bethleem iudeae in diebus herodis regis ecce magi ab oriente uenerunt hierosolymam. dicentes ubi est qui natus est rex iudaeorum uidimus enim stellam eius in oriente et uenimus adorare eum. audiens autem herodes rex turbatus est et omnis hierosolima cum illo et congregans omnes principes sacerdotum et scribas populi
Finishes in the right-hand column:
sciscitabatur ab eis ubi christus nasceretur. At illi dixerunt ei in bethleem iudeae sic enim scribtum est per prophetam et tu bethleem terra iudanequaquam minima es in principibus iuda ex te enim exiet dux qui reget populum meum israhel.

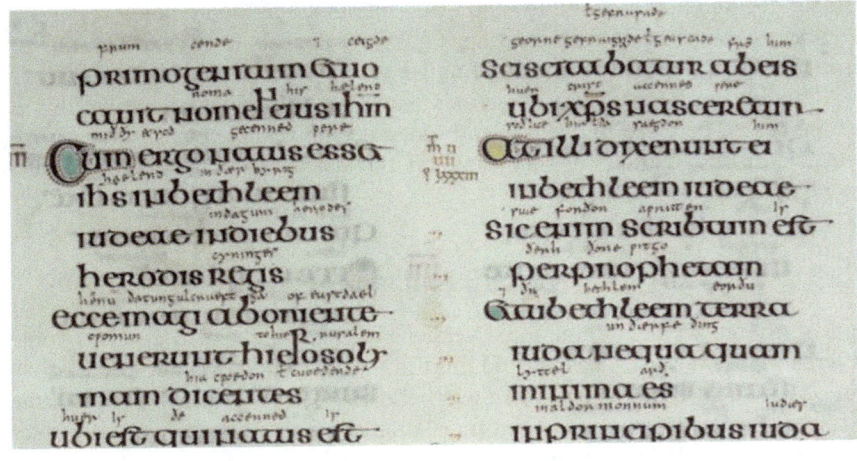

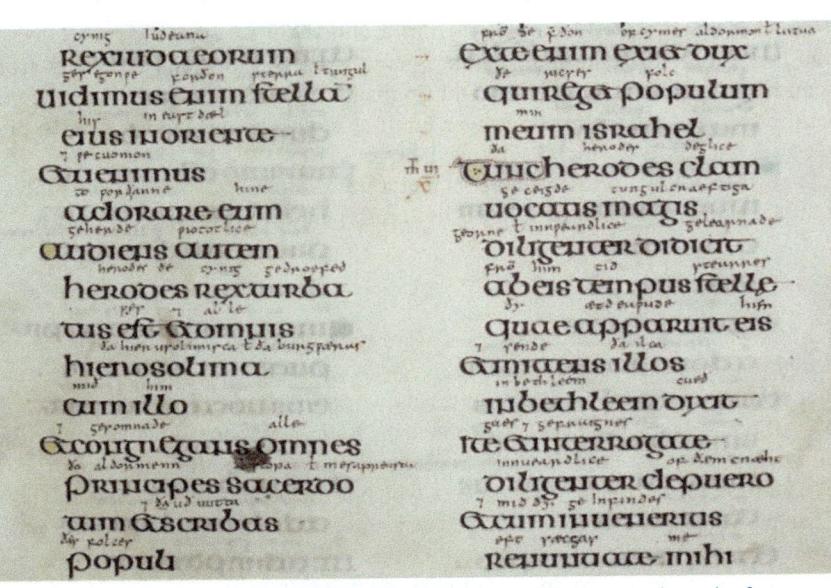

FIGURE 3.6. From the beginning of the Lindisfarne *Matthew*, leaf 30r (Cotton Nero D IV, f. 30. Reproduced with permission from the British Library Board)

(21) Translation of the Latin:
When Jesus was born in the village of Bethlehem in Judea, Herod was king. During this time some wise men from the east came to Jerusalem and said, 'Where is the child born to be king of the Jews? We saw his star in the east and have come to worship him.' When King Herod heard about this, he was worried, and so was everyone else in Jerusalem. Herod brought together the chief priests and the teachers of the Law of Moses and asked them, 'Where will the Messiah be born?' Then said they to him in Bethlehem, in Judea because thus it is written by the prophet. And you Bethlehem, in the land of Judah are

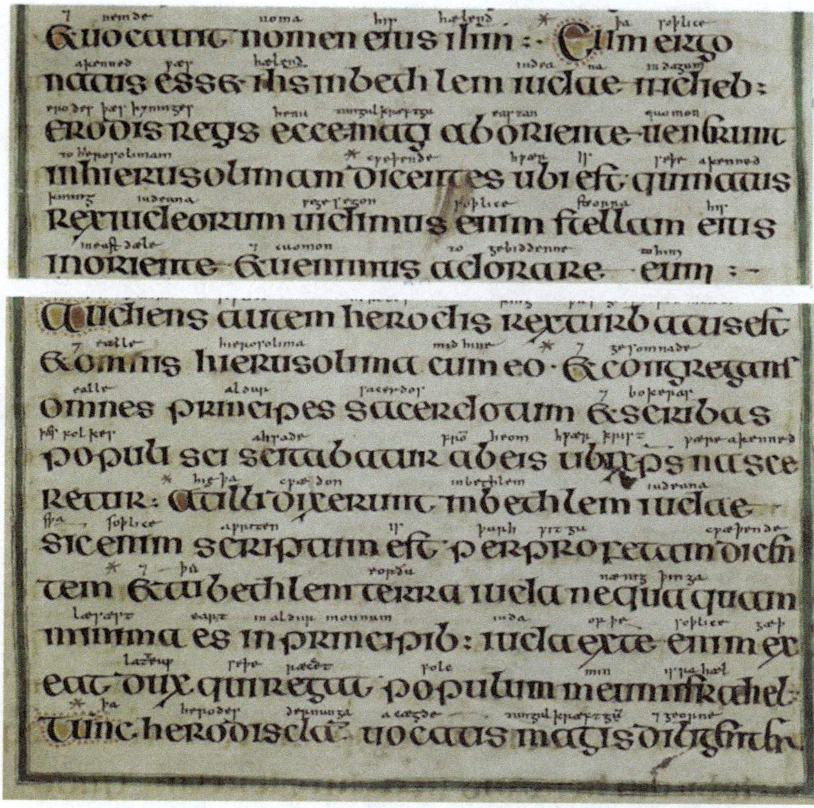

FIGURE 3.7. Rushworth Glosses; with the Latin close but not identical to the transcription in (20) (MS Auctarium D.2.19. Reproduced with permission from the Bodleian Library)

not the least among the princes of Judah. Of you comes forth a ruler who rules my people of Israel.

The glosses to the *Rushworth Gospels* are traditionally divided into Mercian Glosses, said to have been done by Farman, and Northumbrian Glosses, done by Owun. The glosses to the book of Matthew are Mercian, and appear in Figure 3.7. The passage starts above *Cum ergo* in line 1. I have not transcribed the Latin because it is similar to that of Lindisfarne in (20). Note the use of *k* which is not so common in old English.

The West Saxon version from the Corpus Manuscript appears in Figure 3.8 and is a translation from the Latin, not a gloss. It shows some shifts in the letters *s* (*Eornustlice*) and *a* (*acenned*).

The Northumbrian and Mercian Glosses are transcribed in Table 3.6 (as based on Skeat's edition, pp. 28–31) and appear together with the transcription of the West Saxon version. I have not dotted the *y* and have not added nasals where they are abbreviated. The *l* represents Latin *vel* 'or'.

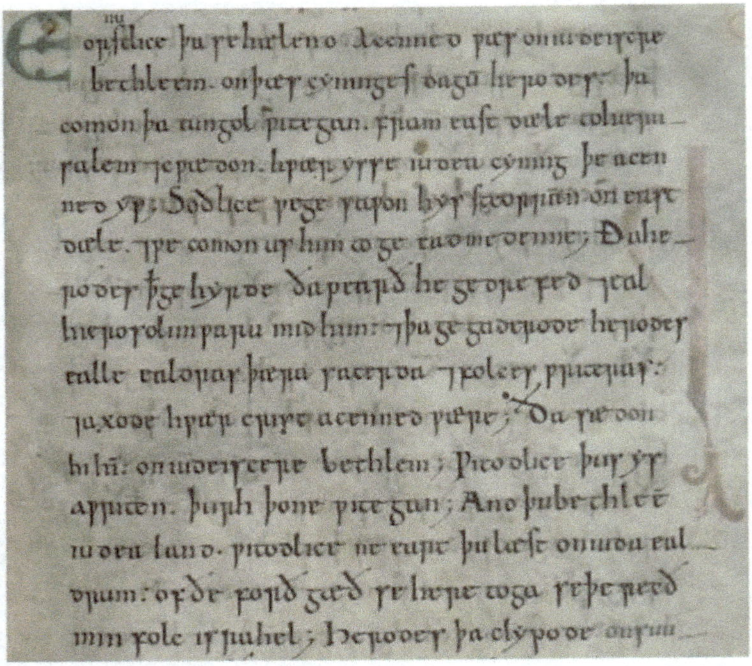

FIGURE 3.8. West Saxon Gospels (Corpus Christi College, Cambridge, 140, f. 3r)

TABLE 3.6. Northumbrian Glosses on the left, Mercian in the middle, and the West Saxon Gospel on the right, based on Skeat ([1881–7] 1970)

miððy ecsoð ʒecenned pere haelend in ðær byriʒ indaʒum herodes cyninʒes heonu ða tunʒulcraeftʒa of east dael cpomun to hierusalem. hia cpoedon *l* cuoeðende huer is ðe accenned is cyniʒ iudeana ʒeseʒon pe forðon sterra *l* tunʒul his in eastdæl 7 pe cuomon to porðianne hine.	þa soþlice akenned pæs hælend iudeana in daʒum erodes þæs kyninʒes henu tunʒulkræftʒu eastan quomon to hierosolimam. cpeþende hpær is seþe akenned is kininʒ **iudeana** pe ʒeseʒon soþlice steorra his in eastdæle 7 cuomon to ʒebiddenne to him.	Eornustlice þa se hælend acenned pæs **on iudeiscre bethleem.** on þæs cyninʒes daʒū herodes. þa comon þa tunʒol piteʒan. fram east dæle tohieru salem 7cpædon. hpær ysse iudea cyninʒ þe acenned ys; Soðlice peʒe sapon hys steorran on east dæle. 7pe comon us him to ʒe eadmedenne;
ʒeherde piototlice herodes ðe cyniʒ ʒedroefed pęs & alle ða ierusolimisca *l* ða burʒpæras mið him. 7 ʒesomnade al le ða aldormenn biscopa *l*	þ þa ʒeherde soþlice herodes kinʒ pæs ʒedroefed in mode 7 ealle hierosolima mid hine. 7 ʒesomnade ealle aldur sacerdos 7 bokeras þæs folkes ahsade frō heom hpær	Ða herodes þʒehyrde ða pearð he ʒe drefed 7eal hierosolimpāru mid him: 7 þa ʒe ʒaderode herodes ealle ealdras þæra sacerda 7 folces priteras : 7axode hpær crist

(Continued)

mesapreasta 7 uð uutta ðæs folces ʒeorne ʒefraiʒnade *l* ʒeascade *l* ʒefrasade frō him huer crist accenned	krist þære akenned. hię þa cpædon in behtlem iudeana spa	acenned þære; Ða sædon hi hī: on iudeiscere bethlem;
þere. soðlice hia *l* ða saeʒdon him suæ forðon apritten is ðerh ðone pitʒo. 7 ðu bethlem eorðu unðærfe ðinʒ lyttel arð in aldormonnum iudæs frō ðe lōon ofcymes aldormon *l* latua ðe ricses folc min.	soþlice apriten is þurh pitʒu cpæþende. 7 þu eorðu næniʒ þinʒa læsæst eart in aldurmonnum iuda of þe soþlice ʒæþ latteup seþe ræccet folc min israhæl.	Þitodlice þus ys apriten. þurh þone piteʒan; And þubethleē iudea land. þitodlice ne eart þu læst on iuda ealdrum: of ðe forð ʒæð se here toʒa se þe recð min folc israhel;

3.4.2 Analysis

I'll discuss the Lindisfarne Glosses first and ignore the word order since that is mostly determined by the Latin original. I provide enlarged parts of the page to make the Old English more readable. After that, we'll look at Rushworth and the Corpus versions. I've modernized the wynn and yogh and some word spacings in the example sentences.

Lindisfarne

The Lindisfarne Glosses are known for having less morphology than their southern and later counterparts. Since the word order mostly follows the Latin, I'll focus on the morphology and where it differs from other Old English texts.

We'll start with the gloss above *Cum ergo*.

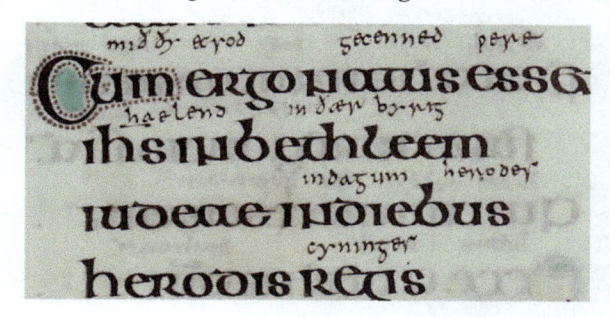

(22) mið ðy   ecsoð gecenned   were
     with that verily brought.forth were
     haelend in ðær   byrig   in dagum herodes cyninges
     savior   in that city   in days   herod   king
     'when Jesus was born in the village of Bethlehem in Judea, Herod was king.'

The case on *dagum*, *herodes*, and *cyninges* is as it would be in other varieties: *dagum* has dative plural, *herodes* genitive, and *cyninges* genitive singular. Note that *Herodes* often ends in *-es* even when it is not genitive, as it is here. There is still an instrumental form of the demonstrative, namely *ðy*. The *ge-* on *gecenned* has not weakened, as we'll see happening in other cases below. Relative to the other versions, we can see interesting morphology with *were* in line 1 which would be *was* in more archaic texts, a sign of morphological simplification. This shows a loss of syntheticity.

The next part starts with the gloss of the Latin *ecce* 'behold', namely *heonu*, with the *o* above the *e*. The passage has a subject *ða tungulcraeftga* 'the astrologers' and a verb *cwomun* 'came'.

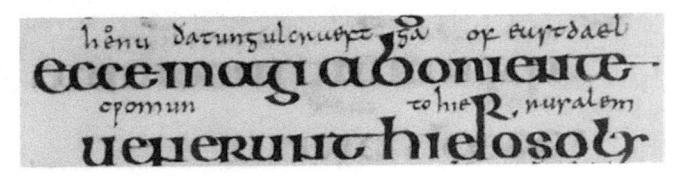

(23) heonu ða   tungulcraeftga of   east   dael cwomun to hierusalem
     behold those   star.crafty   of   eastern part came   to Jerusalem
     'during this time some astrologers from the east came to Jerusalem.'

There are again some peculiarities in the morphology: the endings on *tungulcraeftga* and *cwomun* are not standard, as we find them in the West Saxon version. The noun *tungulcraeftga* is like *tima* which we've seen in Table 3.3, so, from a prescriptive point of view, should have an *-n* ending, and the verb should have a past plural *-on*. There are a few peculiar letters in *tungulcraeftga* and *east*: the *a* is not formed like a *u* but not like an *a* either. Figure 3.1 might help to see what is happening.

The Latin *dicentes* in the next excerpt is glossed with four words, a plural pronoun and two verbs with a coordinator.

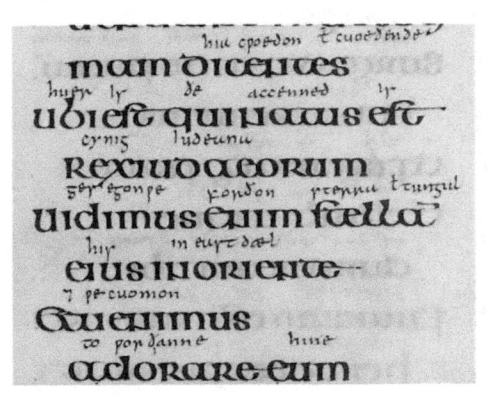

(24) hia cwoedon   ł   cuoeðende huer   is   ðe   accenned
     they said   or   saying   where   is   REL   born
     is   cynig iudeuna   gesegonwe forðon   sterra ł   tungul his
     is   king Jews   saw.we   therefore   star or   wonder his
     in   eastdæl   7   we cuomon to   worðianne   hine.
     in   east   and we came   to   worship   him.

Old English before 1100 71

'they said "where is he who is born king of the Jews?" Because we saw his star in the east and have come to worship him.'

It is noteworthy that the glosser puts the pronoun *hia* in because the Latin lacks it. This addition of *hia* is evidence that the language of the glosser is more analytic than the original.

The next set of words is a direct translation and what looks like a definite article *ðe* is in fact a relative pronoun. The scribal rendering of *a* is again interesting: the pronoun *hia* looks like *hiu*, and *iudeana* and *sterra* look like *iudeunu* and *sterru* in the facsimile. There is evidence for the loss of the endings in the use of *a*- (rather than *ge*-) on *acenned*, reduced from *gecenned*.

In addition to the spelling of the *a*-ending being unclear, the actual ending on *sterra* is not as expected for an accusative (object of *gesegon*). *Sterra* is a noun like *tima* in Table 3.3, so its accusative should it be *sterran* in traditional Old English. Other endings are as expected, e.g. the special masculine accusative *hine*. Note again the two added pronouns *we* with the verbs *gesegon* and *cuomon*, not present in the Latin. This suggests that the glosser isn't comfortable leaving English pronouns out.

Herod continues to be the subject of the next clause, which starts with the verb *geherde*. The word after *Herodes* is *ðe* and then follows *cynig*. The form *ðe* is an early article; if it was a demonstrative, it would be *se*. I have marked the instances of *ða* as DEM here.

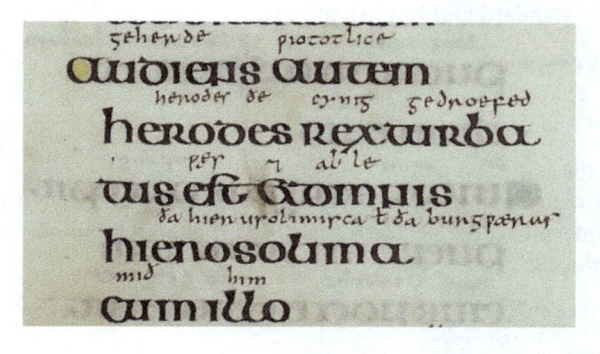

(25) geherde   wiototlice   herodes   ðe   cynig   gedroefed
      heard   certainly   Herod   the   king   worried
      węs   7   al le   ða   hierusolimisca   ł   ða burgwæras mið him
      was   and   all   DEM   Jerusalem   or   DEM citizens with him
      'when Herod heard these things, he was worried and everyone in Jerusalem with him.'

Compare the case on the last pronoun *him* with the other versions. *Mid* is listed in most dictionaries as having either dative or accusative; Mitchell (1985: 505) says the difference is dialectal: the dative in Mercian and Northumbrian and the accusative in West Saxon.

The past participle *ge*- prefix is present twice. The forms *ða* and *burgwæras* are nominative plural, as expected, and the *-sc* on *hierusolimisca* is used to make word meaning 'inhabitant of'. It is the precursor of Modern English *-ish*.

The next part continues with Herod as the subject, though not mentioned, and says who he gathered together.

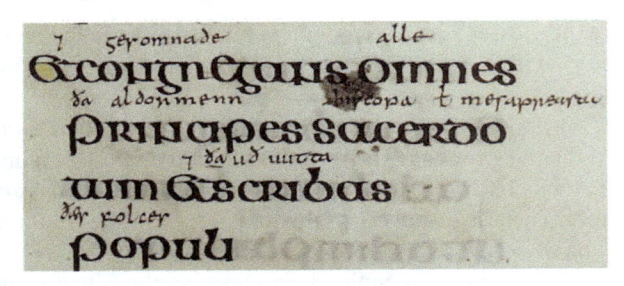

> 7 gesomnade alle
> **& cougnegaus omnes**
> ða aldormenn biscopa ł mesapreasta
> **principes sacerdo**
> 7 ða uð uutta
> **um & scribas**
> ðæs folces
> **populi**

(26) 7   gesomnade   alle   ða   aldormenn   biscopa   ł   mesapreasta
    and gathered   all   those chief   bishops   or   priests
    7   ða   uð   uutta   ðæs   folces
    and those   scribes/scholars   that   people
    'and when he had gathered all the chief priests and scribes of the people.'

This is a fairly straightforward sentence with the verb before the object, following the Latin word order. The cases of *ða*, *ðæs*, and *folces* are as expected: accusative plural *ða*, genitive singular *ðæs*, and the same for *folces*. The forms *biscopa* and *mesapreasta* show reduced endings because the accusative plurals of these would be *-as* (since these are masculine nouns). For instance, Aelfric's *Homilies* shows the standard Old English in (27).

(27) He   þa   gesamnode   ealle   ða   ealdor**biscopas**.
    He   then   gathered   all   those   chief.bishops
    (Innocents: Clemoes; *Catholic Homilies*, 217.15)

The passage ends the left-hand column of that page.

The right-hand column finishes the sentence, giving three synonyms above the Latin for 'asked', all with a perfective prefix *ge-*, although the *acenned* that follows has the reduced form.

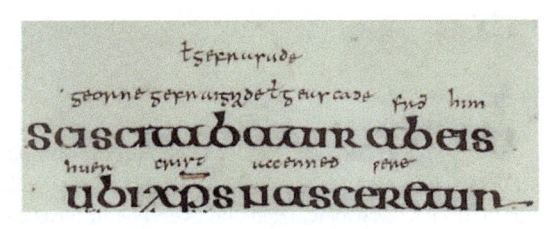

> tgefrnupade
> georne gefrnaigndetg aurcase fra him
> **Sascaubaur abeis**
> huen cnyrt accenned pene
> **ubi xps uascereun**

(28) georne   gefraignade   ł geascade   ł gefrasade   frō   him   huer
    eagerly   asked   or asked   or asked   from   them   where
    crist   accenned   were
    christ   born   was
    'he eagerly asked them where Christ was born.'

The gloss lacks a subject pronoun, which happens more with third person subjects in Old English than with first and second person ones. The subordinate clause adds an auxiliary *were* at the end where the Latin has one synthetic form.

Then comes a sentence with an initial adverb and an interesting coordination.

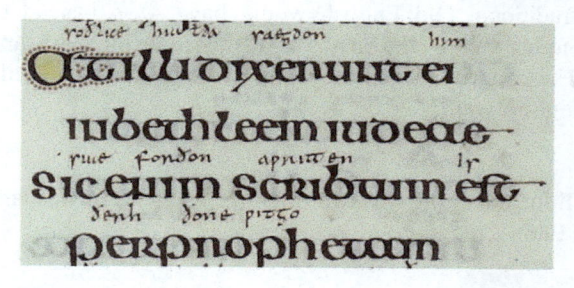

(29) soðlice hia ł   ða   saegdon him   suæ forðon
     Truly they or   those   said   him   so   therefore
     awritten   is   ðerh   ðone   witgo
     written   is   by   the   prophet.
     'truly, they said to him, because thus is it written by the prophet.'

The second word is the subject pronoun *hia*, which may be a translation of the Latin demonstrative subject *illi*. This personal pronoun *hia* is coordinated with the demonstrative *ða* which is evidence for the early ambiguity between personal and demonstrative pronouns. Compared with the Rushworth Glosses, there is an additional demonstrative, namely *ðone*, which appears in the accusative, the 'normal' case after the preposition *ðerh*. As in other sentences, the *ge-* has weakened to *a-* in *awritten* but the ending on *ðone* is as expected.

The last part includes real evidence for a loss of verbal inflection.

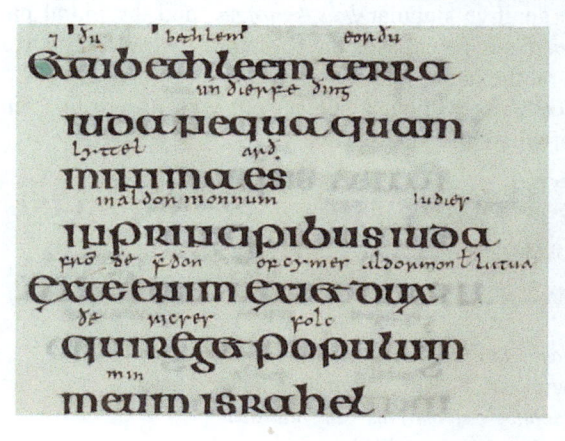

(30) 7   ðu   bethlem   eorðu   unðærfe   ðing   lyttel
     And you   Bethlehem   land   unprosperous   thing   little
     arð in   aldormonnum   iudæs   fro   ðe   fðon
     are among elders   Judah   from   REL   therefore
     ofcymes   aldormon   ł   latua   ðe   ricses folc min.
     comes.forth elder   or   leader   REL   rules   people mine
     'and you Bethlehem, in the land [of Judah], are not the unprosperous little thing among the princes of Judah because from you shall come a ruler who will rule my people.'

There are two third person singular verb forms, namely *ofcymes* 'comes forth' and *ricses* 'rules'. Traditional Old English would have *-ð/-þ* instead of the reduced *-s*. There is another verb *arð*, which is as it is listed in Table 3.6, and two relative particles *ðe*. The case endings on the feminine *eorðu* and the plural noun *aldormonnum* are straightforward.

Rushworth Glosses
The next version we'll look at is the Rushworth Glosses and again we start with the glosses above the Latin *Cum ergo*.

(31) þa soþlice akenned wæs hælend iudeana in dagum erodes
    then truly born was king Jews in days Herod
    þæs kyninges henu tungulkræftgu eastan quomon to hierosolimam.
    that king behold astrologers east came to Jerusalem
    'then truly, the king of the Jews was born in the days of that King Herod.'

The gloss follows the Latin word order and the English morphology. As for the latter, the following endings are as predictable: the genitive plural *-na*, the dative plural *-um*, the genitive singular *þæs kyninges*, and the plural past *-on*. The *a-* prefix on *akenned* is reduced, as is the ending of *tungulkræftgu*. Read the discussion below (23) on the latter.

The second sentence starts without a subject but with a verb first and then follows the question of where the king is.

(32) cweþende hwær is seþe akenned kining iudeana
    saying where is he.REL born king Jews
    we gesegon soþlice steorra his in eastdæle
    we saw truly star his in East
    7 cuomon to gebiddenne to him.
    and came to pray to him
    'they said "where is he who is born king of the Jews?" Truly, we saw his star in the East and came to him to worship.'

The expected markings are found, namely *-ende*, *-ed*, *-ana*, *ge-*, *-on*, *-e*, and another *-on*. The demonstrative *se* serves as the pronoun with *þe* serving as the relative pronoun. Signs of analyticity are the pronoun *we* which is added above the verb where the Latin lacks such a pronoun, the addition of the infinitival marker *to* before *gebiddenne*, and the dative marker *to* before *him*, where again the Latin original lacks these. Old English could also do without the dative *to* so the latter is an indication of change. Note again the lack of an ending on *steorra*.

Next, we have some evidence of Old English word order. Because the Latin verb *audiens* is glossed with an object and adverb preceding it as *þ þa geherde*, we see that the glosser kept Old English in mind as he was glossing. This gloss follows the Old English pattern with a preposed demonstrative object.

(33) þ   þa   geherde   soþlice herodes   king   wæs   gedroefed
     that then heard   truly   Herod king   was   worried
     in   mode   7   ealle   hierosolima   mid   hine
     in   mind   and all   Jerusalem   with   him
     'King Herod, on hearing that, became worried and all Jerusalem with him.'

The last part of the first line also provides some evidence of the syntax of the glosser. In Latin, the words *turbatus est* are glossed as *wæs gedroefed in mode* with the finite verb after the participle and the PP extraposed. The endings are as expected: *mode* shows dative case and *hine* is an accusative pronoun.

The sentence that follows shows some differences with the Lindisfarne version.

(34) 7   gesomnade   ealle   aldursacerdos   7 bokeras   þæs   folkes
     and gathered   all   elders   and scholars that   people
     ahsade   frõ   heom   hwær   krist   wære   akenned.
     asked   from   them   where   Christ   was   born
     'and he gathered all the elders and scholars of the people and asked of them where Christ was born.'

This version has *sacerdos 7 bokeras* as the object of *gesomnade* and, unlike in (26), the endings indicate a clear *-s* plural. That means this less northern version is more synthetic. (The *-os* in *sacerdos* instead of *-as* is quite frequent in Old English.) The order of the auxiliary and verb *wære akenned* is also different.

Next follows the answer to the question.

(35) hię   þa   cwædon   in   bethlem   iudeana
     they   then said   in   Bethlehem Judah

swa soþlice awriten is þurh witgu cwæpende
so truly written is through prophet saying
'they then told him "in Bethlehem" as it is written by the prophet.'

The morphology is what I have been calling traditional Old English, e.g. the past plural *-on* and genitive *-na*, but *awriten* has a weakened *ge-*. The personal pronoun *hie* translates a demonstrative in Latin, again showing that demonstratives and personal pronouns had similar functions. Compared with (29), note the absence of the demonstrative before *witgu*, making this text less analytic than the previous one.

In (36), the subject of the first line is the second person singular *þu* and the first verb we encounter is *eart* which is as expected.

(36) 7 þu eorðu nænig þinga læsæst eart in aldurmonnum iuda
and 2S land not.any thing least are in elders Judah
of þe soþlice gæþ latteuw seþe ræccet folc min israhæl
of 2S truly goes leader 3S.REL stretches people my Israel
'and you are not the least among elders of Judah; from you, a leader will come forth who stretches my people of Israel.'

The third person ending in the second line on *gæþ* is very different from the ending on *ofcymes* in (30). As mentioned in relation to (30), this is the more archaic form. The relative has a demonstrative *se* and *þe*.

West Saxon Gospels

The West Saxon manuscript is one of two West Saxon versions. It is known as manuscript 140, Corpus Christi College, and dates from around 1000.

Because this text involves a translation into Old English and is not glossed above the Latin original, we'll investigate the word order. I have bolded the subjects and underlined the finite verbs of the main clauses, as in sections 3.1 and 3.2, and bracketed the most obvious subordinate clauses. The passage starts with two finite clauses, shown in (37), the first dependent on the other in meaning.

(37) Eornustlice þa **se hælend** acenned wæs on iudeiscre
Indeed then that savior born was in Judah
bethleem on þæs cyninges dagum herodes;
Bethleem in that king days Herod
þa comon **þa tungolwitegan** . fram eastdæle to hierusalem.
then came those astrologers from east to Jerusalem
'when the savior was born in the village of Bethlehem in Judea in the days of king Herod, wise men from the East came to Jerusalem.'

In (37), the clauses are related through the repetition of *þa*. Modern English might instead use a syntactic complementizer, as I have done in using 'when'. The word order in the first clause indicates it is subordinate because the finite verb has not moved to a V2 position. The second clause has V2 and the heavy subject follows it, again typical for Old English. Both clauses have extraposition of PPs.

As for the inflections, there are quite a few that should be familiar: *se, þæs, -es, -um, -on, þa, -an,* and *-e*. As mentioned, some of these endings are more archaic than in the Lindisfarne Glosses, e.g. the *-an* ending on *tungulwitegan* as opposed to *tungulcraeftga* in Lindisfarne. This shows that the West Saxon version is more synthetic.

The next part continues with the subject of 'the astrologers' and informs us what they asked, namely where the king of Judah is.

(38) 7 <u>cwædon</u>. [hwær ys se Iudea cyning [þe acenned ys]]
and said where is that Judah king REL born is
'and they said "where is the king of Judah who has been born".'

The sentence consists of a verb and embedded object clause that includes a relative clause. The word order in the object is V2 because it is a question, somewhat independent of the main clause. The verb and auxiliary are last in the relative clause but there aren't any objects to test if it is really V-last. The grammatical words are *hwær, se, þe,* and *ys*, making this sentence quite analytic. The demonstrative *se* has nominative case, expected because it is part of the subject predicate *se Iudea cyning* and the relative marker is the invariant *þe*.

Next follow two coordinated clauses with an infinitival adverbial included in the second.

(39) Soðlice **we** <u>gesawon</u> hys steorran on eastdæle.
Truly we saw his star in east
7 **we** <u>comon</u> us [him to geeadmedenne];
and we came us him to worship
'truly, we saw his star in the east and have come to worship him.'

The word order in line 1 is V3 with the pronominal subject before the verb, a pattern we have seen in Chapter 2, and V2 in the second coordinated clause. The infinitival clause has a preverbal object *him*.

As for the morphology, compare the endings in (39) with those of (24): *steorran* appears with an *-n* and, unlike the Lindisfarne and Rushworth Glosses, a dative *-e* appears. This makes the West Saxon version more archaic. We also see the use of *him* rather than the *hine* of Lindisfarne, which shows the loss of the distinction between dative and accusative. The pronoun *us* is an ethic dative, used with motion verbs. Its meaning isn't always clear but could be 'for the benefit of' or a measure of intensity.

In the next part, the subject switches to Herod and again, the Modern English would embed the one clause in the other, as I have indicated in the translation and through the underlining/bolding.

(40) Ða herodes þæt gehyrde ða <u>wearð</u> **he** gedrefed
Then Herod that heard then became he worried
7 eal hierosolimwaru mid him:
and all Jerusalem with him
'when Herod heard that, he became worried and all of Jerusalem too.'

The word order seems to indicate that the first clause is subordinate to the second because it is V-final where the second clause is V2. Note the difference between the more dynamic *wearð* in (40) and the more static *wes* and *wæs* in the Lindisfarne and Rushworth versions shown in (25) and (33) above. As I noted in Chapter 2, it is debated if this distinction was really felt by Old English speakers. As also mentioned above, a dative *him* appears after the preposition *mid*, which is typical of the West Saxon dialect.

The next part has a clause and a coordinated other clause with an embedded question.

(41) 7   þa   <u>gegaderode</u> **herodes** ealle   ealdras   þæra   sacerda
     and then gathered   Herod   all   elders   those   priests
     7   folces   writeras   7   <u>axode</u> [hwær   crist   acenned   wære];
     and   people   writers   and asked   where   Christ   born   was
     'and Herod gathered all the elders of those priests and the scholars of the people and asked where Christ was born.'

The first finite verb is in second position and the coordinated verb just introduces the embedded clause, which is verb-final. From a morphological point of view, there are the prescriptively 'correct' accusative plurals *ealdras* and *writeras* and the genitives *þæra sacerda* and *folces*.

Next, I have grouped two independent clauses together in (42).

(42) Ða   <u>sædon</u> **hi**   him : on   iudeiscere   bethlem;   Witodlice   þus
     Then   said   they   him   in   judah   Bethlehem   Truly   thus
     <u>ys</u>   awriten.   þurh   þone   witegan;
     is   written.   through   the   prophet
     'they then told him "in Judah's Bethlehem". Thus, it is truly written by the prophet.'

The first clause is V2 and the second is V3 and lacks a subject. Perhaps interesting in terms of its ending is the accusative *witegan*. This is a noun like *tima* and *steorra* with *-n* in the accusative. The other two versions lack the *-(a)n*.

The last part again has two clauses, with the second including a relative clause.

(43) And   **þu**   bethleem   iudealand.   witodlice   ne   <u>eart</u>   **þu**   læst
     And   2S   Bethlehem Judah   truly   not   are   2S   least
     on   Iuda   ealdrum: of   ðe   forð   <u>gæð</u>   se   **heretoga**
     in   Judah   elders   of   2S   forth   goes   that   leader
     se   þe   recð   min   folc   israhel
     3S   REL   stretches   my   people   Israel
     'and you are not the least among elders of Judah; from you, a leader will come forth who stretches my people of Israel.'

The present tense form *eart* is the same as in Rushworth. Where this West Saxon version (and Rushworth) differs crucially from the Lindisfarne gloss given in (30) is in the endings of the third person singular verb: *gæð* as opposed to *ofcymes*, and *recð* rather than *ricses*. This sets apart Lindisfarne from the other two in being more 'modern'.

3.4.3 Broader view and dialectal differences

Glosses are obviously very different from an actual translation but we can draw conclusions from both kinds of text about the grammar of Old English. Some texts show a loss of morphology and an increase in analytic markings. There are also dialect differences. I start this section with morphology, followed by a discussion of grammatical words, and finally word order.

As we've just seen in (42), the verbal agreement in the West Saxon shows -ð on gæð and -þ on gæþ in (36) in Rushworth. The ending on the verb that corresponds to this in Lindisfarne, namely *ofcymes*, has weakened to -s. I have juxtaposed these in (44abc).

(44) a. from ðe forðon **ofcymes**   *of cymeþ*   Lindisfarne
    b. of þe soþlice **gæþ**   *gæþ*   Rushworth
    c. of ðe forð **gæð**   *gæð*   West Saxon

The perfective prefixes are more frequent in Lindisfarne, at least in this excerpt which has eight *ge-*forms and three with *a-*. In contrast, Rushworth has five *ge-*forms and four *a-* ones and the West Saxon version has four *ge-* and four *a-*forms in this passage. This fits the general trend towards a weakening and loss of *ge-* through time. In this respect, Lindisfarne shows slower change.

As for the marking of nouns, there is a weakening of case in Lindisfarne, as compared with traditional Old English. Thus, *tungulcraeftga* in (23) and *sterra* in (24) lack the *-an* of the West Saxon (37) and (39). Rushworth here follows Lindisfarne in having reduced inflection. There is also a lack of the plural *-as* in Lindisfarne (26) but not in Rushworth (34) and West Saxon (41). The dative with *mid* is non-West Saxon as can be observed in (25).

Lines 6 and 7 of Table 3.6, repeated as (45abc) for the three versions, provide an interesting comparison for the object pronoun. First of all, the Lindisfarne version retains the *hine*, which is a northernism but Rushworth is more analytic in adding a preposition. We can't comment on the word order in (45ab) since it follows the Latin, but (45c) is V2 in the main clause with V-final in the subordinate clause.

(45) a. we cuomon to worðianne **hine.**   Lindisfarne
    b. 7 cuomon to gebiddenne **to him**   Rushworth
    c. we comon us **him** to geeadmedenne.   West Saxon

As mentioned above, the West Saxon in (45c) has an ethic dative, which often accompanies motion verbs.

As we'll see in Chapter 4, the period after 1100 sees an increase in the use of demonstratives and the use of articles. The Lindisfarne and West Saxon versions have a few more demonstratives, e.g. *ðone* before *witgo* in (29) and *se* before *hælend* in (37). The Lindisfarne excerpt possibly shows the earliest use of a definite article in (25).

The personal pronouns are added in Lindisfarne (24) and Rushworth (32) which indicates that finite verbs are felt to need a subject. The personal pronoun is also coordinated with a demonstrative in (29) and this is indicative of the similar status they have in earlier English, namely both could refer to persons. Relative pronouns are most often the simple particle in this passage of Lindisfarne but not in the other two versions (but see Suárez-Gómez 2009 who looks at the entire Gospels and argues that the West Saxon more frequently has a simple pronoun). I have repeated them in (46).

(46) a. **ðe** ricses folc min   *ðe*   Lindisfarne
      b. **seþe** ræccet folc min israhæl   *reþe*   Rushworth
      c. **seþe** recð min folc israhel   *reþe*   West Saxon

As for the word order, we have mainly discussed the West Saxon version because the other two versions usually follow the Latin original. Main clauses favor V2, as in (39), (41), and the first clause in (42). The exception is the second clause in (42) which is V3. As mentioned, some clauses are coordinated in Old English but not in Modern English. Thus, in (37) and (40), the first clause is not V2 which is expected if it is a subordinate. The subordinate last clause in (41) is V-last but the one in (43) is not. It is possible to say that V3 is a southernism but there is only one instance.

As to the style, there are clear markers of subordination in all three texts. Compared with some of the paratactic Middle English texts we'll encounter in the next chapter, these texts are moderately subordinating.

3.5 Poetry from the *Exeter Book*

So far, we have read and analyzed prose texts. The Old English that remains also includes poetic texts and these are more challenging to read. In this section, we'll discuss the last part of a poem known as *The Wife's Lament* and the first part of *The Wanderer*, both elegiac poems from the *Exeter Book*. We've already seen parts of *The Wanderer* in Chapter 2. The poems are without titles in the manuscript. *The Wife's Lament* is the lament of a woman whose lover is elsewhere and *The Wanderer* is a monologue about exile and the transitory nature of life. The word *cearu* 'care, worry' is therefore frequent!

3.5.1 The texts

The excerpt below of *The Wife's Lament* covers the middle of the poem to the end. The facsimile given in Figure 3.9 is taken from Chambers et al. (1933). Because the text is challenging, I have given various renderings in Figure 3.10 and Table 3.7 with the *g* and *w* modernized in the latter. A more modern translation appears as (47). The transcription and translation have used Marsden (2004: 343–4) and Baker (2007: 247–8). In the facsimile, start with the last two words of the first line, namely *heht mec* 'told me'.

(47) They told me to live in a wood grove, under an oak tree in that earthcave. This earthcave is old, and I am full of longing. The valleys are dark; the hills high; cruel towns are overhung with briars, a home without joy. Here, my lord's leaving often overpowers me. There are friends/lovers on earth, beloved while living, sharing a bed, while I walk alone in the light of dawn under the oak-tree

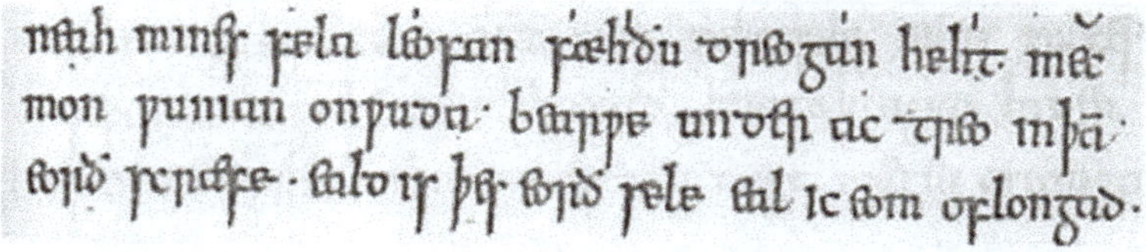

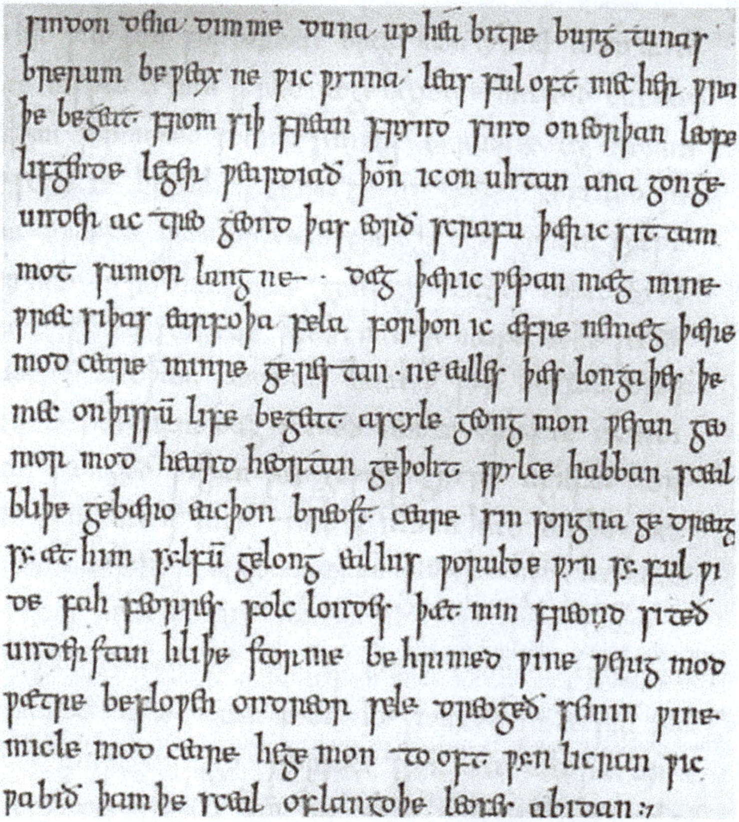

FIGURE 3.9. *The Wife's Lament* from the *Exeter Book*, f. 115r and v (reproduced with permission from the Dean and Chapter of Exeter Cathedral)

and through this earth-cave. There I must sit the long summerday; there I can weep for all my exiles, my many troubles; and so I may never escape from the cares of my sorrowful mind, nor all the longings that have seized my life. May the young man be sad-minded with hard heart-thoughts, yet let him have a smiling face along with his heartache, a crowd of constant sorrows. Let to himself all his worldly joys belong! Let him be outlawed in a far distant land, because my lover sits under stone cliffs chilled by storms, weary-minded, surrounded by water in a sad dreary hall! My beloved will suffer the cares of a sorrowful mind; he will remember too often a happier home. Woe to the one who must suffer longing for a loved one.

[Old English manuscript text]	heht mec mon punian onpuda bearpe under ac treo inþā eorð scræfe. eald is þes eorð sele eal ic eom oflon3ad. sindon dena dimme duna up hea bitre bur3 tunas brerum bepeax ne pic pynna leas ful oft mec her pra þe be3eat from siþ frean frynd sind oneorþan leofe lif3ende le3er peardiað þōn icon uhtan ana 3on3e under ac treo 3eond þas eorð scrafu þær ic sittan mot sumor lan3ne. dæ3 þæric pepan mæ3 mine præc siþas earfoþa fela forþon ic æfre nemæ3 þære mod ceare minre 3erestan. ne ealles þæs lon3aþes þe mec onþissū life be3eat ascyle 3eon3 mon pesan 3eo mor mod heard heortan 3eþoht spyіce habban sceal bliþe 3ebæro eacþon breost ceare sin sor3na 3e drea3 sy æt him sylfum 3elon3 ealhis porulde pyn syful pi de fah feorres folc londes þætmin freond siteð understan hliþe storme behrimed pine peri3 mod pætre beflopen ondreor sele dreo3eð semin pine micle mod ceare he3e mon tooft pyn licran pic pabið þam þe sceal oflan3oþe leofes abidan.

FIGURE 3.10. *The Wife's Lament* and a transcription

A facsimile of *The Wanderer* is given in Figure 3.11.[2] In Figure 3.12, I have provided a transcription of the first twelve and a half lines as they appear in the manuscript.

Table 3.8 again modernizes a few of the letters and provides a translation. The translation in (48) is based on Hogg (1992b: 22–3).

> (48) Often the solitary dweller waits for favor, for the mercy of the creator, although he, troubled in heart, has for a long time, across the sea-ways, had to stir with his hands the ice-cold sea, travel the paths of an exile. Fate is fully determined. Thus spoke the wanderer, mindful of troubles, of cruel battles, of the fall of loyal kinsmen. Often, alone at each dawn, I have had to lament my sorrows; now there is no one alive to whom I dare reveal my thoughts openly. I know too truly that it is a noble virtue in man that he should bind his heart and hold the treasury of his thoughts, think as he will. The weary mind cannot withstand fate nor can the troubled mind provide help. Therefore those eager for glory must bind fast a heavy heart sorrowfully.

3.5.2 Analysis

Having seen the manuscript images and the transcription, we will now discuss the two excerpts. The finite verbs are underlined, the subjects of the main clause are bolded, and brackets are placed around embedded clauses.

The Wife's Lament

This stage of the language is fairly synthetic: the word order is very free and the endings on nouns and verbs are complex.

TABLE 3.7. Transcription and word-by-word gloss of *The Wife's Lament*

heht mec	told me
mon wunian onwuda bearwe under ac treo inþam	man live in wood grove under oak tree in that
eorð scræfe. eald is þes eorð sele eal iceom oflongad.	earth cave. old is this cave dwelling all I am longing.
sindon dena dimme duna up hea bitre burg tunas	are valleys dark hills high biting towns
brerum beweax ne wic wynna leas ful oft mecher wra	briars overgrown place without full often me her cru-
þe begeat from siþ frean frynd sind oneorþan leofe	elly assailed from leaving lord friends are on earth dear
lifgende leger weardiað þonne icon uhtan ana gonge	living bed occupy then I at dawn alone walk
under ac treo geond þas eorð scrafu þær ic sittan	under oaktree through these caves there I sit
mot sumor langne. dæg þæric wepan mæg mine	must summer long day there I weep must my
wræc siþas earfoþa fela forþon ic æfre nemæg þære	wretched journey hardships many for I ever not may those
mod ceare minre gerestan. neealles þæs longaþes þe	troubles my rest. not all those longings that REL
mec onþissum life begeat ascyle geong mon wesan geo-mor	me in this life got ever shall young man be
mod heard heortan geþoht swylce habban sceal bliþe gebæro	sad hearted painful heart's thoughts so have shall happy
eacþon breost ceare sin sorgna gedreag	behavior also then heart-care constant-sorrow host
sy æt him sylfum gelong ealhis worulde wyn sy ful wi	be at herself dependent all his world joy be very far
de fah feorres folc londes þæt min freond siteð	hostile far people land that my friend sits
understan hliþe storme behrimed wine werig mod	under stone slope storm frost-covered friend sad spirited
wætre beflowen ondreor sele dreogeð semin wine	water surrounded sad place endures the my friend
micle mod ceare hege mon to oft wyn licran wic	great sorrow he (is) reminded too often pleasant abode
wabið þam þe sceal oflangoþe leofes abidan.	woe be him REL must for long beloved await.

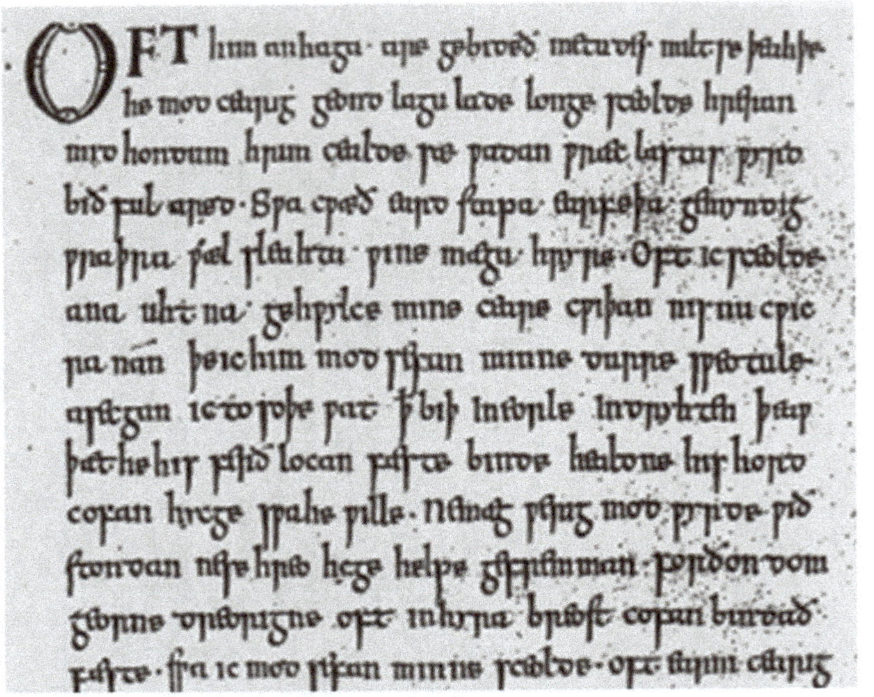

84 Analyzing Syntax through Texts

FIGURE 3.11. The first lines of *The Wanderer* from the *Exeter Book*, f. 76v (reproduced with permission from the Dean and Chapter of Exeter Cathedral)

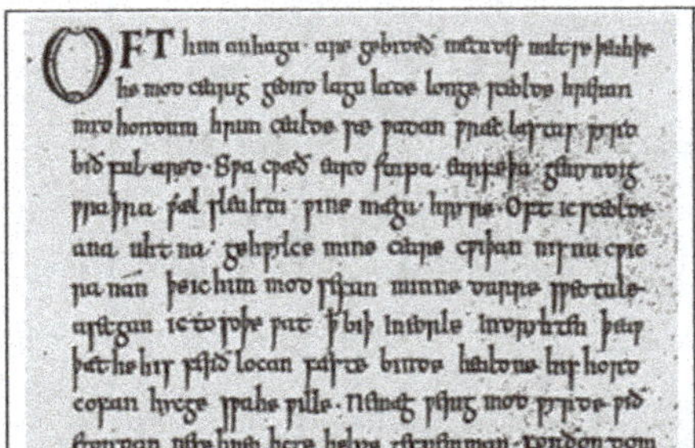

	OFT him anha3a . are 3ebideð metudes miltse þeahþe he mod ceari3 3eond la3u lade lon3e sceolde hreran
	mid hondum hrim cealde sæ padan præc lastas pyrd bið ful ared . Spa cpæð eard stapa earfeþa 3emyndi3 praþra pæl sleahta pine mæ3a hryre . Oft ic sceolde ana uht na 3ehpylce mine ceare cpiþan nisnu cpic ra nan þeichim mod sefan minne durre speotule asec3an ic to soþe pat þ biþ ineorle indryhten þeap
	þæt he his ferð locan fæste binde healdne his hord cofan hyc3e spahe pille.Nemæ3 peri3 mod pyrde pið stondan nese hreo hy3e helpe 3efremman. forðon dom 3eorne dreori3ne oft inhyra breost cofan bindað fæste.

FIGURE 3.12. *The Wanderer* and a transcription

The first sentence starts with a verb, a form of *hatan* 'command'. This verb has an accusative object (marked by the accusative *mec*) and an infinitival clause. The subject is *mon*; the punctuation indicates the end of the full sentence in line 3 of Figure 3.9.

(49) <u>heht</u>   mec   **mon**   [wunian   onwuda   bearwe
     told   me   one   live   in.wood grove

TABLE 3.8. Transcription and word-by-word translation of *The Wanderer*

OFT him anhaga. are gebideð metudes	Often him solitary kindness waits god's
miltse þeahþe he mod cearig geond lagu	mildness though he heart troubles through sea
lade longe sceolde hreran mid hondum	ways long should stir with hands
hrim cealde sæ	frost cold sea
wadan wræc lastas wyrd bið ful ared.	travel exile tracks fate is fully determined.
Swa cwæð eard stapa earfeþa gemyndig	So says earth walker hardship mindful
wraþra wæl sleahta wine mæga hryre.	angry slain slaughters loyal kin fall.
Oft ic sceolde ana uht na gehwylce	Often I should alone morning each
mine ceare cwiþan nisnu cwic	my cares say not.is.now alive
ra nan þeichim mod sefan minne durre	none REL I.him thoughts mine dare
sweotule asecgan ic to soþe wat þ biþ	clearly tell I too truly know REL is
ineorle indryhten þeaw þæt he his ferð	in man noble virtue that he his mind
locan fæste binde healdne his hord	enclosure fast bind hold his thought
cofan hycge swahe wille.Nemæg werig	room think as he wants. Not.can weary
mod wyrde wið stondan nese hreo hyge	mind fate with stand nor.the troubled mind
helpe gefremman. forðon dom georne	help provide. therefore glory eager
dreorigne oft inhyra breost cofan	sorrowful often in.their breast room
bindað fæste.	bind fast.

    under   ac   treo   in   þam   eorð   scræfe].
    under   oak   tree   in   that   earth   cave
    'they told me to live in a wood grove, under an oak tree in that earthcave.'

The verb *heht* is the past tense of the verb *hatan* and there are many different views on what the function of V-first is. To me, it sounds more animated; Lass (1994: 221) thinks the use of V-first signals new information. Endings that we have encountered before are the infinitival *-an* and the dative *-e* endings. The noun *wuda* is the dative singular of the masculine *wudu* (see Table 2.3); *treo* is neuter and could have been marked as a dative which would have been *treowe*.

The next sentence consists of two juxtaposed clauses: 'this cave is old and I am full of longing'.

(50) eald   <u>is</u>   **þes**   **eorð**   **sele**   eal   ic   <u>eom</u>   oflongad .
      old   is   this   earth   cave   all   I   am   out.longed
      'this cave is old and I am full of longing.'

The first clause is V2 and the second is V3, which in this case could also indicate that it is subordinate. There are no morphological peculiarities: *eorð* in (49) and (50) is treated as part of a compound but is normally a weak noun, as we'll see in (53).

In the next sentence, I have only marked *dena* as subject because the finite verbs are left out in the coordinate clauses that follow.

(51) <u>sindon</u> **dena**   dimme   duna   upheabitre   burg   tunas   [brerum beweax ne
      are   valleys   dark   hills   high.biting   town   towns   briars   overgrown

> wic   wynna   leas]
> place delight lacking
> 'the valleys are dark; the hills high; cruel towns are overhung with briars, a home without joy.'

The finite verb is again in initial position. The morphology shows some of the predictable endings, for instance, *-as*, *-um*, and *-ne*. The paradigms in Table 2.6 show that the *-on* on *sindon* is not a past but a present. *Dena* is the plural of the feminine *denu*; see *lufu* in Table 2.3. The adjective *dimme* is the strong form of a plural feminine because it goes with *duna* which is the plural of the feminine *dun*. Finally, Table 2.3 gives us some ideas for the feminine noun *wicwynna*: it must be a plural genitive because *leas* is an adjective that gives genitive to its noun.

The next clause lacks a subject even though the verb *begeat* is finite. The word order is Verb-last with a PP *from siþ frean* extraposed.

> (52) *ful* *oft* *mec* *her* *wraþe* <u>*begeat*</u> *from* *siþ* *frean*
> very often me here cruelly seized from journey lord
> 'here, my lord's leaving often overpowered me.'

Mec is a special accusative, which mainly occurs in older and poetic texts. The *mec*, *siþ*, and *frean* are properly inflected: *mec* is the first person singular accusative, because the first person was seized; *siþ* is a masculine noun that must be part of a compound, or else it would be *siþes*; and *frean* is a masculine weak noun so that ending is correct according to Table 3.3.

In (53), there are two independent sentences where in Modern English we might embed the second one.

> (53) **frynd** <u>sind</u> oneorþan **leofe** **lifgende** leger <u>weardiað</u>
> friends are on.earth dear living bed occupy
> 'there are friends/lovers on earth, while living, they occupy a bed.'

The word order shows V2 in the first part and V-last in the last part. The subject *frynd* is the masculine irregular plural of the noun *freond*; *sind* is without *-on* this time; *eorþan* shows the weak noun in the dative; the present participle *lifgende* modifies *leofe*; and *weardiað* is third person present plural.

The next sentence would also be subordinate in Modern English and perhaps is in Old English. The punctuation would be consistent with that analysis because the finite verb *gonge* occurs in a relatively late position, i.e. after two adverbials. The sentence concludes with two extraposed PPs following the verb.

> (54) *þonne* **icon** *uhtan* *ana* <u>*gonge*</u> *under* *ac* *treo* *geond* *þas eorð scrafu*
> then I.at dawn alone walk under oak tree through these caves
> 'while I walk alone in the light of dawn under the oak-tree and through this earth-cave.'

From a morphological point of view, *uhtan* is a weak noun in (54). The *-n* ending on this noun shows that it is compatible with being the dative singular form of the masculine *uhta*. Also interesting is the ending on the plural *scrafu*, which is a neuter noun and hence an *-um* ending might be expected. The manuscript shows no indication of this ᚦᚱᚪᚱᵘ. *Treo* could also have been marked as dative *treowe*, but isn't ᚱᛁᛒ.

The next passage starts with two sentences next to each other that are parallel in meaning and structure and it ends with an adverbial.

(55) *þær   ic   sittan   mot   sumor langne. dæg*
     there   I   sit   must   summer long   day
     þæric   wepan   mæg   mine wræc   siþas   earfoþa   fela
     there.I   weep   must   my   wretched journeys hardships many
     [forþon   ic   æfre   nemæg   þære   mod   ceare   minre   gerestan].
     for.that   I   ever   not.may those heart troubles mine   rest.
     'there I must sit the long summerday; there I can weep for all my exiles, my many troubles; and so I may never escape from the cares of my sorrowful mind.'

The finite verb in the first part of (55) comes after an adverb, subject, and lexical verb and that is very similar to the second part, adding to the parallel. The adverbial clause introduced by *forþon* has the finite verb *mæg* in the middle and the lexical verb *gerestan* occurs in final position. If we go back to the image of the manuscript in Figure 3.12, we observe that the negative *ne* immediately precedes the auxiliary without any spacing ᚾᛖᛗᚫᚷ. This is a case of negative contraction.

The adverbial *sumor langne dæg* is marked as an accusative. Other case marked phrases are *mine wræcsiþas*, *earfoþa fela*, and *þære modceare minre*. First (and second person) possessives are inflected like indefinite strong adjectives. Take the noun *wræcsiþas*. It is a compound of *wræc* 'misery' and *siþ* 'journey' and marked for the accusative plural through *–as*, and *mine* is consistent with that. The neuter noun *earfoþe* is the basis of *earfoþa fela*, a genitive plural, which either modifies *siþas* or is another object of *wepan*. The next clause has a genitive object *þære modceare minre* to go with the verb *gerestan*.

In (56), we have a fragment that goes with the previous sentence; I have separated it to improve readability. The relative clause is V-final. The negative and *ealles* are not contracted this time.

(56) *ne   ealles þæs   longaþes   [þe   mec onþissum life   begeat]*
     not   all   that longing   REL   me   in.this   life   got.
     'nor all of the longing that have seized my life.'

There is another *mec*, an indication that this manuscript has a robust accusative dative distinction; *þæs longaþes* is a genitive singular, and *þissum* and *life* show dative endings. The relative is the single *þe*.

The passage in (57) starts with a verb that is contracted with an adverb.

(57) *ascyle   geong   mon   wesan geomor mod   heard   heortan   geþoht*
     ever.shall   young   man   be   sad   heart   painful heart   thought
     [swylce   habban   sceal   bliþe   gebæro   eacþon   breost
     so   have   shall   cheerful behavior   also.then   heart
     ceare   sin   sorgna   gedreag]
     care   constant   sorrow   host

'may the young man be sad-minded with hard heart-thoughts yet let him have a cheerful behavior along with his heartache, a crowd of constant sorrows.'

The subject of the first part is an indefinite *geong man* although the speaker has a particular man in mind and could have used a demonstrative. The adverbial clause is subject-less and all the verbs occur in the beginning. The verb *scyle* is a subjunctive modal, to contrast it with the indicative modal *sceal* in the next clause. The infinitives that go with them are marked by *-an*.

The problem in understanding the remainder of the passage starts after *wesan*. The noun *mod* is a neuter nominative, here a compound with the adjective *geomor*, which functions as subject predicate. The noun *heorte* is a feminine weak noun and could therefore be genitive, dative, or accusative singular. If we take it as a dative, the man is sad with a painful heart. But then the masculine singular noun *geþoht* is unconnected. Could it be that *geþoht* is a subject with *heortan* as its genitive, so that the heart's thought is painful? These two possible analyses are provided in Table 3.9.

In the next line, we encounter more challenges: *bliþe gebæro* and *breost ceare sin sorgna gedreag*. *Gebæro* could be a feminine or neuter noun that doesn't change in the accusative, so the man should have a cheerful behavior. The noun *ceare* is a feminine accusative as well (or genitive or dative) and could be a second object to *habban* and *gedreag* another accusative, either an apposition to the other accusatives or its own object. The noun *sin sorgna* is feminine and here it has a genitive plural, so it goes with the *gedreag*.

The next sentence starts with a verb, another subjunctive *sy* that is repeated in the second clause. The sentence can be interpreted as having two wishes for the young man.

(58) *sy*   æt   him   sylfum   gelong   ealhis   woruldewyn
      be   at   him   self   dependent   all.his   world.joy
      sy   ful   wi de fah   feorres   folc   londes
      be   very far   hostile far   people   land
      'let all his worldly joys belong to himself! Let him be outlawed in a far distant land.'

TABLE 3.9. Two analyses of a part of (57)

(a)	ascyle	geong mon	wesan	geomor mod		heard heortan		geþoht
		Subject	V	Subject Predicate		dative modifier to 'mon'		?
(b)	ascyle	geong mon	wesan	geomor mod	(and)	heard	(V)	heortan geþoht
		Subject 1	V	Subject Predicate 1		Subject Predicate 2		Subject 2
	Ever.shall	young man	be	sad heart		painful		heart thought

TABLE 3.10. More on (57)

habban	sceal	*bliþe gebæro*	eacþon	*breost ceare*	*sin sorgna gedreag*
V		object		object	object
have	shall	cheerful behavior	also.then	heart care	constant sorrow host

The reflexive is clearly split into a pronoun *him* and an adjective *self*, inflected for dative case. The subject is unexpressed in both clauses. The *feorres folc londes* functions as adverbial.

Next comes a dependent clause that starts with a conjunction *þæt* which could express a reason behind (58).

(59) *þæt min freond siteð understan hliþe [storme behrimed]*
that my friend sits under.stone slope storm frost-covered
wine werig mod wætre beflowen ondreor sele
friend sad spirited water surrounded sad place
'because my lover sits under stone cliffs chilled by storms, weary-minded, surrounded by water in a sad place!'

It could also be an adverbial that explains why he will suffer, and that's the translation I have given.

The first line is relatively straightforward: the subject *min freond* precedes the present tense verb *siteð* after which a PP *understan hliþe* and a participle clause *storme behrimed* follow. Both *storme* and *hliþe* are dative singulars. The second line is another set of appositives: the friend is sad and is surrounded by water in a sad place.

In (60), we hear why he is weary-minded. It starts with a verb in the present tense followed by the subject, which has both a demonstrative and possessive pronoun.

(60) <u>dreogeð</u> *se* **min wine** *micle mod ceare*
endures that my friend much heart sorrow
hege <u>mon</u> *to oft wynlicran wic*
he.reminded too often pleasant abode
'my beloved will suffer many sorrows of the heart; he will remember too often a happier home.'

The feminine noun *cearu* is one we have seen before; its *-e* ending isn't very helpful in that it can be genitive, dative, or accusative singular, nominative or accusative plural. *Cearu* is obviously the object of the verb *dreogeð* but it could have accusative or genitive case. The case sometimes makes a difference in the meaning, with the genitive being only partially affected. Here the *micle* tells us in fact how much the object is affected. The second line is independent with its own subject *he*, a finite verb *gemon*, an adverb *tooft*, and the object *wynlicran wic*.

The last line starts with an adjective, a verb, and an object that is modified by a relative clause.

(61) <u>wabið</u> *þam [þe sceal oflangoþe leofes abidan]*
woe.be him REL must longing beloved await
'woe shall come to the one who waits longingly for a loved one.'

Note that the (dative) demonstrative *þam* can be used to refer to persons and also that the genitive *leofes* is the object of *abidan*. Compared with other sentences, this one is straightforward.

The Wanderer

The morphology and syntax of this text are very similar to those of the poem just discussed, possibly simpler in having fewer ambiguities where nominal case marking is concerned.

There are a few periods in this excerpt that indicate a new sentence, e.g. the period in line 4 before *swa*. I have taken the four words preceding that period as an independent conclusion to it all, so I list it as (63).

(62) Oft   him   anhaga   are   <u>gebideð</u>   metudes   miltse   [þeahþe
Often him   solitary   grace   experiences   God's   mildness   though.REL
he mod   cearig geond   lagu lade longe   sceolde   hreran   mid   hondum
he heart   troubled through   sea   ways   long   should   stir   with   hands
hrim   cealde   sæ   wadan   wræc   lastas]
frost   cold   sea   travel   exile   tracks
'often the solitary dweller experiences the grace, the mercy of the creator, although he, troubled in heart, has for a long time, across the sea-ways, had to stir with his hands the ice-cold sea, travel the paths of an exile.'

The first sentence runs as a unit of three clauses with the first one as the main clause. The structure of the first clause doesn't look like a main clause because the finite verb *gebideð* appears in a position after an adverb, pronoun, and object. The second clause is introduced through the complex subordinator *þeahþe* and has a modal *sceolde*, and an infinitive *hreran*. The infinitival clause centered around *wadan* is possibly coordinated.

We see expected inflections on verbs, e.g. third person singular present tense *gebideð*, and case on nouns, e.g. genitive singular on *metudes*, dative plural on *hondum*, and accusative plural on *lastas*. In the first line, I take *anhaga are* and *metudes miltse* to be the genitive objects of *gebideð*, i.e. what is experienced or waited for.

The next clause has the finite verb in second position and the non-finite *ared* in last position and is an independent conclusion of the beginning: fate is fully set!

(63) wyrd   <u>bið</u>   ful   ared.
fate   is   fully   set
'fate is fully determined.'

The past participle *ared* derives from the verb *arædan* 'to appoint, settle'.

The next sentence has a V2 clause with the subject, *eardstapa*, following the verb. The phrase starting with *gemyndig* 'mindful' is a modifier to the subject and the rest of the sentence depends on what *eardstapa* is mindful about (and in the genitive case), namely hardships, the slaughters, and the fall of kinsmen.

(64) Swa   <u>cwæð</u>   **eard stapa**   earfeþa   gemyndig   wraþa   wæl
So   says   earth walker   hardships   mindful   hostile   slaughter/slain
sleahta   wine   mæga hryre.
slaughters   friend   kin fall
'thus spoke the wanderer, mindful of hardships, of cruel slaughters, of the fall of kinsmen.'

As for the endings, *eardstapa* is a unique word in the corpus of Old English and its shape looks like a nominative weak noun. The adjective *gemyndig* needs genitive objects, which *earfeþa* and *sleahta* are. *Wæl* is a compound with *sleahta*, *wine mæga* is a compound marked masculine plural, but the masculine *hryre* could be a genitive *hryres*.

The next clause starts after a period in line 5 of Figure 3.10; this passage consists of two loosely juxtaposed clauses.

(65) *Oft   ic   sceolde   ana   uhtna gehwylce   mine   ceare   cwiþan*
    Often   I   should   alone morning each   my   cares   say
    *nis   nu   cwic ra   **nan**   [þeichim   modsefan minne*
    not.is now alive   none   REL.I.him thoughts mine
    durre   sweotule asecgan]
    dare   clearly   tell
    'often, alone at each dawn, I have had to lament my sorrows; now there is no one alive to whom I dare reveal my thoughts openly.'

The first clause has the finite modal *sceolde* in third position (because the subject is a pronoun) and the non-finite verb *cwiþan* in last position, exactly as expected. The second clause starts with a negative contracted with the finite verb, *nis*, and then a light adverb and a negative subject *nan*, showing negative concord. This subject is modified by a relative clause, which has the modal following the subject and the lexical verb last. The words *þe*, *ic*, and *him* are very close in the manuscript.

The endings are regular: the weak noun *ceare* is the object of *cwiþan* and *modsefa* is the object of *asecgan*. *Modsefan* is a compound where the last part *sefa* is a weak masculine noun. Both objects therefore have a form that can be accusative but is not unambiguously so.

In (66), the subject pronoun starts the sentence but is not immediately followed by the finite verb *wat*.

(66) ***Ic***   *to   soþe   wat   [þ   biþ   ineorle   indryhten   þeaw*
    I   to   truth know   that is   in.noble   noble   custom
    [þæt   he   his   ferð   locan   fæste   binde healdne his   hord   cofan]]
    that   he   his   mind   enclosure fast   bind   hold   his   treasure chamber
    hycge   [swa   he   wille].
    think   as   he   wants
    'I know too truly that it is a noble virtue in man that he should bind his heart and hold his thoughts. Think as he wants to.'

This verb has a clausal object (*þ biþ ineorle indryhten þeaw*), which in turn has a clause functioning as the subject (*þæt he his ferðlocan fæste binde*). The *healde his hord cofan* may be a coordinate to *binde* and I have analyzed *hycge swa he wille* as an independent interjection.

As for the verb forms, *wat* is an irregular present tense verb, *biþ* is a form of the copula that stresses the desirability of the future state, and the verbs *binde* and *healde* are subjunctives, as is *hycge*, all stressing that the situation is in the future. *Wille* is ambiguous between indicative and subjunctive. It looks like there are two weak nouns. The accusative singular *his ferðlocan* is the object of *binde* (but its *-an* ending can of course be many other things) and the accusative singular or plural *hordcofan* is the object of *healed*. The punctuation is clearly marked after *wille*. The scribe may be using it emphatically, as in (60).

Finally, the last part of the excerpt consists of three clauses, the first two of which are loosely coordinated. The clause starting with *forðon* can be seen as independent although not V2.

(67) Nemæg **werig mod** wyrde wið stondan [nese hreo hycge helpe
     Not may weary mind fate   withstand   not.that troubled mind help
     gefremman]. Forðon **dom georne** dreorigne oft in hyra breost cofan
     provide   Therefore glory.eager sorrowful oft in their heart chamber
     <u>bindað</u> fæste.
     bind   fast
'the weary mind cannot withstand fate nor can the troubled mind provide help. Therefore those eager for glory must bind fast a heavy heart sorrowfully.'

The first clause starts with a negative adverb, followed by the finite verb and the subject, which is in turn followed by the object and the lexical verb. This is a 'model' Old English sentence: V2 (for the finite verb) and V-final (for the lexical verb). What follows is a related negative that depends on the modal *mæg* for its interpretation. The manuscript shows evidence of negative contraction but without another negative reinforcing it, as (65) did; see the snip for the contraction. nǣmæȝ

Some case endings are as follows: *mod* is nominative neuter singular, appropriate for a subject, *wyrde* is feminine singular but could be genitive, dative, or accusative, and *hyge* is masculine nominative singular, usual for a subject. The noun *help* is feminine and could be dative or accusative in form; *breastcofa* is weak so again could represent a number of forms, here dative.

3.5.3 Status and dialect

The poetry of the *Exeter Book* we have studied in section 3.5.2 is West Saxon but much more archaic and synthetic than the prose we have seen before. Word order in poetry is of course much freer than in prose. We find many instances of Verb-first in *The Wife's Lament* that enliven the narrative; see (49), (51), and (58). Most main clauses are V2, as in (50), (53), (61), (63), (64), and (67), and many subordinate clauses have the verb in a later position, as in (56) and (59). There is PP extraposition, as before, e.g. in (52). I have repeated some of these patterns as (68).

(68) a. **heht**   mec mon   wunian onwuda   bearwe   (49) V1
        told   me   one   live   in.wood   grove
     b. eald   **is** þes   eorð   sele   (50) V2
        old   is   this   earth   cave
     c. þe   mec onþissum   life   **begeat**   (56) V-last
        REL   me   in.this   life   got
     d. ful oft   mec her   wraþe   begeat   **from** siþ frean (52) PP-Extr
        very often me   here   cruelly seized   from journey lord

The morphology is traditional in that endings appear on all nouns, for instance, the special accusative *mec* in (49), (52), and (56), and all forms of nouns, e.g. the weak noun *heortan* in (57) and the dative plural *hondum* in (62). Articles are absent and demonstratives less frequent, e.g. before *ac treo* in (49) and before *dena* and *duna* in (51). So, this stage is synthetic. Relatives are simple, i.e. just the particle in (56), (61), and (65).

As for the verbs, many forms of 'to be' appear, verbs are fully inflected, e.g. *weardiað* in (53), and many are subjunctive, as in (58). That said, there are also a lot of modals, e.g. *mæg* in (55), *scyle* in (57), *sceal* in (61), and *mæg* in (67). The prefixes on past participles are intact, as in *oflongad* in (50), *gerestan* in (55), and *abidan* in (61).

A southernism that is already evident is the negative concord in (65) and the contraction of the negative and the finite verb, as in (55), (65), and (67).

3.6 Conclusion

In this chapter, we have examined several kinds of Old English text types, prose narrative, sermon, glossed biblical, biblical, and poetry. We have seen some texts that were very synthetic, e.g. the poems in section 3.5, and other texts that were less so, e.g. *Orosius*, in section 3.2. The former are from a manuscript that was written in the second half of the tenth century whereas the manuscript in which *Orosius* appears is from the early tenth. So, the time of the manuscript is not indicative of how archaic the stage of the language is.

For each of the texts, an analysis has been given along with a discussion on the word order, morphology, and whether or not it is possible to determine the dialect.

Exercises

A Look at the text in Figure 3.13 from Alfred's *Cura Pastorale*. Try to find words you recognize.

B Identify some letters that characterize the insular script.
The transcription is provided in Appendix III.

C We discussed sentence (1) above. Comment on the word order and the endings that you recognize. Then check the discussion around (39).

(1) Soðlice we gesawon hys steorran on eastdæle . 7 we comon us him to geeadmedenne

D Now, look at (2), which we haven't yet discussed, and comment on word order endings, etc. From what time or stage in the language is this? Justify your answer.

(2) Þe cildra biddaþ þe, eala lareow, þæt þu tæce us sprecan forþam ungelærede we syndon & gewæmmodlice we sprecaþ.

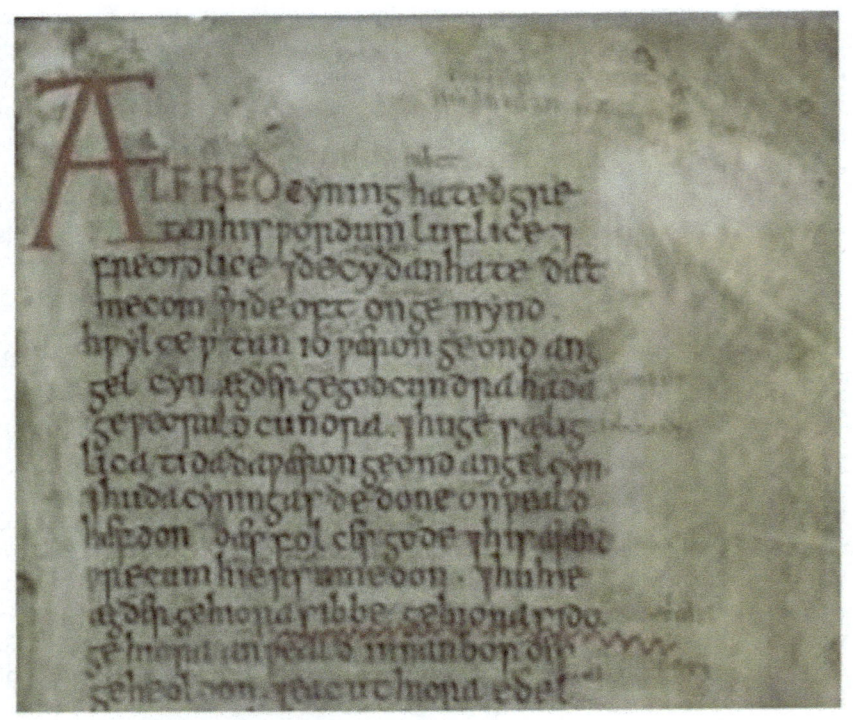

FIGURE 3.13. *The Pastoral Care* (Corpus Christi College, Cambridge, 12, f. 1r)

Further reading

Roberts (2005) is a wonderful resource about the intricacies of the different scripts. Walkden (2014) includes a chapter of the position of the verb in early Germanic, with a great review of the previous literature. Moore and Marckwardt (1951: ch. 6) provide an excellent overview of the development of inflection. As for Old English verbal morphology, the volume edited by Diewald et al. (2013) contains chapters on some intricacies with verbs, for instance Cloutier on *hatan* (see *heht* (46) above), Petré on passive auxiliaries, and Bolze on the glossing/ translation of the verb *to be* in the Lindisfarne and West Saxon Gospels. The online lessons at The University of Texas at Austin Linguistics Research Center[3] would be a good place to go after finishing this chapter because the texts are given with a glossary but not with a syntactic analysis.

Diewald, Gabriele, Leena Kahlas-Tarkka and Ilse Wischer (eds) (2013), *Comparative Studies in Early Germanic*, Amsterdam: John Benjamins.
Moore, Samuel and Albert Marckwardt (1951), *Historical Outlines of English Sounds and Inflections*, Ann Arbor: George Wahr.
Roberts, Jane (2005), *Guide to Scripts*, London: British Library.

Walkden, George (2014), *Syntactic Reconstruction and Proto-Germanic*, Oxford: Oxford University Press.

Notes

1. See also 'De Temporibus Anticristo, edited by Arthur Napier, Homily 42', available at <http://webpages.ursinus.edu/jlionarons/wulfstan/AdsoOE.html> (last accessed 9 May 2017).
2. An online edition of *The Wanderer*, ed. and trans. Tim Romano, 1999, is available at <http://www.aimsdata.com/tim/anhaga/WandererMain.htm> (last accessed 9 May 2017).
3. 'Old English Online', The University of Texas at Austin Linguistics Research Center, available at <http://www.utexas.edu/cola/centers/lrc/eieol/engol-0-X.html> (last accessed 9 May 2017).

4

Early Middle English 1100–1300

In this chapter, we follow a similar format as in Chapter 3. There will be images of the original manuscripts with a transcription and (free) translations; word-by-word renderings are only given when the text is more difficult. The texts follow each other in chronological order, unlike in Chapter 3 where the less complex texts are discussed first.

The early manuscripts continue to use the insular or Anglo-Saxon minuscule. Later, we observe Carolingian and then Gothic scripts. The Gothic script makes the writing look very dense: the lines thicken although the letters narrow and lengthen, and ligatures and conjoined letters abound. This script is later adopted for the printing press in England by Caxton as we'll notice in the next chapter. Figure 4.1 provides the lower case letters of this script.

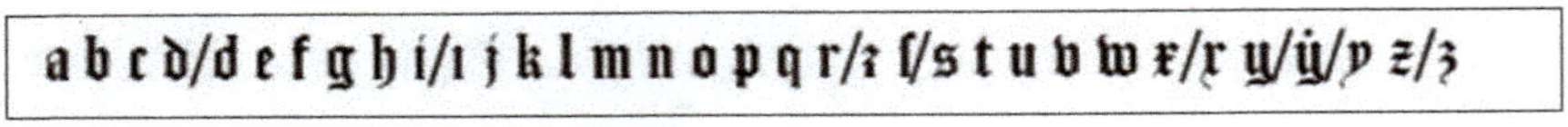

a b c ð/d e f g h i/ı j k l m n o p q r/ꝛ ſ/s t u b w ꝛ/r y/ẏ/v z/ʒ

FIGURE 4.1. The Gothic script (from <http://guindo.pntic.mec.es/jmag0042/LATIN_PALEOGRAPHY.pdf>, last accessed 4 June 2017. Reproduced with permission from Juan-José Marcos)

The outline of this chapter is as follows. Section 4.1 starts with a prose text we've encountered in Chapter 2, namely the *Peterborough Chronicle*. It is a twelfth-century text from the Northeast Midlands. Section 4.2 examines *Seinte Katerine*, a West Midlands text that is more archaic than the *Peterborough Chronicle* although it is a century later. Section 4.3 continues with *The Owl and the Nightingale*, a text whose date of composition is not known and whose geographical origin is probably southern. Section 4.4 turns to *The Lion*, from *The Physiologus* or *Bestiary*, a text from the Northeast Midlands from around 1300, and section 4.5 analyzes Richard Rolle's *Psalter*, a northern text from an author born in the late thirteenth century. Section 4.6 presents a conclusion.

4.1 The *Peterborough Chronicle*

The *Peterborough Chronicle* is one of nine manuscripts that tell the history of England and of its people. None of the manuscripts is the original and some are left only in part. The Peterborough version was produced in Peterborough, seventy-five miles north of London, in the Danelaw area. It is also referred to as Laud 636 and now kept in the Bodleian Library. The language of the *Peterborough Chronicle* is traditionally seen as representing the change from Old to Middle English and is often seen as representative of changes contact with Scandinavians brought.

There had been a fire in the abbey in 1116, which destroyed an earlier version, and the scribes therefore copied the chronicle from other sources up to 1122 and after that started to write their own entries. Thus, the main change in this text comes around the entry for the year 1122, when the scribe stops copying from an earlier source and starts adding new information; a second change starts with the year 1132 when the second scribe takes over. There are also some additions that the first scribe makes throughout the text that are original to him and not due to an older source. In order to show the changes that happen throughout this text, I will first examine an excerpt from the beginning of the chronicle (the Introduction), then an excerpt from when the first scribe adds his own observations (the year 1130), and finally I will look at when the second scribe is writing (the year 1137).

In 4.1.1, the manuscript images of the three excerpts are provided with a transcription and a translation; in 4.1.2, an analysis of the texts appears, and in 4.1.3, I comment on the general nature of the text as a whole and compare it with a more southern version, the *Parker Chronicle*, which is the oldest surviving one.

4.1.1 The text

A facsimile of the *Peterborough Chronicle* has been available since 1954 (Whitelock 1954) and it has also been digitized. For the translation, I have benefitted from the one available at *The Online Medieval and Classical Library*.[1] Figure 4.2 shows the start and Table 4.1 provides a transcription (again with some letters modernized) and a translation.

Figure 4.3 shows the 'middle' stage of the *Peterborough Chronicle*. If you look at the actual manuscript image, you'll notice the year in a different color on the right side: mcxxx, i.e. 1130. Some letters have been added later.

A transliteration follows each line in the column on the left-hand side of Table 4.2 and a translation appears in the column on the right. Note the special abbreviations, e.g. for 'bishop' and 'William'; note also the use of some capitals for names but not all.

The last stage of the *Peterborough Chronicle* is that from 1132 on. I have given the entry for the year 1137 in Figure 4.4. Notice the year in the top left written using roman numerals. There are also some abbreviations, e.g. *k* and *Steph* in the first line and the 3 is replaced by *g*. A transliteration and translation follow in Table 4.3.

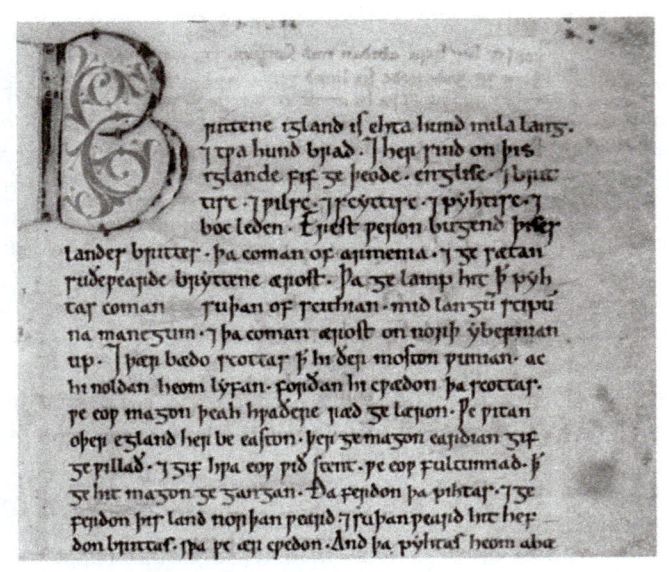

FIGURE 4.2. The Introduction to the *Peterborough Chronicle* (Laud Misc. 636, f. 1r. Reproduced with permission from the Bodleian Library)

TABLE 4.1. The first page of the *Peterborough Chronicle* (transliteration and translation)

Brittene iʒland is ehta hund mila lanʒ. 7 tpa hund brad. 7 her sind on þis iʒlande fif ʒe þeode. enʒlisc. 7 Brit tisc. 7 pilsc. 7 scyttisc. 7 pyhtisc. 7 boc leden. Erest peron buʒend þises landes brittes. þa coman of armenia. 7 ʒe sætan suþepearde bryttene ærost. þa ʒe lamp hit þ pyh tas coman suþan of scithian. mid lanʒũ scipũ na maneʒum. 7 þa coman ærost on norþ ybernian up. 7 þær bædo scottas þ hi ðer moston punian. ac hi noldan heom lyfan. forþan hi cpædon þa scottas. pe eow maʒon þeah hwaðere ræd ʒelæron. Þe pitan oþer eʒland her be easton. þer ʒe maʒon eardian ʒif ʒe pillað. 7 ʒif hpa eop pið stent. pe eop fultumiað. þ ʒe hit maʒon ʒeʒanʒan. Ða ferdon þa pihtas. 7 ʒe ferdon þis land norþanpeard. 7 suþanpeard hit hef don brittas. spa pe ær cpedon.	The island Britain is 800 miles long and 200 miles broad. And there are on the island five nations; English, Brittish, Welsh, Scottish, Pictish, and Latin. First were living on this land Britons, who came from Armenia, and peopled Britain southward. Then happened it, that the Picts came south from Scythia, with long ships, not many. and, then coming first in the northern part of Ireland, they told the Scots that they must dwell there. But they would not give them leave; because the Scots told them that they could not all dwell there together; But, said the Scots, we can nevertheless give you advice. We know another island here to the east. There you may dwell, if you will; and whosoever withstandeth you, we will assist you, that you may gain it. Then went the Picts and entered this land northward. Southward the Britons possessed it, as we before said.

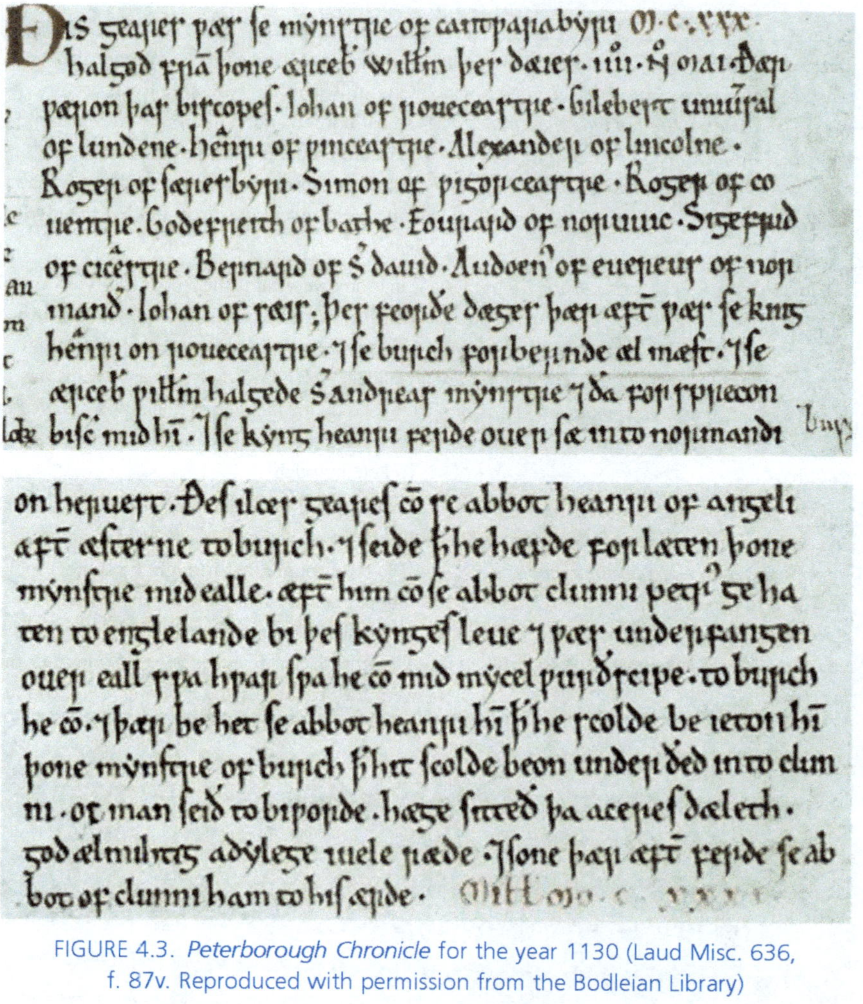

FIGURE 4.3. *Peterborough Chronicle* for the year 1130 (Laud Misc. 636, f. 87v. Reproduced with permission from the Bodleian Library)

TABLE 4.2. *Peterborough Chronicle* for the year 1130

Ðis ȝeares pæs se mynstre of cantparabyri M.C.XXX. halȝod frā þone ærceb Þillm þes dæies iiii No MAI. Ðær pæron þas biscopes. Iohan of roueceastre. Ȝilbert uniusal of lundene. heanri of pinceastre. Alexander of lincolne . Roȝer of særesbyri . Simon of piȝorcestre. Roȝer of co uentre. ȝodefreith of bathe. Eouuard of noruuic. Siȝefrid of cicaestre. Bernard of S dauid. Audoen of euereus of nor mand . Iohan of sæis;	This year was the monastery of Canterbury consecrated by the Archbishop William, that fourth day before the nones of May. There were the Bishops John of Rochester, Gilbert Universal of London, Henry of Winchester, Alexander of Lincoln, Roger of Salisbury, Simon of Worcester, Roger of Coventry, Geoffry of Bath, Evrard of Norwich, Sigefrith of Chichester, Bernard of St David's, Owen of Evreux in Normandy, John of Sieyes.

(Continued)

TABLE 4.2. *Continued*

Ðes feorðe dæ3es þær æft þæs se kin3 heanri on roueceastre. 7 se burch forbernde æl mæst. 7se ærceb pillm hal3ede S andreas mynstre 7 ða forsprecon bisc mid hī. 7 se kyn3 heanri ferde ouer sæ into normandi on heruest.	The fourth day after this was Henry the King in Rochester, when the town was almost burned and William the Archbishop consecrated the monastery of St Andrew, and the aforesaid bishops with him. And the King Henry went over sea into Normandy in harvest.
Ðes ilces 3eares cõ se abbot heanri of an3eli æft 3 æsterne to burch. 7 seide þ he hæfde forlæten þone mynstre mid ealle. æft him cõ se abbot clunni petr 3e ha ten to en3lelande bi þes kyn3es leue 7 þæs underfan3en ouer eall spa hpar spa he cõ mid mycel purðscipe. to burch	This same year came the Abbot Henry of Angeli after Easter to Peterborough, and said that he had relinquished that monastery withal. After him came the Abbot of Clugny, Peter by name, to England by the king's leave; and was received by all, whithersoever he came, with much respect. To Peterborough
he cõ.7 þær be het se abbot heanri hī þ he scolde be ieton hī þone mynstre of burch þ hit scolde beon underðed into clun ni. oc man seið to biporde. hæ3e sitteð þa aceres dæleth. 3od ælmihti3 adyle3e iuele ræde. 7 sone þær æft ferde se ab bot of clunni ham to his ærde.	he came; and there the Abbot Henry promised him that he would procure him the ministry of Peterborough, that it might be subject to Clugny. But it is said in the proverb, The hedge abideth, that acres divideth. May God Almighty frustrate evil designs. Soon after this went the Abbot of Clugny home to his country.

FIGURE 4.4. *Peterborough Chronicle* for the year 1137 (Laud Misc. 636, f. 89r. Reproduced with permission from the Bodleian Library)

4.1.2 Analysis: from the beginning to the end of the *Peterborough Chronicle*

In this section, we'll examine certain features of the transcribed text from Tables 4.1 to 4.3: the use of demonstratives and – in the last excerpt – articles, the word order and morphology, and the paratactic nature of clause combining which was already mentioned in Chapter 2.

Early Middle English 1100–1300

TABLE 4.3. *Peterborough Chronicle* for the year 1137

Ðis gære for þe k Steph ofer sæ to normandi 7 ther þes under fangen forþi ð hi uuenden ð he sculde ben alsuic alse the eỏ þes. 7 for he hadde get his tresor.ac he todeld it 7 scatered sotlice. Micel hadde henri k gadered gold 7 syluer. 7 na god ne dide me for his saule thar of. Þa þe king S to englal cõ þa macod he his gadering æt *Oxeneford*. 7 þar he nam þe ƀ *Roger of Serebi* 7 *Alex* ƀ *of lincol* 7 te canceler Rog hise neues. 7 dide ælle in psun. til hi iafen up he re castles.	This year, (the) King Stephen crossed the sea to go to Normandy and was received there because they thought he was like the uncle (i.e. his uncle). And because he still had his treasury, but he divided and scattered it stupidly. King Henry has gathered much gold and silver and no good did men with it for his soul. When King Stephen came to England, he held a gathering at Oxford and there he took bishop Roger of Salisbury and Alexander bishop of Lincoln and the chancellor Roger, his nephews. And put all in prison until they gave up their castles.

The first excerpt starts as (1), with a description of the island.

(1) Brittene igland is ehta hund mila lang. 7 twa hund brad. 7 her sind on **þis** iglande fif geþeode. englisc.7 brittisc. 7 wilsc.7 scyttisc. 7 pyhtisc. 7 boc leden. 'the island Britain is 800 miles long and 200 miles broad. And there are on the island five nations; English, British, Welsh, Scottish, Pictish, and Latin.'

Two finite verbs, *is* and *sind*, make two finite clauses and these two clauses are coordinated. The word order in both is V2.

As was mentioned in Chapter 2, demonstratives are scarcer in older texts than articles are in Modern English. In (1), there is one proximal demonstrative (shown in bold) to emphasize that the island was already mentioned. There are no other demonstratives or articles whereas the translation has two articles and could have a few more. Table 4.4 provides the paradigm for the proximal demonstrative and, as you can see, the shape of the dative *þis* (after the preposition *on*) in (1) is uncommon from an Old English point of view.

As for the nominal endings in (1), *Britten* is a feminine noun and so is *mil*, so the Old English genitive *-a* surfaces as a weakened *-e* on *Brittene* but *mila* has the expected nominative plural *-a* ending. The neuter noun *iglande* is the object of

TABLE 4.4. Proximal demonstratives in Old English

	masculine	feminine	neuter	plural
NOM	þes	þeos	þis	þas
GEN	þisses	þisse	þisses	þissa
DAT	þissum	þisse	þissum	þissum
ACC	þisne	þas	þis	þas

a preposition so the dative *-e* is therefore appropriate. As always, some spelling variation can be found!

The next sentence explains who inhabited the island. We'll first look at the demonstratives.

(2) Erest weron bugend **þises** landes brittes. þa coman of armenia. 7 gesætan suþewearde bryttene ærost. þa gelamp hit þ pyhtas coman suþan of scithian. mid langum scipum na manegum.
'first were living on this land Britons, who came from Armenia, and peopled Britain southward. Then happened it, that the Picts came south from Scythia, with long ships, not many.'

The proximal *þises* in (2) is again used for reference to the already-mentioned island, but no other demonstrative is used with a noun. A literal translation of the first part is 'first were living on this island Britons'. Because the languages/tribes mentioned in (1) are adjectival, they are not seen as a proper mention of the actual people, the Britons. There is also a *þa*, before *coman*, which has the shape of a nominative plural demonstrative and could be seen as starting an independent sentence or as a relative marker heading a relative clause.

As for the structure, if we take *þa* to be a personal pronoun, there are three independent sentences in (2), as indicated by the periods in the manuscript. A Modern English reader might think of the first part as a V2 main clause with a relative clause that contains two coordinated clauses. The sentence starting with *þa gelamp* is V2 with an extraposed subject clause, namely *þ pyhtas coman suþan of scithian mid langum scipum na manegum*. Some dative plural endings from Figure 4.2 are reproduced in a snip that shows the abbreviated nasal

mið langū scipū.

The verb in the first clause signals past imperfective, indicating a duration, but the rest of the passage is marked as simple past. The *-an* on *coman* and *gesætan* would be *-on* in Old English. There are some traditional case endings, as in *landes*, *pyhtas*, *langum scipum*, and *manegum*, namely a genitive *-es*, a nominative plural *-as*, and three dative *-um* plurals. The ending on *Brittes* would be *-as* in Old English. The demonstrative *þises* indicates an adverbial that is genitive.

Next follows (3). I have given a slightly different translation from Table 4.1. We'll again first consider the personal and demonstrative pronouns.

(3) 7 þa coman ærost on norþ ybernian up. 7 þær bædon **scottas** þ hi ðer moston wunian. ac hi noldan heom lyfan. forþan hi cwædon **þa scottas**. we eow magon þeah hwaðere ræd gelæron.
'and, then coming first in the northern part of Ireland, they told the Scots that they must dwell there. But they would not give them leave; because the Scots told them we prevail though we can give you advice.'

The first occurrence of *scottas*, who have not been mentioned before, lacks a demonstrative but the second occurrence has a *þa*. The third person plural pronouns are *hi* and this becomes relevant in determining the dialect and age of a manuscript. The plural pronoun 'they' first appears in the same geographical area as the *Peterborough Chronicle*, namely in the *Ormulum*, so it is interesting that it doesn't yet appear in the *Peterborough Chronicle*.

Taking note of the periods, the structure of the passage is quite paratactic, namely consisting of five clauses. There is a simple V2 clause followed by another V2 clause which itself includes a V-last complement clause. The clause starting with *ac* could be part of the preceding clause, as could the *forþan*-clause which in turn has a clausal object, namely *we eow magon þeah hwaðere ræd gelæron*.

As for the morphology, *scottas* is nominative plural, *wunian* has an infinitival ending, and *bædon, moston, cwædon*, and *magon* have plural past endings. There are some endings that are less expected from an Old English point of view, namely *coman* and *noldan* (rather than *-on*) and *gelæron* (rather than *-an*).

In (4), the *Pihtas* are also preceded by a demonstrative since they have been mentioned before, as does *þis land*. The *Brittas* are possibly indefinite and therefore without *þa*.

(4) We witan oþer egland her be easton. þer ge magon eardian gif ge willað. 7 gif hwa eow wið stent. we eow fultumiað. þ ge hit magon gegangan. Ða ferdon **þa pihtas**. 7 geferdon **þis land** norþanweard.7 suþanweard hit hefdon **brittas**. swa we ær cwedon.

'we know another island here to the east. There you may dwell, if you will; and whosoever withstandeth you, we will assist you, that you may gain it. Then went the Picts and entered this land northward. Southward the Britons possessed it, as we before said.'

The many periods show a separation between clauses. The sentence is paratactic for a written register, at least from a Modern English point of view. It starts with a V2 sentence with a possible relative clause following it, i.e. *þer* can be thought of as 'where' or as 'there' starting an independent sentence. What is the clause structure of the remainder of the passage?

Modern English would have two main clauses with the first containing a main (*we eow fultumiað*) and two subordinate clauses (*gif hwa eow wið stent* and *þ ge hit magon gegangan*) and the second includes three coordinate ones followed by an adverbial (*swa we ær cwedon*). It is unclear if (4) was seen as so subordinate and connected though in the English of the chronicle.

There are the verbal plural present verbs *witan* (*witon* in OE) and *magon*, the infinitive *eardian*, the present tense plural third person verbs *willað* and *fultumiað*, the present plural *magon*, the infinitive *gegangan*, and a number of past tense plurals, namely *ferdon, geferdon, hefdon*, and *cwedon*. The plural nominative *-as* is visible on *pihtas* and *brittas*.

For the transitionary period (the First Continuation), we consider the beginning of the entry of the year 1130. There is a real increase in demonstratives and these demonstratives are often phonologically lighter.

(5) Ðis geares wæs **se** mynstre of cantwarabyri halgod fram **þone** ærceb Willm **þes** dæies iiii No MAI. Ðær wæron **þas** biscopes. Iohan of roueceastre. Gilbert uniuersal of lundene. heanri of winceastre. Alexander of lincolne. Roger of særesbyri . Simon of wigorceastre. Roger of co uentre. Godefreith of bathe.

Eourard of noruuic. Sigefrid of cicaestre. Bernard of S dauid. Audoen of euereus of nor mand . Iohan of sæis;
'this year was the monastery of Canterbury consecrated by the Archbishop William, that fourth day before the nones of May. There were the Bishops John of Rochester, Gilbert Universal of London, Henry of Winchester, Alexander of Lincoln, Roger of Salisbury, Simon of Worcester, Roger of Coventry, Geoffry of Bath, Evrard of Norwich, Sigefrith of Chichester, Bernard of St. David's, Owen of Evreux in Normandy, John of Sieyes.'

As far as I can see, all nouns are preceded by demonstrative pronouns: *Ðis geares, se mynstre, þone ærcebiscop, þes dæies,* and *þas biscopes. Gear* and *mynstre* are neuter and *(ærce)bishop* and *dæg* masculine, but some genders are fluid, e.g. *mynstre* is treated as masculine here and in (7) but listed in most dictionaries as neuter.

Some other interesting morphology and lack thereof can be seen in the presence of adverbial genitive on *geares* and *dæies,* the lack of genitive case on *Ðis* and *þes,* and the absence of *ge-* on *halgod.* The demonstratives *se* and *þone* are, as in Old English, nominative masculine singular and accusative masculine singular, respectively, but the nominative plural *þas* would be *þa* in Old English.

In (6), I have bolded all nouns with their preceding demonstratives.

(6) **Ðes feorðe dæges** þæræfter wæs **se king heanri** on roueceastre. 7 **se burch** forbernde ælmæst. 7 **se ærceb willm** halgede **S andreas mynstre** 7 ða **forsprecon bisc** mid him. 7 **se kyng heanri** ferde ouer sæ into normandi on heruest.

'the fourth day after this was Henry the King in Rochester, when the town was almost consumed by fire and William the Archbishop consecrated the monastery of St. Andrew, and the aforesaid bishops with him. And the King Henry went over sea into Normandy in harvest.'

The only noun that isn't preceded by a demonstrative is *Sancti Andreas mynstre* 'St. Andrew's monastery' but this is because *Sancti Andreas* functions as demonstrative. Inside PPs, such as *ouer sæ* and *on heruest,* a demonstrative is typically absent.

The word order of all five clauses is V2. One can think of them as loosely coordinated, as the periods also indicate. The morphology of *dæges* is as expected because it is a genitive adverbial but its demonstrative *Ðes* is not, *se king* is nominative, as is s*e burch, se ærceb,* and *se kyng.*

In (7), again all the count nouns are preceded by demonstratives. The only exception seems to be inside the quoted proverb.

(7) **Ðes ilces geares** com **se abbot heanri of angeli** æft æsterne to Burch. 7 seide þ he hæfde forlæten **þone mynstre** mid ealle. æft him com **se abbot clunni** petrgeha ten to englelande bi **þes kynges** leue 7 wæs underfangen ouer eall swa hwar swa he com mid mycel wurðscipe. 7 to burch he com. 7 þær behet **se abbot heanri** him þ he scolde beieton him **þone mynstre of burch** þ hit scolde beon underðed into clun ni. oc man seið to biworde. **hæge** sitteð **þa aceres** dæleth. **god ælmihtig** adylege **iuele ræde**. 7 sone þæræft ferde **se abbot of clunni** ham to **his ærde.**

'this same year came the Abbot Henry of Angeli after Easter to Peterborough, and said that he had relinquished that monastery withal. After him came the Abbot of Clugny, Peter by name, to England by the king's leave; and was received by all, whithersoever he came, with much respect. To Peterborough he came; and there the Abbot Henry promised him that he would procure him the ministry of Peterborough, that it might be subject to Clugny. But it is said in the proverb, The hedge abideth, that acres divideth. May God Almighty frustrate evil designs. Soon after this went the Abbot of Clugny home to his country.'

There is a lot of V2, abundant coordination, and morphologically similar features to what we saw before, e.g. *Ðes*.

Next we turn to the last part, the entry from 1137; see (8) and (9), which are from the start of the entry for this year. We can look at the snip below (8) to see what precedes the nouns *k Steph* and *eom* here.

(8) Ðis gære for **þe k Steph** ofer sæ to normandi 7 ther wes under fangen forþi ð hi uuenden ð he sculde ben alsuic alse **the eom** wes. 7 for he hadde get his tresor. ac he todeld it 7 scatered sotlice. Micel hadde henri k gadered gold 7 syluer. 7 na god ne dide me for his saule thar of.

'this year, (the) King Stephen crossed the sea to go to Normandy and was received there because they thought he was like the uncle (i.e. his uncle). And because he still had his treasury, but he divided and scattered it stupidly. King Henry has gathered much gold and silver and no good did men with it for his soul.'

Preceding the nouns, we see the use of articles, *þe* and *the* in (8) and *te* in (9).

(9) Þa þe king S to Englal com þa macod he his gadering æt Oxeneford. 7 þar he nam þe b Roger of Serebi & Alexander biscop of lincol 7 te canceler Roger hise neues. 7 dide ælle in prisun. til hi iafen up here castles.

'when King Stephen came to England, he held a gathering at Oxford and there he took bishop Roger of Salisbury and Alexander bishop of Lincoln and the chancellor Roger, his nephews. And put all in prison until they gave up their castles.'

Note that names such as *þe k(ing) Steph(ne)* and *Henri k(ing)* show that the article is in complementary distribution with the preposed name, i.e. the name is article-like and the name and article cannot therefore co-occur.

Other differences with older texts are a lack of a genitive *-s* on *gære* in (8) and visible endings on nouns. In addition to articles, grammatical words have increased in number and variety, e.g. new conjunctions like *forþi ð* and *for* in (8) and *til* in (9), and an increase in light verbs, such as in *macod his gadering* and *dide in prison* in (9). Verbs still have some prefixes, such as *under fangen* and *todeld* in (8), but have lost *ge-* in *gadered* in (8) and *macod* and *iafen* in (9). There is also a particle, *up* in (9) to replace the erstwhile prefix.

The word order is still solidly V2 and many loosely connected clauses occur. A multiple negative appears in (8) as well.

4.1.3 Status and dialect

According to Clark (1970: xlvii), the morphology in the *Peterborough Chronicle* 'shows the East-Midland basis ... even more clearly than phonology does'. For instance, there are some plural present indicative forms in *-en* though not found in the excerpts discussed in section 4.1.2. Other morphological evidence of change is the loss of *-as* on *Brittes* in (2), changes in the shape of demonstratives, as in (1), the appearance of a feminine pronoun *she*, as in (10), the loss of the participial *ge-* prefix in (5), (8), and (9), and completely new complementizers, namely *for* and *till* in (8) and (9).

(10) *He brohte his wif to Engleland. & dide hire in þe castel on Canteberi. God wimman scæ wæs. oc scæ hedde litel blisse mid him.*
'he brought his wife to England and put her in a castle in Canterbury. **She** was a good woman but **she** had little bliss with him.' (*Peterborough Chronicle* for the year 1140)

Dekeyser (1986) examines relative markers in the *Peterborough Chronicle* and shows that the demonstrative option is lost, that *þe* is receding, and *þat* is increasing, especially in the final continuation. In (1) to (9), there happen not to be any relative clauses except possibly the ones introduced by *þa* in (2) and *þer* in (4), but that depends on one's analysis.

In Chapter 3, we saw the first possible occurrence of a definite article in the *Lindisfarne Gospels*. The *Peterborough Chronicle* is the other text to use a definite article really early on.

As far as the word order is concerned, Kroch and Taylor (1997) argue that V2 is strong in the North and that clitic fronting and V3 occur in the South. There are other versions of the chronicle, e.g. the southern Parker one, that can be compared. If Kroch and Taylor are correct, there should be a difference between the Parker and the Peterborough, and there is some, as in (11), where the Parker has V3 and the Peterborough V2.

(11) a. *Her on þysum geare **for** se micla here* V3
Here in this year went the big army
'in this year, the large army went.' (*Parker Chronicle* for the year 893)
b. *Her **for** se myccla here* V2
Then went the big army
'then, the large army went.' (*Peterborough Chronicle* for the year 893)

Many other constructions exhibit no difference, however, as in (12), where pronouns are preposed in the Parker and the Peterborough. Sentence (13) is actually the opposite from what we would expect, with the southern text having V2 and the northern one having more V3.

(12) a. *Her hiene bestæl se here into Werham* (*Parker Chronicle* for the year 876) V3

b. *Her hine bestæl se here into Wærham* (*Peterborough Chronicle* for the
year 876) V3
'in this year, the army stole away to Warham.'
(13) a. *Her gefeaht Ecgbryht cyning ...* (*Parker Chronicle* for the
year 833) V2
b. *Her Ecgbriht cining ge feaht ...* (*Peterborough Chronicle* for the
year 833) V3
'in this year Ecgbriht fought ...'

In conclusion, the language in this text is Old English in the early entries but Middle English in the last entries. Many of the synthetic markers have disappeared and analytic ones, such as articles and conjunctions, are appearing in the later texts. The style is highly paratactic. The dialect is Northeast Midlands in its morphology but not in its word order.

4.2 Seinte Katerine

The Katherine Group includes prose descriptions of the lives of three saints, *Seinte Katerine*, *Seinte Iuliene*, and *Seinte Marherete*, as well as two treatises, *Hali Meiðhad* and *Sawles Warde*. The texts appear in several versions; here, the Bodley 34 manuscript is used. The language is a West Midlands variety, from Herefordshire, dated between 1200 and 1220.

4.2.1 The texts

Figures 4.5 and 4.6 are taken from Ker (1960); the edited version most often used is d'Ardenne (1977) and it appears in the left-hand column in Table 4.5. The translation in the right-hand column is loosely based on Einenkel (1884). The script used by the scribe is early Gothic.

4.2.2 Analysis

The English of this text is a little more challenging than that of the *Peterborough Chronicle*. I have therefore bolded the subjects again and underlined the finite verbs of the main clauses; subordinate clauses appear in brackets.

In (14), *þeos meiden* is Katerine and it is the subject of the sentence.

(14) **þeos meiden** <u>lette</u> lutel of þ [he seide]. ant smirkinde smeðeliche <u>ȝef</u> him þullich onswere.
'this maiden thought little of that (which) he said and smilingly lightly gave him such answer.'

Two clauses are coordinated in (14) and the first contains a relative clause which is V2 or V-last. The verb is in second position in the first clause and in third position in the coordinated clause. The coordinated sentence leaves the subject unexpressed because it shares it with the first.

A demonstrative pronoun *þeos* and quantifier *þullich* appear before the nouns rather than articles. The demonstrative is a nominative feminine singular,

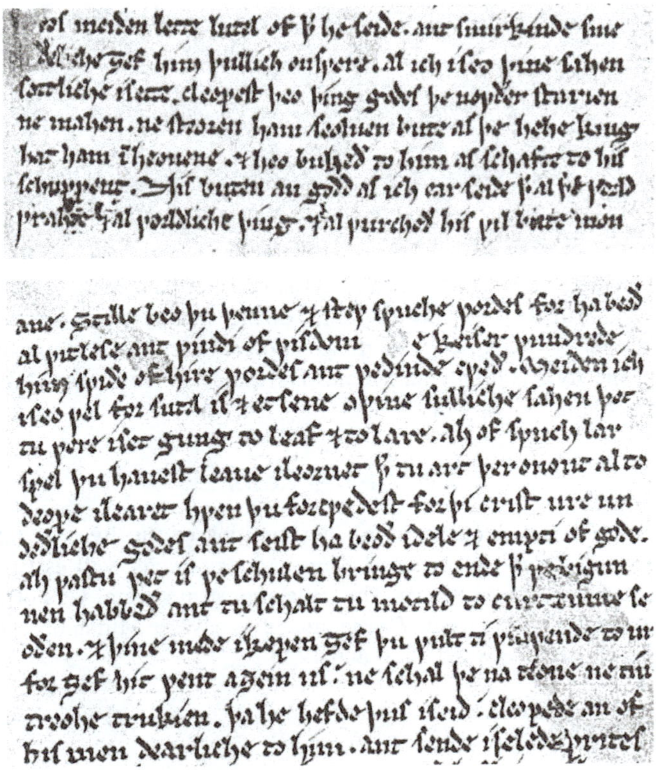

108 *Analyzing Syntax through Texts*

FIGURE 4.5. *Seinte Katerine* (Bodley 34, f. 3v and f. 4r. Reproduced with permission from the British Library Board)

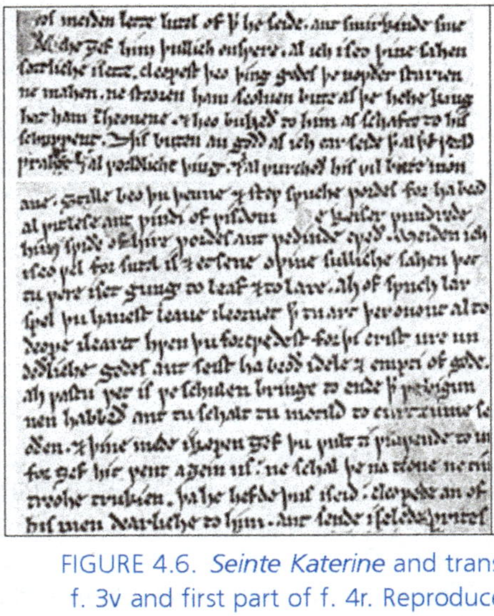

	þeos meiden lette lutel of þ he seide. ant smirkinde sme ðeliche ʒef him þullich onspere. al ich iseo þine sahen sottliche isette. cleopest þeo þing godes þe nopðer sturien ne mahen. ne steoren ham seoluen bute as þe hehe king hat ham in heouene. 7 heo buheð to him as schafte to his schuppent. Nis buten an god as ich ear seide þ al þe porld prahte 7 al porliche þing. 7 al purcheð his pil bute mon ane. Stille beo þu þenne 7 step spuche pordes for ha beoð al pitlese ant pindi of pisdom þe keiser pundrede him spiðe of hire pords ant pedinde cpeð. Meiden ich iseo pel for sutel is 7 etsene oþine sulliche sahen þet tu pere iset gung to leaf 7 to lare. ah of spuch lar spel þu hauest leaue ilearnet þ tu ert þer onont al to deope ilearet hpen tu forcpedest forþi crist ure un deðliche godes ant seist ha beoð idele 7 empti of gode. ah pastu þet is þe schulen bringe to ende þ þebegun nen habbeð and tu schalt tu motild to curt cume se oðen. 7 þine mede ikepen ʒef þu pult ti pilipende to ure. for ʒef hit pent aʒein us. ne schal þe na teone ne tin treohe trukien. þa he hefde þus iseid. cleopode an of his men dearliche to him. ant sende iselede iprites …

FIGURE 4.6. *Seinte Katerine* and transcription (Bodley 34, the last part of f. 3v and first part of f. 4r. Reproduced with permission from the British Library Board)

TABLE 4.5. Transcription and translation of f. 3v and f. 4r of *Seinte Katerine*

þeos meiden lette lutel of þ he seide. ant smirkinde smeðeliche 3ef him þullich onswere. al ich iseo þine sahen sottliche isette. cleopest þeo þing godes þe nowðer sturien ne mahen. ne steoren ham seoluen bute as þe hehe king hat ham in heouene. 7 heo buheð to him as schafte to his schuppent. Nis buten an god as ich ear seide þ al þe world wrahte 7 al worliche þing. 7 al wurcheð his wil bute mon ane. Stille beo þu þenne 7 stew swuche wordes for ha beoð al witlese ant windi of wisdom þe keiser wundrede him swiðe of hire words ant wedinde cweð. Meiden ich iseo wel for sutel is 7 etsene oþine sulliche sahen þet tu were iset gung to leaf 7 to lare. Ah of swuch lar spel þu hauest leaue ilearnet þ tu ert þer onont al to deope ilearet hwen tu forcwedest forþi crist ure un deðliche godes ant seist ha beoð idele 7 empti of gode. ah wastu wet is we schulen bringe to ende þ webegun nen habbeð and tu schalt tu motild to curt cume se oðen. 7 þine mede ikepen 3ef þu wult ti wiliwende to ure. for 3ef hit went a3ein us. ne schal þe na teone ne tin treohe trukien. þa he hefde þus iseid. cleopode an of his men dearliche to him. ant sende iselede iwrites ...	This maiden thought little of what he said. and smilingly gave him such answer. I see all your savings are foolishly put out. Call (you) those things Gods that neither stir nor have power to move themselves except as the high king commands them in heaven. And they bow to him as creation to his creator. Not is (there) but one God as I before said that made all the world and all worldly things and all do his will except man alone. Be still then and stop such words because they are all witless and empty of wisdom. The emperor wondered very much at her words and said angrily 'Maiden, I see very well because it is clear and plain of your strange sayings that you were set young to belief and to learning. But of such learning you have, dear, learned that you are thereon too deeply learned when you blaspheme, for your Christ, our immortal gods and say they are idle and empty of good. But know you what is we should bring to end that we begun have and you shall, you disputator, come to court then and your meed keep if you want your will turn to ours. Because if it goes against us not shall you no pain nor torture lack.' Then he had thus said (he) called one of his men privately to him and sent sealed writings ...

according to Table 4.4, and this fits the function it has of modifying a feminine subject. The object *þullich onswere*, however, should get accusative and this is only compatible with *onswere* being neuter, not feminine as it is in Old English.

Note the *-inde* on the present participle *smirkinde*, which shows southern influence, while the *on-* in *onswere* is a northernism.

The answer that is given follows in the next fragment in (15) and continues in the full sentence in (16).

(15) **al [ich iseo]** *þine sahen sottliche isette.*
   'all I see (is) your savings foolishly put out.'

The fragment has a subject that contains a relative clause, a deleted copula, and a subject predicate modified by a participle clause *sottliche isette* with a prefix *i-* typical for past participles in the Midlands. There is also an *i-* in the present *iseo* and which we'll see later in this text in (19) and in other texts. It is not usually remarked upon in grammars but I think it must be an analogical extension to the finite forms of the participle prefix.

I have analyzed the passage in (16) as containing two independent sentences, the first with a relative and adverbial clause inside. It could also be a coordinated sentence.

(16) <u>cleopest</u> þeo þing godes [þe nowðer sturien ne mahen. ne steoren ham seoluen [bute as þe hehe king hat ham in heouene]]. 7 **heo** <u>buheð</u> to him as schafte to his schuppent.
'call (you) those (or these) things gods that neither stir nor have power to move themselves except as the high king commands them in heaven. And they bow to him as creation to his creator.'

There are quite a number of verbs in (16) with varied endings. The first verb has a second person *-est* ending and lacks a subject pronoun *þu* 'you'. The verbs inside the relative clause are all finite plurals which end in *-en*, typical for the Midlands. The third person plural ending on *buheð* shows there is variation between *-en* and *eð*. The demonstrative *þeo* is not as it appears in Old English; in fact, the form *þeo* appears neither in Table 2.11 nor in Table 4.4. The plural third person pronoun is still *heo* for the nominative and *ham* for the accusative. Later, these change to *they* and *them*, respectively, in this dialect as well. The reflexive *seoluen* forms the reflexive but is still separate from the pronoun, as shown in the snip ⟨ham seoluen⟩.

In (17), there is a contracted negative auxiliary that starts the statement.

(17) <u>N**is**</u> buten **an god** [as ich ear seide] [þ al þe world wrahte 7 al worliche þing]. 7 al wurcheð his wil bute mon ane.
'there is but one God as I before said that made all the world and all worldly things and all do his will except man only.'

I regard the passage as consisting of two coordinated clauses. The word order is V2 in the main clause (if we count the contracted negative as the first element), V-last in the first subordinate, and V-last with an extraposed object *al worliche þing* in the second clause. The last clause is V2 or SV.

There is a definite article before *world* and a relative *þ*. The *an* preceding *god* is a numeral here but indefinite articles are present in this text.

The next clause starts with a coordinated imperative followed by an adverbial introduced by *for*.

(18) Stille <u>beo</u> **þu** þenne 7 <u>stew</u> swuche wordes [for ha beoð al witlese ant windi of wisdom].
'be (you) quiet then and stop such words because they are all witless and empty of wisdom.'

There are no case endings; the noun *word*, which is neuter in Old English and, in that stage, has no ending in the nominative or accusative plural, now shows the *-es* as an indication of a generalized plural. As for the third person plural pronouns, Einenkel (1884: 1) makes the observation that the plural *ha* is used for less exalted third persons than *heo*. Compare (18) with (16) and see if this observation makes sense.

In (19), the emperor states his amazement at Katerine's words.

(19) *þe keiser <u>wundrede</u> him swiðe of hire words ant wedinde cweð. Meiden ich iseo wel [for sutel is 7 etsene opine sulliche sahen [þet tu were iset gung to leaf 7 to lare]].*
'the emperor was very much amazed at her words and said angrily "Maiden, I see very well because it is clear and plain of your strange sayings that you were set young to belief and to learning".'

Quotes may have periods around them and are possibly not seen as integrated in another clause the way Modern English does. The word order is SV in the main clause and also in the quote. The adverbial starting with *for* has a clausal subject *þet tu were iset gung to leaf 7 to lare* which in Modern English would prompt an expletive *it* before *sutel*.

Other points of interest are a reflexive *him* after *wundrede* that isn't reflexive in the modern sense, another *-inde* participle, an *i-* prefixed past participle *iset* and present tense *iseo*, and possibly a dative *-e* on *lare*.

The next passage is really hard to comprehend but I think the core is that 'you have learned something' and then the something is further explained.

(20) *Ah of swuch lar spel þu <u>hauest</u> leaue ilearnet [þ tu ert þer onont al to deope ilearet [hwen tu forcwedest forþi crist ure un deðliche godes ant seist [ha beoð idele 7 empti of gode]]].*
'but of such learning you have, dear, learned that you are too deeply learned when you blaspheme, for your Christ, our immortal gods and say they are idle and empty of good.'

The brackets indicate an object, an adverbial, and another object. All of these clauses, as well as the main clause, have an SV order. This shows a shift away from the V2/V-last word order of older English.

There are second person singular endings on verbs, *hauest, ert, forcwedest,* and *seist*, third person plural *beoð*, and two participles with *i-*, namely *ilear(n)et*. Note variation between *þu* and *tu*, and the use of *ha* rather than *heo*.

The address continues in (21) and I have again put brackets in to mark subordinate clauses.

(21) *ah <u>wastu</u> [wet is [we schulen bringe to ende [þ we begin nen habbeð and tu schalt tu motild to curt cume se oðen. 7 þine mede ikepen [ʒef þu wult ti wiliwende to ure]]].[[for ʒef hit went aʒein us]. ne schal þe na teone ne tin treohe trukien].*
'but do you know what (it) is we should end that we begun have and you shall, you disputator, come to court then and keep your meed if you want your will turn to our. Because if it goes against us not you shall lack no pain nor torture.'

An adverb *ac*, or conjunction depending on your point of view, starts the sentence and the verb is second followed by the pronominal subject. Apart from this first VS and the last (*schal þe*), all other word orders are SV. The subject *tu* is attached to the verb *was*, as the snip shows ▫▫▫. The passage is again verb-heavy: *wast, schulen, bringe, beginnen, habbeð, schalt, cume, ikepen, wult, wende, went, schal,* and *trukien.* These forms show endings we've already seen, e.g. *-st, -en,* and *-eð.* Another interesting feature is the negative concord in the last part and the lack, from a Modern English perspective, of dummy *do* in the initial question.

I have not marked the subject and finite verbs of the main clause in (22) because the first clause may be subordinate to the second.

(22) þa he hefde þus iseid. cleopode an of his men dearliche to him. ant sende iselede iwrites ...
'then he had thus said. (He) called one of his men privately to him and sent sealed writings ...'

The first clause has an SV order for the finite verb and a V-last order for the non-finite *iseid.* This first clause could be the first constituent in the second clause. With the left out subject to the finite verb *cleopode,* it is hard to tell. Other features involve what we've seen before, e.g. the *i-* on participles.

4.2.3 Status and dialect

Seinte Katerine shows conjunctions such as *for* appearing in (18) and (19) and frequent complex embedded clauses, as in (20) and (21). The style is therefore hypotactic. The word order differs from older English in often being SV, as in (20), so that makes for a non V2 structure. There are still V-last clauses, e.g. in (17) and (22). These orders are juxtaposed in (23).

(23) a. Ah of swuch lar spel þu **hauest** ... ilearnet   (20) SV
       but of such learning you have   learned
    b. as ich ear **seide**   (17) V-last
       as I before said
    c. þa he **hefde** þus **iseid**   (22) SV and V-last
       then he had thus said

Verbal inflections are mainly full, e.g. second person singular *-est* in (16) and (20), but the plural *-en* in (15) and the *eþ* in (18) both occur. The present participle, as in (14), ends in *-inde,* which is a southernism. The *i-* marks past participles, like *iseon* and *isenden,* and occasionally a finite verb.

There is some case left on nouns, e.g. *heouene* in (16) is dative but the ending on *words* in (18) is just plural. The feminine *heo* in (16) and *ha* in (18) and plural *ham* in (16) are used, typical for early southern texts. The relative markers are *þe* in (16) and zero in (15) and there is a definite article in (16). The reflexive is making inroads, e.g. *ham seoluen* in (16), but *him* in (19). There is negative concord in (21).

The dialect is more southern than northern, as is typical for the West Midlands. I have already indicated the *-inde* ending and there is the absence of the third person plural *they* and the feminine *she* as all typical for southern texts. The *-en* plural in so early a text, however, marks it as non-southern. As to its style, it shows quite some subordination through relative and adverbial clauses.

4.3 The Owl and the Nightingale

The date of composition of *The Owl and the Nightingale* is unclear, as is its geographical origin (see Fulk 2012: 253). In section 4.3.3, I will suggest a southeastern origin but some have suggested Worcestershire, which is south of Birmingham and more western. Its genre is that of a debate poem, where two birds insult each other and try to win the debate. This genre was known from French and Latin sources but the loans (such as *plait* and *plaiding*) from these languages are infrequent and this suggests an English origin.

4.3.1 The text

The Owl and Nightingale is preserved in two manuscripts, Cotton Caligula A IX and Jesus College, Oxford, MS 29. The Cotton edition is used in Figure 4.7, taken from Ker (1963). It is from the middle of the thirteenth century. A transcription can be found at *Bibliotheca Augustana*,[2] which I have adapted in Table 4.6; and a translation appears below each sentence, which I have adapted from *Wessex Parallel WebTexts*.[3]

The script is Gothic. In some Middle English texts, the shape of the thorn *þ* (the rendition of the interdental fricative) shifts; it loses its top extension and looks like the wynn. Many times, *th* appears instead. I will change the thorn to *th* and the wynn to *w*.

4.3.2 Analysis

The first part of (24) shows the use of periods to indicate breaks or clauses and the structure is very paratactic. I have again indicated subjects in bold and underlined finite verbs.

(24) **Ich** was in one sumere dale. in one suthe di3ele hale. iherde **ich** holde grete tale an hule and one ni3tingale.
'I was in a valley in springtime, in a very secluded corner, and heard an owl and a nightingale holding a great debate.'

It could be that the first clause is subordinate to the second if we think of it as 'while I was in a valley, I heard ...'. The evidence for the second clause being the main clause is that it would then be V2 with the first clause in first position.

The language of this stage is analytic, with pronouns and articles in place. The use of *one* is that of an indefinite article rather than a numeral. I think the -*e* endings are just the silent -*e* not dative endings. Note the *i*- on the past tense *iherde*, an extension we've also seen in *Seinte Katerine*.

(25) starts as SV (or V2).

(25) **That plait** was stif 7 starc 7 strong. sum wile softe 7 lud among. an aither a3en other sval. 7 let that vuele mod ut al. 7 either seide of otheres custe that alre worste that hi wuste: 7 hure 7 hure of othere songe hi holde plaiding suthe stronge.
'that argument was fierce, passionate, and vehement, sometimes soft, sometimes loud; and each of them swelled with rage against the other and let out all her

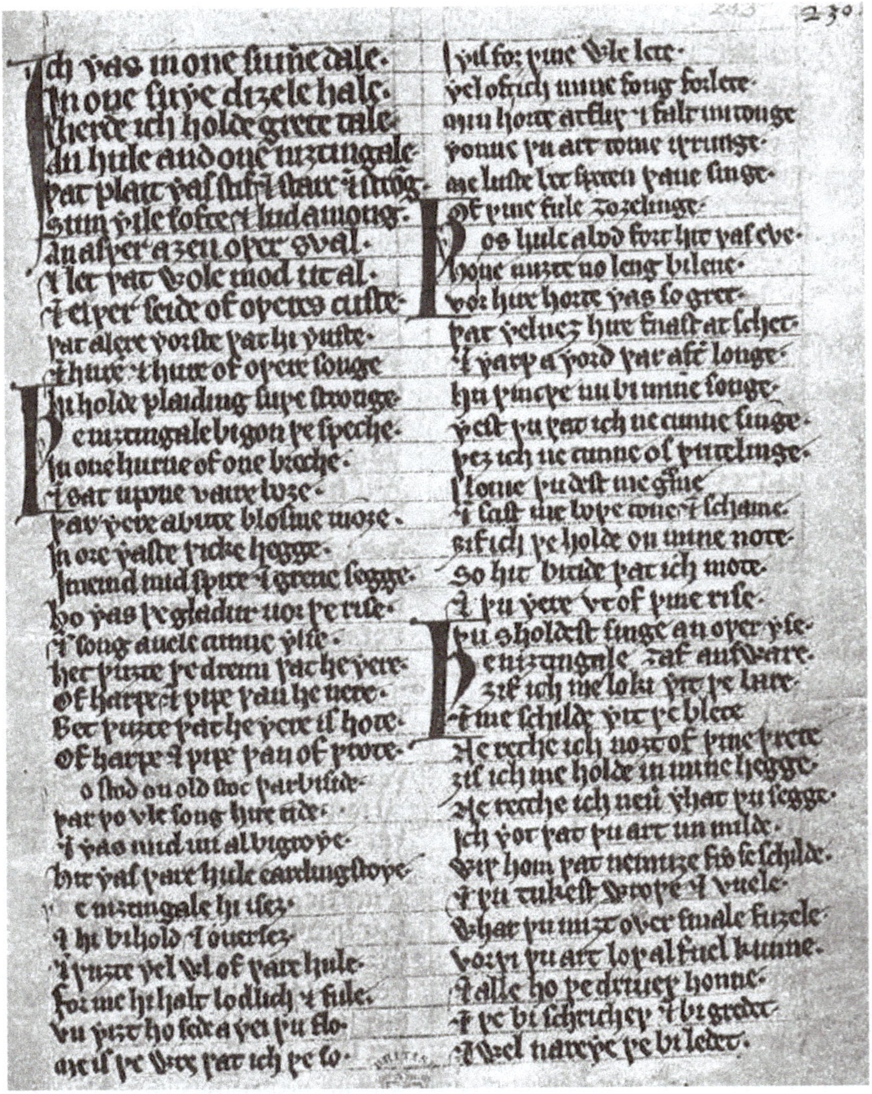

FIGURE 4.7. *The Owl and the Nightingale* (Cotton Caligula A IX, f. 233. Reproduced with permission from the British Library Board)

anger, and said the very worst she could think of about the other's character, and at intervals they argued vehemently against each other's song.'

When the subject is present, we can observe that the word order is SV, e.g. *that plait was, hi wuste,* and *hi holde.*

As for the morphology, the third person plural pronoun is *hi* and a present participle ends in *-ing* which are southern traits. One genitive is marked (*others*) and another is not (*othere*) so this stage is not very synthetic.

TABLE 4.6. *The Owl and the Nightingale*, lines 1–68

Ich was in one sumere dale.	Iwis for thine vule lete.
in one suthe di3ele hale.	wel [oft ich] mine song forlete.
iherde ich holde grete tale	min horte atflith 7 falt mi tonge
an hule and one ni3tingale.	wonne thu art tome ithrunge.
That plait was stif 7 starc 7 strŏg.	me luste bet speten thane singe.
sum wile softe 7 lud among.	of thine fule 3o3elinge.
an aither a3en other sval.	Thos hule abod fort hit was eve.
7 let that vuele mod ut al.	hone mi3te no leng bileue.
7 either seide of otheres custe	vor hire horte was so gret.
that alre worste that hi wuste:	that welne3 hire fnast atschet.
7 hure 7 hure of othere songe	7 warp a word thar after longe.
hi holde plaiding suthe stronge.	Hu thincthe nu bi mine songe.
The ni3tingale bigon the speche.	West thu that ich ne cunne singe.
in one hurne of one breche.	the3 ich ne cunne of writelinge.
7 sat upone vaire bo3e.	Ilome thu dest me grame
thar were abute blosme ino3e.	7 seist me bothe tone 7 schame.
in ore waste thicke hegge.	3if ich the holde on mine uote.
imeind mid spire 7 grene segge.	so hit bitide that ich mote.
Ho was the gladur uor the rise.	7 thu were vt of thine rise.
7 song auele cunne wise.	thu sholdest singe an other wise.
bet thu3te the dreim that he were	The ni3tingale 3af answare.
of harpe 7 pipe than he nere.	3if ich me loki wit the bare.
bet thu3te that he were ishote	7 me schilde wit the blete
of harpe 7 pipe than of throte.	ne reche ich no3t of thine threte
[Th]o stod on old stoc thar biside.	3if ich me holde in mine hegge.
thar tho vle song hire tide.	ne recche ich neuer what thu segge.
7 was mid iui al bigrowe.	Ich wot that thu art unmilde.
hit was thare hule eardingstowe.	with hom that ne mu3e from the schilde.
[Th]e ni3tingale hi ise3.	7 thu tukest wrothe 7 vuele.
7 hi bihold 7 ouerse3.	whar thu mi3t, over smale fu3ele.
7 thu3te wel vul of thare hule.	Vorthi thu art loth al fuel kunne.
for me hi halt lodlich 7 fule.	7 alle ho the driueth hone.
Vn wi3t ho sede awei thu flo.	7 the bischricheth 7 bigredet.
me is the wurs that ich the so.	7 wel narewe the biledet.

In (26), there are a lot of periods but not as many clauses.

(26) **The ni3tingale** <u>bigon</u> the speche. in one hurne of one breche. 7 sat upone vaire bo3e. **thar** <u>were</u> abute blosme ino3e. in ore waste thicke hegge. imeind mid spire 7 grene segge.

'the nightingale began the argument in the corner of a clearing, and perched on a beautiful branch. There was plenty of blossom around it, in an impenetrable thick hedge, with reeds and green sedge growing through it.'

There is a coordinate first clause (*bigon 7 sat up*) and another independent clause (*thar were* ...) that has a possible dummy *thar* as subject, a novelty in Early Middle English. There is an *i-* on the past participle *imeind* and a voiced *v-* starting *vaire*. The latter two features will be relevant to determine the dialect.

(27) has a paratactic character. It starts with a verb *was* coordinated with another verb *song*. Then follow two instances of the impersonal verb *thu3te* each without a subject but each with a clausal object.

> (27) **Ho** <u>was</u> the gladur uor the rise. 7 song auele cunne wise. bet thu3te the dreim
> [that he were
> of harpe 7 pipe [than he nere]]. bet thu3te [that he were ishote. of harpe 7 pipe than of throte].
> 'she was the happier because of the branch and sang in many different ways. Rather (it) seemed the music was from a harp or a pipe than not; rather (it) seemed it was shot from harp and pipe than from a throat.'

Note the use of the feminine *ho* and the neuter *he* to refer to the music. The use of *uor* ( ) is that of a preposition 'because of'.

There is a contracted negative *nere* ( )and another *i-* on the past participle *ishote*.

The first letter of (28) is hard to read in the manuscript and this unclarity is indicated by the brackets.

> (28) *[Th]o* <u>stod</u> **on old stoc** thar biside. thar **tho vle** <u>song</u> hire tide. 7 was mid iui al bigrowe. **hit** <u>was</u> thare hule eardingstowe.
> 'then stood an old stump nearby where the owl sang her Hours, and which was all overgrown with ivy. It was the owl's dwellingplace.'

The initial adverb makes this sentence clearly V2 and not SV. The second SV clause could be independent in Middle English, as I have indicated through the underlining of the finite verb *song*, but the Modern English translation embeds it as a relative clause. The coordinate clause that starts with *7* modifies *stoc*. The last clause is a simple SV clause.

I am not clear what the demonstrative *tho* before *vle* is; it could be a changed feminine nominative *þeo* 'this'. There is a feminine genitive singular demonstrative *thare* before the later *hule*. Note also the past participle *bigrowe*, and compound *eardingstowe*.

The initial letter in (29) is unclear in the manuscript, again indicated by the brackets.

> (29) *[Th]e ni3tingale* hi <u>ise3</u>. 7 hi bihold 7 ouerse3. 7 thu3te wel vul of thare hule. [for me hi halt lodlich 7 fule].
> 'the nightingale looked at her, and scrutinized her and despised her, and thought foul of the owl because she is regarded as ugly and dirty.'

The main clause is composed of a string of coordinate verbs. When the object of these verbs is a pronoun, it precedes the verb (*hi ise3* and *hi behold*). The adverbial clause starting with *for* has an impersonal subject *me* followed by the object pronoun *hi* and then the verb and the object predicate. (29) strongly shows that pronouns hold on to their earlier pre-verbal position.

Morphologically interesting, there is another finite verb *ise3* marked with *i-* and a possible genitive *thare*.

The next passage quotes what the nightingale said.

(30) *Vn wi3t* **ho** sede *[awei thu flo]. me* is *the wurs [that ich the so].*
'evil creature, she said, fly away. To me (it) is worse that I see you so.'

Note the absence of quotation marks, which is typical for Old and Middle English texts, and the predominance of SV word order, although an 'it' is left out (from a Modern English perspective) and the last clause is V-last because of the pronoun preceding the verb.

The following sentence starts with three adverbials (*Iwis, for thine vule lete,* and *wel oft*) and then a subject (*ich*), object (*mine song*), and verb (*forlete*) follow. The coordinate sentence that comes next is fairly standard in word order and the last clause has an impersonal verb *luste*.

(31) *Iwis for thine vule lete. wel oft* **ich** *mine song* forlete. **min horte** atflith *7 falt mi tonge wonne thu art to me ithrunge. Me* luste *bet speten thane singe. of thine fule 3o3elinge.*
'certainly I often have to stop singing because of your ugly face. My heart flees away and my tongue folds, when you are thrust on me. I'd rather spit than sing about your wretched howling.'

There are a lot of morphological options in Middle English, e.g. infinitivals end in *-en* and *-e* (*speten* in (31) has *-en* and *singe* has *-e*) and *mine* and *mi* both occur before a noun starting with a consonant. The third person singular ending on the verb in (31) is *-th*.

In (32), the main verbs with their subjects have been indicated. Punctuation is plentiful in marking most (sub)ordinate clauses.

(32) **Thos hule** abod *[fort hit was eve].* **hone** mi3te *no leng bileue. [vor hire horte was so gret. [that welne3 hire fnast at schet. 7 warp a word thar after longe]].*
'this owl waited until it was evening. She couldn't hold back any longer, because she was so angry that she could hardly breathe, and finally she spoke.'

The word order is SV throughout and negative concord appears in the second main clause between *ne* and *no*. The demonstrative *thos* is most likely the proximal.

There is a *fort* instead of *til* and a conjunction *vor*. The *fort* and *vor* obviously show variation in the voicing of their initial consonant. We'd have to check if the preposition always has the *f-* and the conjunction the *v-*. In any case, the use of *v-* presents evidence of southeastern influence.

In (33), I have given a long passage in which the first verb is impersonal and the next V-initial. The other word orders are SV with one preverbal object (*the holde*).

(33) *Hu* thincthe *nu bi mine songe.* Wenst **thu** *[that ich ne cunne singe.[the3 ich ne cunne of writelinge]].* Ilome *[thu dest me grame 7 seist me bothe tone 7 schame]. [3if ich the holde on mine uote.[so hit betide [that ich mote]]. 7 thu were vt of thine rise].* **thu** sholdest *singe an other wise.*

'how does my song seem to you now? Do you think that I can't sing just because I can't twitter? You often insult me and say things to upset and embarrass me. If I held you in my talons – if only I could! – and you were off your branch, you'd sing a very different tune!'

The passage shows quite some embedding as well, as indicated by the brackets. The morphology on the verb is elaborate in its frequent -*(e)st* endings, appropriate for the second person singular present tense.

There is again a rather long passage in (34) in which everything after *answare* is a quote which I have not put brackets around.

(34) **The ni3tingale** <u>3af</u> *answare. 3if ich me loki wit the bare. 7 me schilde wit the blete ne reche ich no3t of thine threte 3if ich me holde in mine hegge. ne recche ich neuer what thu segge. Ich wot that thu art unmilde. with hom that ne mu3e from the schilde. 7 thu tukest wrothe 7 vuele. whar thu mi3t, over smale fu3ele. Vorthi thu art loth al fuel-kunne. 7 alle ho the driueth hone. 7 the bischricheth 7 bigredet. 7 wel narewe the biledet.*

'the nightingale answered: as long as I keep out of the open, and protect myself against being exposed, I'm not bothered about your threats; as long as I stay put in my hedge, I don't care at all what you say. I know that you're ruthless towards those who can't protect themselves from you, and that you bully small birds cruelly and harshly. That is why all kinds of birds hate you, and they all drive you away, and screech and scream around you, and attack you.'

The answer starts with a coordinate adverbial (from 3*if* to *blete*) and then a negative *ne*, a verb, a subject, and another negative. Then follows another adverbial (3*if ich me holde in mine hegge*) that is not marked by a preceding period and that seems to go with the second *ne recche ich.* The clauses after this are SV.

Other interesting aspects are *me* functioning as a reflexive, the negative concord (e.g. *ne reche ich no3t* and *ne recche ich neuer*), the conjunction *vorthi*, the use of *hom* and *ho*, and the *-th* on *driveth*.

4.3.3 Status and dialect

As mentioned in the beginning of section 4.3.2, the style is relatively paratactic, as in (24) and (27), but there is some embedding, as in (33). The word order is varied, though often SV, as in (25) and (26), with a possible V2 in (28). Pronouns still precede the verb, as in (29), and possibly some V-last orders occur, as in *thu art to me ithrunge* in (30). I juxtapose examples of these in (35).

(35) a. Vn wi3t ho **sede** awei thu flo   (30) SV
Evil creature she said away you fly
'fly away, you evil creature!'
b. [Th]o **stod** on old stoc thar biside   (28) V2
Then stood an old oak thare besides
'an old oak stood beside.'
c. wel oft ich mine song **forlete**   (31) V-last
very often I my song leave
'very often I leave my song.'

Early Middle English 1100–1300 119

    d. [Th]e ni3tingale hi **ise3**   (29) Pre-V pronouns
       The nightingale her saw
       'the nightingale saw her.'

There is a lack of reflexives ending in *-self*, but a presence of indefinite articles *one/an* in (24) and of possible dummy pronouns, as in (26). This presence makes the stage analytic.

In the beginning of this chapter, I mentioned that the date of composition is not known, nor is the geographical region. I would argue that this is a southern text on the basis of the (still) elaborate verbal endings (a *-th* for plural present and *-est* for second person singular), the presence of *ho* for third person feminine singular and *hi* for third person plural, and the occurrence of multiple negation in (32) and (34). The variation between *uor* and *for* suggests a southeastern origin.

4.4 The Lion

The Physiologus, in which *The Lion* appears, is also known by the name of *The Bestiary* and dates from around 1300. It was probably written at Norwich, which makes it an East Midlands text.

4.4.1 The text

The manuscript resides in the British Library under the name of Arundel 292.[4] A good edition by Wirtjes (1991) is what I have used for the transcription in Table 4.7, as well as Wright (1960). As you can see in line 2, the *g* and *r* have changed their shape, and line 3 shows that the *f* has moved upwards. Wright (1960: 8) calls this a 'book hand with court-hand flavor' and Roberts (2005: 154) 'Gothic *littera textualis rotunda media*'. The special characteristics are the splitting of the upper parts of, for instance, the *l* and the *h* in line 1. Capitals are marked in black and some in red. The first part describes the lion (*Natura leonis*) and the second gives an explanation (*Signification*).

The transcription in Table 4.7 uses the *p* (wyn) for the *w* and the ð (eth) for the *th* but does not distinguish between the *i* with and without a forward stroke, which became the later English dot on this letter. This scribe puts strokes on the *i* when there are *n*, *m*, or *u* letters around that make it hard to read. See *him* in line 3. I am providing a word-by-word translation and will give a more fluent translation in the analysis section.

4.4.2 Analysis

The sentences in this excerpt are very loosely connected, i.e. paratactic, as is clear from the abundance of periods in the manuscript which sometimes just mark phrases. I have added many sentences together so as not to create too many separate passages. I have not used brackets to show clause structure to indicate the main clauses because I might be changing the original meaning too much. For the same reason bolding of the subject and underlining of the main verb have

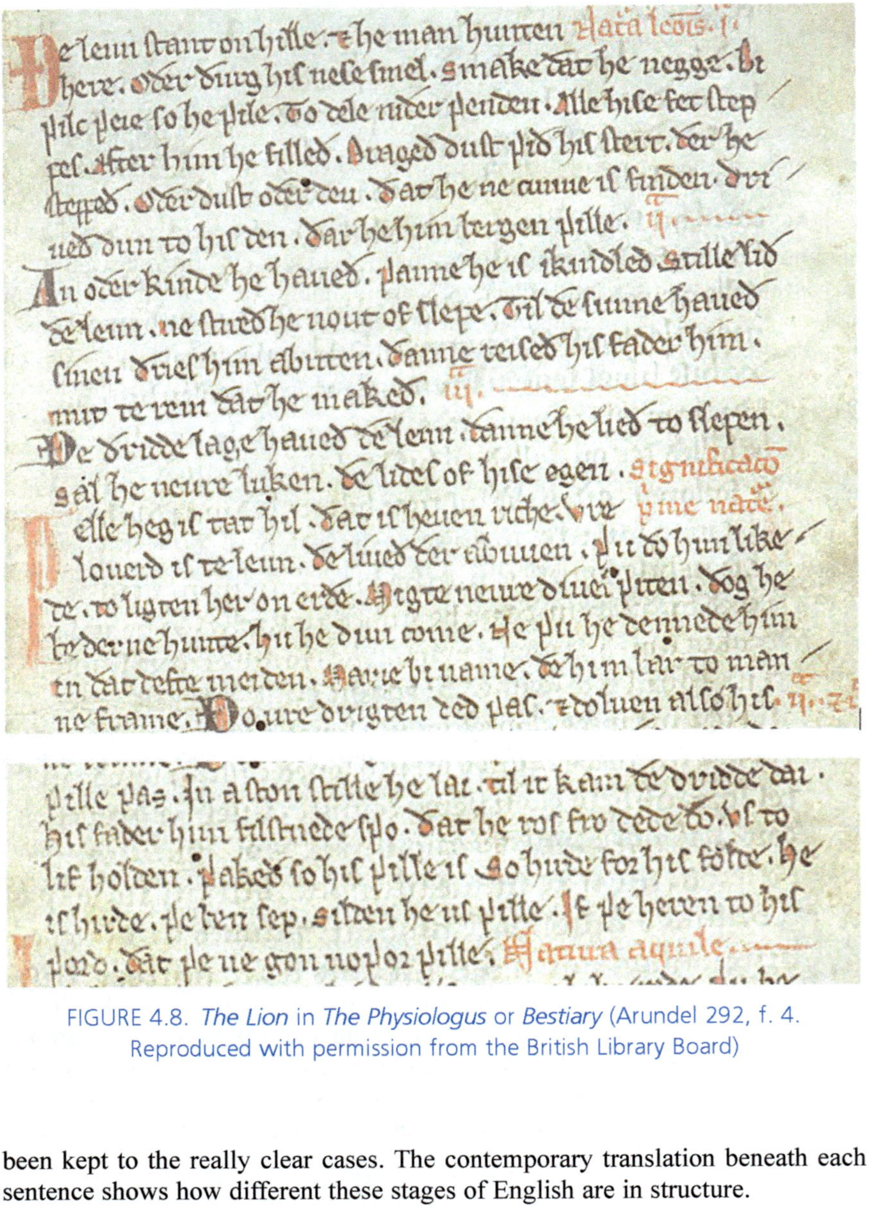

FIGURE 4.8. *The Lion* in *The Physiologus* or *Bestiary* (Arundel 292, f. 4. Reproduced with permission from the British Library Board)

been kept to the really clear cases. The contemporary translation beneath each sentence shows how different these stages of English are in structure.

(36) starts out by introducing the lion.

(36) *Ðe leun stant on hille. 7 he man hunten here. Oðer ðurg his nese smel. Smake ðat he negge. Bi wilc weie so he wile. To dele niðer wenden.*
'the lion stands on a hill. If he hears a man hunt or, through his sense of smell, perceives that he comes near, he will go to lower parts.'

The passage starts with a description of six clauses each ending with a period. As for the word order, SV seems to be prevalent, with some OV and Adverbial-V

Early Middle English 1100–1300

TABLE 4.7. Transcription and word-by-word rendition of *The Lion*

Ðe leun stant on hille. 7 he man hunten **Nat(ur)a leðis** here. Oðer ðurg his nese smel. Smake ðat he negge. Bi pilc peie so he pile. To dele niðer penden. Alle hise fet step pes. After him he filleð. Drageð dust pið his stert . Ðer he steppeð. Oðer dust oðer deu. ðat he ne cunne is finden. Dri ueð dun to his den. ðar he him bergen pille.	The lion stands on a hill and (if) he man hunt hears. Or through his smell.sense (may) smell that he nears. By which way so he will. To parts lower turn. All his feet's steps after him he fills. (He) drags dust with his tail. there he steps. Either dust or dew. that he not can them find. (he) drives down to his den. there he himself hide wants.
An oðer kinde he haueð. panne he is ikindled Stille lið ðe leun. Ne stireð he nout of slepe. Til ðe sunne haueð sinen ðries him abuten. Ðanne reiseð his fader him. mit te rem ðat he makeð. Ðe ðridde lage haueð ðe leun. ðanne he lieð to slepen. Sal he neure luken. ðe lides of hise egen. **Significaciõ**	Another characteristic he has. when he is born quiet lies the lion. (he) stirs not from sleep till the sun has shone thrice about him. then rouses his father him. with the cry that he makes. The third law applies to the lion. then he lies to sleep. Shall he never lock. the lids of his eyes.
Welle heg is tat hil. Ðat is heuen riche. Vre **prime nature.** louerd is te leun. Ðe liueð ðer abuuen. pu ðo him like te. To ligten her on erðe. Migte neure diuel piten. ðog he be derne hunte. Hu he dun come. Ne pu he dennede him in ðat defte meiden. Marie bi name. Ðe him bar to man ne frame. Ðo ure drigten ded was. 7 doluen also his pille pas. In a ston stille he lai. til it kam ðe dridde dai.	Very high is that hill. that is heaven's kingdom. Our lord is the lion. that lives there above. How then he wanted. to come down to earth. Might never devil know. though he be craftily hunting. how he came down. Not how he sheltered himself in that humble maiden. Mary by name. which him bore to man's advantage. Then our lord dead was. and buried as his will was. In a stone still he lay. till it came the third day (when)
His fader him filstnede spo. ðat he ros fro dede ðo. vs to lif holden. pakeð so his pille is So hirde for his folde. He is hirde. pe ben sep. Silden he us pille. If pe heren to his pord. Ðat pe ne gon nopor pille.	His father him helped so. that he rose from dead then. (so as to) us to life hold. (he) wakes so his will is So (like) shepherd for his flock. He is shepherd. we are sheep. Shield he us wants. if we listen to his words. that we don't go nowhere astray.

orders, as in *man hunten* and *niðer wenden*. Since the clauses mainly involve subjects and verbs, we can't say a lot.

Some nouns have an article (*Ðe leun*) but some lack one (*man*). The verbal endings are a mix of one present indicative (*stant*), several subjunctives emphasizing possibility (*here, smake, negge, wile*), and two infinitives (*hunten* and *wenden*). The latter have *-en* endings and differ from the Old English *-an* forms. Possible dative case endings could be the *-e* on *hille* (on hille), *weie*, and *dele*.

(37) contains eight periods but can easily be seen as one contemporary sentence.

(37) *[Alle hise fet steppes. After him he filleð]. [Drageð dust wið his stert]. [ðer he steppeð. Oðer dust oðer deu].[ðat he ne cunne is finden].[Driueð dun to his den]. [ðar he him bergen wille].*

'he fills all his footsteps behind him and drags dust with his tail where he steps, either dust or dew, so that he cannot be found; and hastens down to his den where he wants to hide.'

The first period appears after the topicalized object. The next group of words shows that the word order is clearly SV, because after the initial object, an adverbial follows but then the subject *he* and the verb *filleð*. This SV word order appears in all other clauses; only in the last clause is the auxiliary *wille* last and the reflexive object pronoun *him* preverbal.

The set of clauses in (37) is verb-'heavy' and the verbal endings are third person singular indicative (*filleð*, *drageð*, *steppeð*, *driueð*), two modals (*cunne*, *wille*), and two infinitives (*finden*, *bergen*). The form *is* after *cunne* could be the third person plural pronoun (Wirtjes 1991: 56).

The next set of clauses is given in (38).

(38) *An oðer kinde he haueð. wanne he is ikindled Stille lið ðe leun. ne stireð he nout of slepe. Til ðe sunne haueð sinen ðries him abuten. ðanne reiseð his fader him. mit te rem ðat he makeð.*
'the lion has another characteristic. When he is born, he lies still and doesn't stir in his sleep till the sun has shone thrice around him. Then his father wakes him with the noise that he makes.'

It starts again with a preposed object *an oðer kinde* followed by a subject and a verb. The second clause shows a sign of embedding because it uses a *wh*-word *wanne*. There is postposition of the subject *ðe leun* in the third clause. The verb *stireð* appears after the negative *ne* in initial position in the negative clause which shows negative concord because of the additional negative *nout* as shown in the snip ne ſtiueð he nout. Then comes an adverbial clause, introduced by *til*, with SVO order and a V2 main clause that starts with *ðanne*. The last part of the sentence is a PP adverbial that contains a relative clause.

There are articles before *leun*, *sunne*, and *rem* and the verbs show third person present indicative endings (*haueð*, *is*, *lið*, *stireð*, *haueð*, *reiseð*, *makeð*), a participle (*ikindled*), and an infinitive (*sinen*). The relative marker is *ðat*.

I have grouped the next set of clauses in (39) using brackets because I think there is a sign of embedding in the word order.

(39) *Ðe ðridde lage <u>haueð</u> **ðe leun**. [ðanne he lieð to slepen]. <u>Sal</u> **he** neure luken. ðe lides of hise egen.*
'the lion has a third characteristic. When he lies down to sleep, he never closes the lids of his eyes.'

The first clause is V2 with the object *ðe ðridde lage* in the first position and the verb *haueð* next. The second clause is an independent one in terms of the punctuation but dependent in meaning on the third and fits as first constituent in the third clause. The last part, *ðe lides of hise egen*, is the object of the verb *luken*. As for the morphology, again there are numerous articles and the verbal endings are also similar to those we've seen before, namely the indicatives *haueð* and *lieð*, the modal *sal*, and the infinitive *luken*.

And then comes what the reader should get out of the description, i.e. the signification.

(40) *Welle heg <u>is</u> **tat hil.*** *[ðat is heuen riche].* ***vre louerd*** <u>is</u> *te leun. [ðe liueð ðer abuuen].*
'very high is that hill that is the heavenly kingdom. Our Lord is the lion that lives above.'

The first clause puts the subject predicate (*Welle heg*) first, the verb *is* in second position, and the subject last. The subject is enriched by a relative clause, although *ðat* could also be a demonstrative making the sentence independent. Its word order is V2 so that is a possible analysis. The second part is very similar in structure, but with a subject first, the verb *is*, and then the subject predicate which is modified by a relative clause. Here, *ðe liueð ðer abuuen* has to be a relative because of the relative marker *ðe*, although the word order is also V2.

The use of demonstratives and articles before nouns is 'modern' and the verbal endings show only indicative third person endings, namely three copula verbs (all of the form *is*) and one intransitive (*liueð*).

The next passage combines seven clauses and a phrase, all set apart by periods. The main clause is bolded in the translation. This structure is not paratactic as I outline below.

(41) *[Wu ðo him likete. [to ligten her on erðe].* <u>Migte</u> *neure **diuel** witen. [ðog he be derne hunte].[Hu he dun come. Ne wu he dennede him in ðat defte meiden. Marie bi name.[ðe him bar to man ne frame]]].*
'how then he wanted to come down to earth, **the devil might never know**, though he is a crafty hunter, and how he came down to earth and how he sheltered himself in that humble maiden, called Mary, which bore him to man's advantage.'

The first clause contains the impersonal verb *likete* which in Old and Middle English means 'be pleasing' and the next clause gives us the subject of 'pleasing', namely to come down to earth. These two initial clauses are the object of the third clause, which is the main clause. Counting the initial clauses as the first position, the verb *migte* is in second position. After this main clause, we see an interjection about the nature of the devil (*ðog he be derne hunte*) and the clausal object is then continued with *hu he dun come*. The next clause, which continues the object of *witen*, is a negative and the phrase, *Marie bi name*, is delineated by periods and appositive to *meiden*. The last clause is a relative introduced by *ðe*, again modifying *meiden*.

The verbal forms are past (*likete, dennede, bar*), infinitive (*to ligten, witen*), modal (*migte*), and subjunctive (*come*). There may also be a remnant of a plural genitive in *manne*.

Then follow four clauses that can be rendered as one in Modern English, which I have done in the translation (with the main clause in bold) and shown with the brackets.

(42) *[Ðo ure drigten ded was. 7 doluen [also his wille was]]. In a ston stille **he** <u>lai</u>. [til it kam ðe dridde dai].*

'when our lord was dead and buried, according to his will, **he lay in a grave** until the third day arrived.'

I take the first clause to be a subordinate adverbial, clear from it being V-final. *Doluen* is coordinate to *ded*, and *also his wille was* is adverbial to that. What I have made into the main clause in the translation has a PP in first position, an adjective in second position, the subject in third, and the verb last. This clause still counts as SV because all the other phrases are fronted before the SV sequence. The final clause is dependent and its verb is an existential where *it* is a dummy subject and *ðe dridde dai* is the real subject.

There are articles in predictable places, namely *a ston* and *ðe dridde dai*, and the verbs are past indicative, i.e. *was* occurs twice, and *lai* and *kam*. The past participle *doluen* no longer has the earlier prefix *ge-* or *i-*.

The last part of this excerpt can be rendered as three Modern English sentences but as five in Middle English.

(43) **His fader** him <u>filstnede</u> swo. [ðat he ros fro dede ðo.[vs to lif holden]]. <u>wakeð</u> so his wille is So hirde for his folde. **He** <u>is</u> hirde. **we** <u>ben</u> sep. Silden **he** us <u>wille</u>. [If we heren to his word.[ðat we ne gon nowor wille]].

'his father helped him rise from dead to keep us alive. He wakes as his will is, like a shepherd for his flock. He is the shepherd; we are sheep; he will shield us. If we listen to his words, we won't go astray.'

Word order is still very much in flux. Pronouns precede the verb in the first clause, the second clause is V2; and the third is V-last. The fourth starts with a left out subject and the adverbial that follows is SV. Then come two juxtaposed V2 clauses (*He is hirde* and *we ben sep*) and a preposed infinitive (*silden*) with the auxiliary last. The last two clauses are most likely subordinate to the preceding.

This fragment contains another multiple negative in the last clause. Verbal endings are past indicative (*filstnede*, *ros*), infinitive (*holden*, *silden*), present indicative (*wakeð*, *is*, *ben*), and modal (*will*). Wiltjes considers *heren* and *gon* as subjunctives but they could also be indicative and *ben* could be a future.

4.4.3 Status and dialect

As mentioned, the style is paratactic because sentence connections are through juxtaposition rather than through embedding. The word order still shows traces of V-final, especially with pronominal objects, and, typical for a text before 1400, there are V2 orders but this is not strict. In (44), a list of the main word orders is provided.

(44) a. Ðe ðridde lage **haueð** ðe leun   (39) V2
       The third feature has the lion
    b. In a ston stille he **lai**   (42) SV
       In a grave still he lay
    c. Hu he dun **come**   (41) V-last
       How he down came

d. His fader **him** filstnede swo (43) Pre-V pronouns
   His father him helped

A sign that we are dealing with a Middle and not Old English text is that only *ðe* and *ðat* function as relatives, as in (40) and (38), respectively, and that there are frequent articles. This makes the texts analytic. Negative concord, as in (38) and (43), is more typical of a later text, but is not consistently used in this text, as the single negatives in (37), (39), and (41) show.

We can observe that this is not a southern text because the verbal and nominal endings have changed and, in a text of this age, a southern text wouldn't yet have this. Although the third person singular *-eð* is still frequent, the distinction between some indicatives and subjunctives is hard to see, e.g. *heren* in (43). Infinitival endings are always *-en*, an indication of the early date. The *-e* endings on nouns no longer mark case. For instance, in (42), *ston* appears after a preposition, where Old English would have had *stone* because this noun is masculine. Wirtjes (1991: xxii) lists a few 'traces of a prepositional case' and that is possible in *hille* in (36).

The use of *til* in (38) and (42) is more typical of a northern text and also compatible with an East Midlands provenance. The use of *sal* and *sep* rather than *shall* and *shep* is northern; the appearance of *ston* and *swo* rather than *stan* and *swa*, southern. The prefix *i-* on past participles is typical in the South but occurs rarely in *The Physiologus* as a whole, though once in our excerpt. These mixed northern and southern characteristics are typical for Midlands texts; the loss of morphology more typical for the East Midlands. It turns out our text is dated from 1300 and has the Northeast Midlands as its origin, according to Wirtjes (1991).

4.5 Richard Rolle's *Psalter* Preface

Richard Rolle was born in North Yorkshire in 1290 so his texts are from past 1300 but, because there are few northern early Middle English writers, I discuss him in this chapter. Most of his writings are hard to date. He was a preacher and hermit and wrote mainly in Latin. The *English Psalter* whose Preface is discussed here was written for a woman (who needed it in the vernacular) and survives in many versions. A psalter is a book of psalms and possibly other devotional writing.

There are several northern versions: Oxford 64,[5] which Bramley (1884) uses for his edition; Bodley, Hatton 12, which Allen (1931) edited; and MS 148, the one used below, for which I have not found an edited copy. I have used Allen's translation as a basis for mine.

4.5.1 The text

The northern version of the text reproduced in Figure 4.9 is taken from MS 148 from the Huntington Library. The transcription follows in Tables 4.8 and 4.9. Many nasals are abbreviated on the preceding vowels and so are conjunctions. The hand is Gothic and the translation is based on Allen's edition.

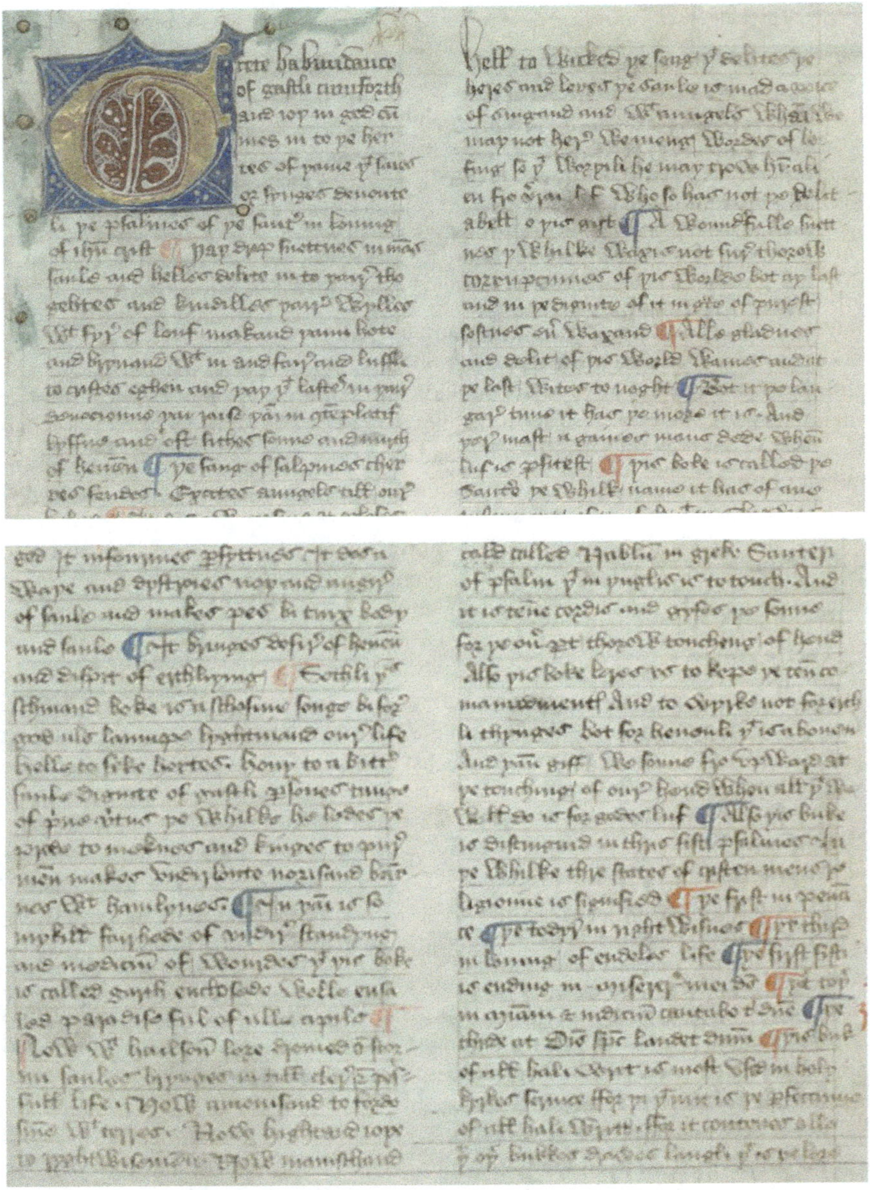

FIGURE 4.9. Richard Rolle's *Psalter* (HM 148, f. 23. Reproduced with permission from the Huntington Library)

4.5.2 Analysis

The Preface of Richard Rolle's *Psalter* has capitals that serve as markers of clauses. They are also preceded by paragraph marks in color, easy to see in Figure 4.9. In the analysis section, I'll again mark the finite verb of main clause, its subject, and embedded sentences.

TABLE 4.8. Transcription and translation of the first column of the Preface of Richard Rolle's *Psalter*

Grete habundance	A great abundance of spiritual comfort and
of gastly cumforth	joy in God comes into the hearts of those that
and ioy in god cū	devoutly say or sing the psalms in the loving
mes in to þe her	of Jesus Christ. They drop sweetness in the
tes of thaime þt saies	souls of man and pour delight into their
or synges deuoute	thoughts and kindle their wills
li þe psalmes of þe sant in louing	
of ihū crist. Þai drop suettnes in mās	
saule and helles delite in to paire tho	
gehtes and kindilles þaire wylles 10	
wt fyre of louf makand þaim hote	with the fire of love, making them hot and
and brynand wt in and faire and luffli	burning within and beautiful and lovely
to cristes eghen and þay þt lastes in þaire	to Christ's eyes and they that persevere in
deuocionus þai rays þāi in cotēplatif	their devotion they raise themselves up in
lyfne and oft sithes soune and mirth	contemplative life and often times exalts
of heuēn. Þe sang of salpmes cher	them to the melody and celebration of
ues fendes. Excites aungels till oure	heaven. The song of psalms chases away
helpe. It dos a waye sine it pleses	fiends and stirs angels to our help. It drives
god it informes perfyttnes it dos a	out discontent and it pleases God. It informs
waye and dystroies noy and angire 20	perfection; it does away and destroyes harm and anger
of saule and makes pes bi twix body	of soul and makes peace between body and
and saule. It bringes desire of heuēn	soul. It brings desire of heaven and contempt
and dispit of erthliynge. Sothli þis	for earthly things. Truly, this radiant book is
schinand boke is a schosime songe bifor	a choice song before God, as a lamp lighting
god als laumpe lyghtnand oure life	our life, health for a sick heart, honey for
helle to seke hertes. hony to a bitt	a bitter soul, a high mark of honor among
saule dignite of gastli persones tunge	spiritual people, a voicing of private virtues,
of priue vrtus þe whilke he lodes þe	which forces down the proud to humility and
proud to meknes and kinges to pure	makes kings bow in reverence to poor men,
mēn makes vndirelouto fosterand bār 30	nurturing
nes wt hamlynes. In þāi is so	children with gentleness. In the psalms,
mykill fairhede of vndirstandynge	there is such great beauty of meaning and of
and medicin of wordes þt þis boke	medicine from the words that this book is
is called garth enclosede welle ensa	called 'a garden enclosed', a sealed fountain,
led paradise ful of alle apils	a paradise full of apples. Now see: with
now wt hailesom lare drowed ā stor	wholesome instruction, it brings agitated and
mi saules brynges in till clere ā pes	tempestuous souls into a fair and peaceful
full life. Now amonisand to fordo	way of life, now warning them to repent of
sinne wt terres. Now hightand ioye	sin with tears, now promising joy for the
to ryghtwismōn. Now manischand 40	virtuous, now threatening

TABLE 4.9. Transcription and translation of the second column of the *Psalter*'s first page

Hell to wicked þe song þt delites þe heres and leues þe saule is mad a voice of singand and wt aungels whāiwe may not here we menge wordes of lo fing so þt worpili he may trow hī ali en fro verai lif who so has not þe delit abett o þis gyft. A wonudfulle suett nes þ whilke waxis not sure thorogh corrupcnnes of þis worlde bot ay last and in pedignite of it in grace of purest	hell for the wicked. The song which gives delight to hearts and instructs the soul has become a sound of singing: with angels whom we cannot hear we mingle words of praise so that anyone would be right to reckon himself exiled from true life if does not in this way experience the delight of this gift of wonderful sweetness which never grows sour with the corruption of this world but is everlasting 50 in its own superlative quality and is always increasing in the grace of purest
softnes on waxand. Alle gladnes and delit of þis world waines and at þe last wites to noght. Bot it þe lan gere time it has þe more it is. and þere mast a gaines mans dede whēn luf is perfitest. Þis boke is called þe sautere þe whilk name it has of ane instrument of musyk þt in Ebru is cald called. Hablum in greke Sauter of psalm þt in inglis is to touch. And	softness. All the pleasures and delights of earthly loves vanish away and at last vanish away to nothing, but the longer the gift persists, the greater it is, and is greatest of all, quite the opposite of cursed human love affairs, when love is most perfected. This book is called the Psalter, a name which it takes from a musical instrument known in Hebrew as nablum, the Greek forms is 60 psaltery, derived from psalm, and in English its meaning is to touch.' and
it is tēne cordis and gyfes þe sonne for þe ouerer thorogh touching of hend Also þis boke leres us to kepe þe teñ co maundments and to wyrke not for erth li thynges bot for heuonli þt is abouen and pān giff we soune fro vpward at þe touchinge of oure hend when all þt we wele do is for godes luf. Also þis buke is distinguid in thris fifti psalmes In þe whilke thre states of cristen mens re	this consists of ten strings and gives out sound from the upper part when it is touched by hand. This book also teaches us to keep the ten commandments and to work not for the sake of earthly things, but for the heavenly which is above. And so we emit sound from our superior natures at the touch of our hands when everything which we intend to do is for the love of God. Moreover this book is 70 divided into three times fifty psalms, in which are symbolized three phases of progress in the faith of a Christian man.
ligionne is signified. Þe first in peñā ce. Þe todþer in right wisnes. Þe thrid in louing of endelas life. Þe first fifti is ending in miserere mei deus. Þe toper in [misericordiam & iudicium cantabo tibi domine]. Þe	the first covers the penitential, the second virtuous living and the third praise of eternal life. The first fifty end with 'have mercy on me, O God,' the second with 'I will sing of mercy and judgement unto thee, O lord,' and

(Continued)

TABLE 4.9. *Continued*

thrid at [Dies spiritus laudet onm̄]. Þis buk of all hali writ is most oysed in holy kyrkes seruice ffor þi þt initis þe perfeccioun	the third with 'Let everything that has breath praise the lord.' This book of holy scriptures is mostly used in the services of the holy church because it is the epitome
of all hali writ. ffor it contenes alle þt oþer bukkes draghes langli þt is þe lore 80	of the divine writing. Because it contains what all the other books treat at length, namely the teaching ...

Sentence (45) consists of two clauses, both V2; the first is the main clause and the second a relative within it. It starts out with a long subject.

(45) **Grete habundance of gastly cumforth and ioy in god** <u>cumes</u> in to the hertes of thaime [that saies or synges deuouteli the psalmes of the sant in louing of ihū crist].
'a great abundance of spiritual comfort and joy in God comes into the hearts of those that devoutly say or sing the psalms in the loving of Jesus Christ.'

The use of articles is modern and the agreement on the present tense verb with third person subjects is *-s* whether it is a singular subject (*habundance ... cumes*) or a plural one (*thaime that saies*). This is a clear mark of a northern text. Other northern characteristics are the use of the third person plural pronoun *thaime* and the continuation of the *-a-* sound in *gastly* where southern texts shift to *-o-*.

Sentence (46) is also V2 throughout. Its structure is that of a coordinate clause, with the first including a coordinate present participle clause, which is in brackets, and the second including a relative clause, also in brackets.

(46) **Thai** <u>drop</u> swettnes in mans saule and helles delite in to thaire thogehtes and kindilles thaire wylles with the fyre of louf [makand thaim hote and brynand with in and faire and luffli to cristes eghen] and thay [that lastes in thaire deuocionus] thai rays thaim in contemplatif lyfne and oft sithes soune and mirth of heuen.
'they drop sweetness in the souls of man and pour delight into their thoughts and kindle their wills with the fire of love, making them hot and burning within and beautiful and lovely to Christ's eyes and they that persevere in their devotion they raise themselves up in contemplative life and often times to the sound and celebration of heaven.'

This text shows genitive case *-s* on *mans* and *helles* and the *-en* plural on *eghen*. It has *-s* for all third person verbs except the first verb *drop*, and *-and* endings for present participles, typical for northern texts. Note the simple pronoun *thaim* used as reflexive.

The next sentence has a period but no capital letter so I treat it as a coordinate one.

(47) **The sang of salpmes** <u>cheses</u> fendes. Excites aungels till oure helpe.
'the song of psalms chases away fiends and stirs angels to our help.'

The word order is SV in the first clause and not known in the second since it lacks a subject. Again, all the verbs end in -s and so do plural nouns. The preposition *till* is northern.

(48) is very analytic with its *it* subjects that ensure SV word order but very paratactic and that makes it a challenge to analyze. I have not marked the main clause subjects and verbs because they would have a contemporary bias.

> (48) It dos a waye [sine it pleses god] it informes perfyttnes it dos a waye and dystroies noy and angire of saule and makes pes bi twix body and saule.
> 'it drives out because it pleases God. It informs perfection; it does away and destroys harm and anger of soul and makes peace between body and soul.'

Morphologically speaking, there are again only -s endings on verbs.

In (49), there is a simple main clause, SVO in word order. The multiple use of *of* makes it analytic.

> (49) It bringes desire of heuen and dispit of erthlithynge.
> 'it brings desire of heaven and contempt for earthly things.'

The next sentence is more complex. It starts with an adverb *sothli* and then has the subject and the verb showing that it is an SV structure and not V2. After the two embedded adverbial clauses (indicated with brackets), there follows a period. It may mean that an 'it is' is left out or the *hony* ... is a continuation of the subject predicate in the first clause.

> (50) Sothli **this schinand boke** is a schosime songe bifor god [als laumpe lyghtnand oure life helle [to seke hertes]]. hony to a bitt saule dignite of gastli persones tunge of priue vertus [the whilke he lodes the proud to meknes and kinges to pure men makes vndirelouto fosterand barnes with hamlynes].
> 'truly, this radiant book is a choice song before God, as a lamp lighting our life, health for a sick heart, honey for a bitter soul, a high mark of honor among spiritual people, a voicing of private virtues, which forces down the proud to humility and makes kings bow in reverence to poor men, nurturing children with gentleness.'

Northernisms are the -*and* participles and the continued use of the -*(e)s* third person ending. The use of *barnes* for 'children' still survives in the North of England, according to the OED (s.v. *bairn*) and *ham* is northern as well.

In (51), the word order in the main clause is V2 but in its relative second clause it is SV.

> (51) In thaim is **so mykill fairhede of vndirstandynge and medicin of wordes** [that this boke is called garth enclosed wel ensa led paradise ful of alle apils] now with hailesom lare drowed and stormi saules *brynges* in till clere and pes full life.
> 'in them, there is so much beauty of understanding and of medicine from the words that this book is called a garden enclosed well, a sealed paradise full of apples. Now with wholesome instruction (it) brings agitated and stormy souls in to a clear and peaceful life.'

The part starting with *now* is hard to comprehend. I think the subject of *brynges* is *this boke* and this is an independent clause which I haven't marked. A northernism we haven't yet seen in this text is the lack of palatalization on *mykill* 'much'.

Sentence (52) is a continuation of (51) in the form of an adverbial clause. I have put a period in the translation after 'wicked'. I have put brackets around the subordinate clauses, but the entire passage is a 'stream-of-consciousness'.

(52) Now amonisand to fordo sinne with terres. Now hightand ioye to ryghtwismon. Now manischand Hell to wicked the song [that delites the heres and leres the saule] is mad a voice of singand and with aungels [whaimwe may not here] we menge wordes of lofing [so that worthili he may trow him ali en fro verai lif [who so has not the delit abett o this gyft]].
'now warning them to repent of sin with tears, now promising joy for the virtuous, now threatening hell for the wicked. The song which delights the hearts and instructs the soul has become a sound of singing: with angels whom we cannot hear we mingle words of praise so that anyone would be right to reckon himself exiled from true life if does not in this way experience the delight of this gift.'

The next sentence is again a fragment, a noun phrase with a relative clause. It is very analytic in the number of grammatical words.

(53) A wonudfulle suetnes [the whilke waxis not sure thorogh corrupcnnes of this worlde bot ay last and in thedignite of it in grace of purest softnes on waxand].
'a wonderful sweetness which never grows sour with the corruption of this world but is ever lasting in its own dignity of purest softness that is growing.'

The first part of (54) is straightforward: it is a coordinate sentence where both parts are SV. The second part starts with the conjunction *bot* 'but'. This clause has an unusual word order, e.g. a doubling of the subject *it*.

(54) **Alle gladnes and delit of this world** <u>waines</u> and at the last wites to noght. Bot it the langere time it has the mare it is. and there mast a gaines mans dede when luf is perfitest.
'all the pleasures and delights of this world wane and at last wither to nothing. But the longer the gift persists, the greater it is, and is greatest against man's deeds when love is most perfected.'

It is again typically northern in its verbal endings and the use of *mast* for *most*. It is also very analytic again with its use of expletive *there*.

In (55), we start with an SV main clause that includes a number of relative clauses the *wh*-form of which is quite modern. *Whilk* is the unpalatalized form typical for a northern text. Although *wh*- pronouns are used as interrogatives in Old English, *which* only gets used as a relative around the end of the twelfth century and *who* only in the thirteenth century.

(55) **This boke** <u>is</u> called the sautere [the whilk name it has of ane instrument of musyk [that in ebru is cald called Hablum in greke Sauter of psalm [that in

inglis is to touch]]. And it is tene cordis and gyfes the sonne for the ouerer thorogh touching of hend.
'this book is called the Psalter, a name which it takes from a musical instrument known in Hebrew as nablum, the Greek forms is psaltery, derived from psalm, and in English its meaning is 'to touch' and this consists of 10 strings and gives out sound from the upper part through the touch of the hand.'

In (56), the word order is SV. I have added brackets delineating possible subordinate clauses but that is hard to do from a Modern English point of view.

(56) Also **this boke** <u>leres</u> us [to kepe the ten comaundments and to wyrke not for erth li thynges bot for heuonli [that is abouen]] and than [giff we soune fro vpward at the touchinge of oure hend [when all [that we wele do] is for godes luf]].
'in addition, this book teaches us to keep the ten commandments and to work not for the sake of earthly things but for heavenly (ones) which is above. And if we emit sound from upwards at the touch of our hands when everything which we intend to do is for the love of God.'

The last passage starts with a main clause with SV word order that contains another *whilke*-relative. After that, the remainder says what the three parts of the book contain and where they end.

(57) Also **this buke** <u>is</u> distinguid in thrisfifti psalmes [In the whilke thre states of cristen mens religionne is signified]. The first in penance. The todther in right wisnes. The thrid in louing of endelas life. The first fifti is ending in ... The tother in ... The thrid at ... This buk of all hali writ is most oysed in holy kyrkes seruice [ffor thi that initis the perfeccioun of all hali writ]. [ffor it contenes alle [that other bukkes draghes langli]] that is the lore.
'also, this book is subdivided into three (sets of) fifty psalms, in which are symbolized three phases of progress in the faith of a Christian man: the first covers the penitential way of life, the second covers virtuous living and the third deals with praise of eternal life. The first fifty conclude with [Latin deleted], the second with [Latin deleted] and the third closes with the words [Latin deleted]. This book of holy scriptures is one of the most used in the services of holy church because in it is the epitome of the divine writing. Because it incorporates what all the other books treat at length. That is the teaching ...'

Morphologically interesting are the use of *is* agreeing with a plural subject *thre states*, some complex conjunctions typical of late Old English, such as *ffor thi that*, but also simple ones, such as *ffor* and *that*.

4.5.3 Status and dialect

The word order is mainly SV; there is one V2 left in (51) and that may be an inversion. For completeness, I have summarized the possibilities in (58).

(58) a. In thaim **is** <u>so mykill fairhede</u>   (51) V2
       'in them, there is so much beauty.'

b. Thai **drop** suettness 'they drop sweetness.'	(46) SV
c. none	V-last
d. none	Pre-V pronouns

As for the morphology, endings have regularized in that there are mainly plural nouns ending in -*s* (and one in -*en*) and verbal present endings are -*s*. There is no case left on either nouns or demonstratives. There are no special reflexive pronouns (yet), many -*li* adverbs, e.g. in (45) and (46), one modal *may* in (52), and *wh*-relative pronouns, e.g. in (50), (52), and (57).

The stage is analytic with expletives, the use of *of* and *to*. Its style varies from one subordinate clause, as in (45), to quite paratactic, as in (47) and (48).

As mentioned, the text is full of northernisms, namely the *-and* participles, the use of the *-(e)s* third person ending for singular and plural, the preposition *till* in (51), *mykill* in (51), *ham* in (50), and *mast* in (54). It is indeed northern in origin, dated early 1300s.

4.6 Conclusion

The period of Early Middle English shows both a paratactic style (in the *Peterborough Chronicle, Owl and Nightingale,* and *Lion*) and one with more subordinate clauses (in *Seinte Katerine* and the Preface of Rolle's *Psalter*). New conjunctions appear, e.g. *till* and *for*, and there is an increase in the use of demonstratives and articles. Case endings on nouns disappear in most texts but endings on verbs remain in certain dialect areas. The latter may be responsible for the fact that auxiliaries continue to be used in similar ways as in Old English. So, nominal analyticity increases but verbal less so.

Exercises

A The image in Figure 4.10 is taken from the *Parker Chronicle*, mentioned in section 4.1.

Try to decipher a few words and the periods before looking at the transcription in Table 4.10. Is there evidence that the scribe that starts on line 8 is a different one from the earlier lines?

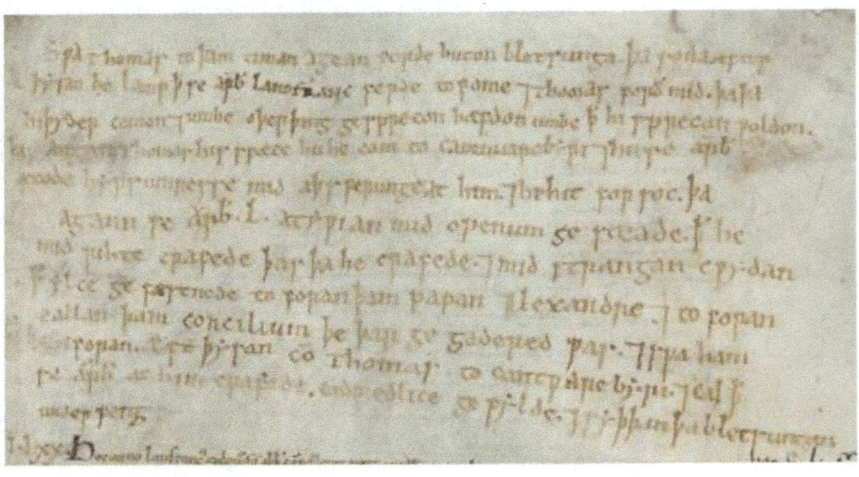

FIGURE 4.10. Last entry in the *Parker Chronicle* for the year 1070 (Corpus Christi College, Cambridge, 173, f. 31v and f. 32r)

Early Middle English 1100–1300   135

B Look at the transcription of this text in Table 4.10 and provide evidence for its analytic or synthetic stage.

TABLE 4.10. Transcription of the last entry in the *Parker Chronicle* (adapted from <http://asc.jebbo.co.uk/a/a-L.html>, last accessed 9 May 2017)

Her landfranc se þe pæs abb an Kadū cō to æn3la lande se efter feapū da3um pearð arceb onkantpareberi3. he pæs 3e haded .iiii. kl septēbris on his a3enū biscpsetle frā eahtebisco pum his under ðioddum ða oþre ðe þær næron þurh ærendra kan 7 þurh 3prite atipdon hpi hi ðær beon ne mihton. on þā 3eare THOMAS se pæs 3coran biscp to eferpic cō to cantpareberi3 þ man hine ðær 3hadede efter þan ealdan 3punan. Ða ða landfranc crafede fæstnun3e his 3hersūnesse mid aðsperun3e

þa forsoc he. 7 sæde þ he hit nahte to donne. Þa 3e praðede hine se arcb landfranc. 7 be bead þā biscopan ðe þar cumene pæran be ðas Arb L hæse þa serfise to donde. 7 eallan þan munecan þ hi scoldan hi unscrydan. 7 hi be his hæse spa didan. Spa Thomas to þam timan a3ean ferde buton bletsun3a. Þa sona æfter þysan be lamp þ se arl Landfranc ferde to rome 7 thomas forð mid. Þa þa hi þyder comon 7 umbe oþer þin3 3esprecon hæfdon umbe þ hi sprecan poldon. þa an3an thomas his spæce hu he com to cantuuarebyri 7huse arb axode hyrsumnesse mid aþsperun3e at him. 7hehit for soc. Þa a3ann se arb. L. atypian mid openum 3e sceade. þ he mid rihte crafede þas þa he crafede . 7 mid stran3an cpydan þ ylce 3e fæstnode to foran þam papan Alexandre. 7 to foran eallan þam concilium þe þar 3e 3adered pas. 7 spa ham foran. Æfter þysan cō Thomas to cantparebyri 7 eal þ se arb at him crafede. eadmedlice 3e fylde. 7 syþþan þa bletsun3an underfen3.

C The image in Figure 4.11 is from the other manuscript of *The Owl and the Nightingale*, known as Jesus College, Oxford, MS 29, and is taken from Ker (1963). It is later than the one we looked at. Is this version more paratactic or less than the one examined above in section 4.3; is it more northern or southern?

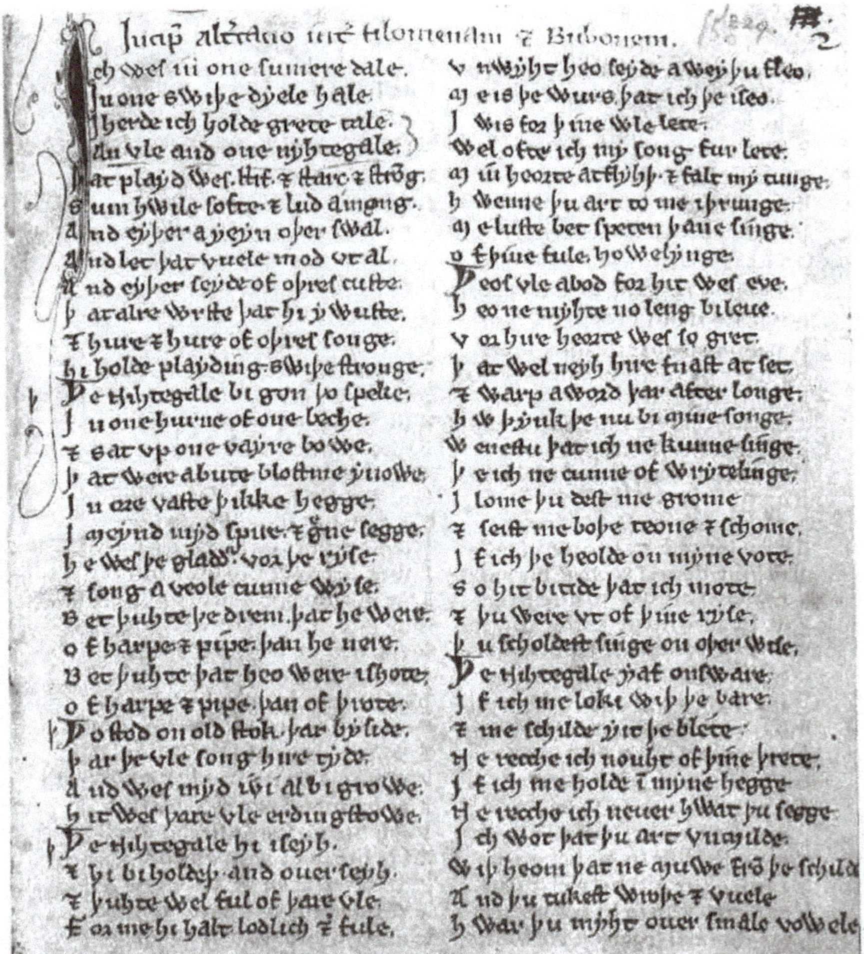

FIGURE 4.11. *The Owl and the Nightingale* (Jesus College, Oxford, MS 29, f. 156r)

D *Havelok* is a story about a Danish prince, Havelok, who is sheltered in his youth in England by a fisherman called Grim and then assumes the rule of Denmark. Preserved in the Bodleian Library as Laud Misc. 108, it is from the end of the thirteenth century and from the Northeast Midlands. The excerpt describes Havelok's arrival in England and his stay with Grim. A translation appears in Appendix III.

What can you say about negatives, articles, and word order?

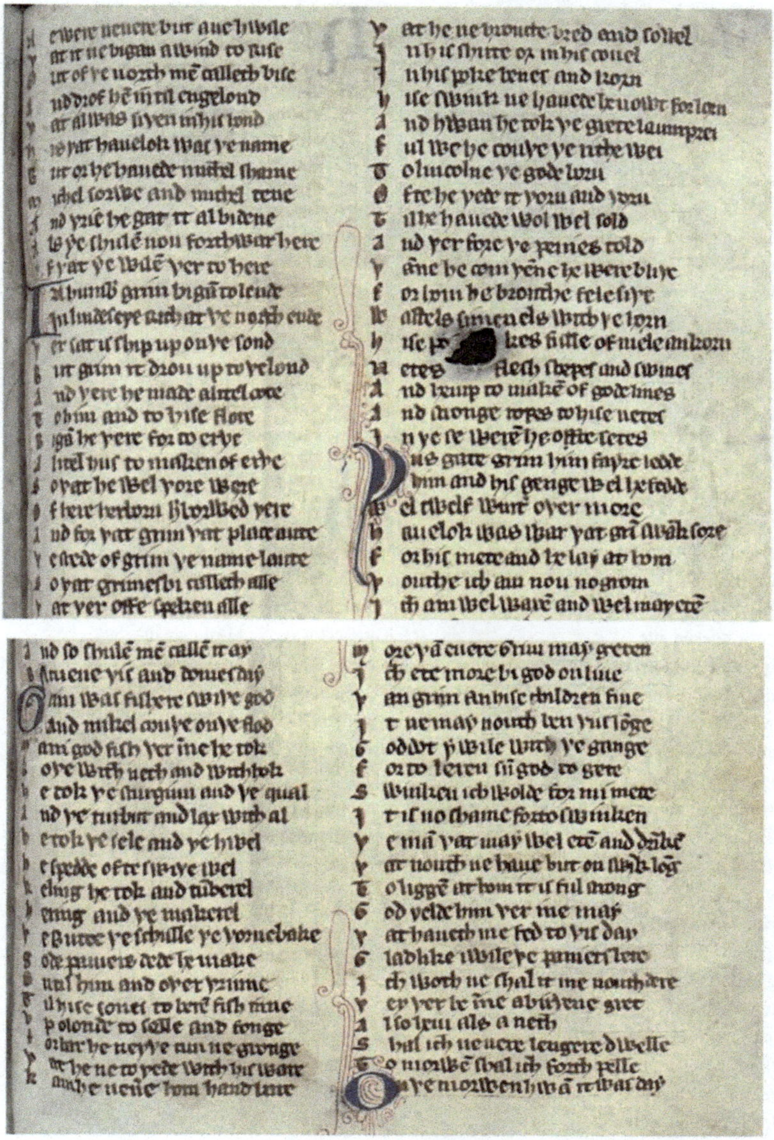

FIGURE 4.12. *Havelok*, lines 722–811 (Laud Misc. 108, f. 208r.[6] Reproduced with permission from the Bodleian Library)

138 *Analyzing Syntax through Texts*

E What stage is this text in, in terms of analytic or synthetic?

In the transcription in Table 4.11, I have used the wynn for the *th* even though sometimes it represents a thorn.

TABLE 4.11. *Havelok,* lines 722–811 (adapted from Herzman et al. 1997[7])

Newere neuere but ane hwile	Þat he ne broucte bred and sowel
Þat it ne bigan a wind to rise	In his shirte or in his cowel
Out of þe norþ mē calleth bise	In his poke benes and korn
And drof hē intil engelond	Hise swink he hauede he nowt forlorn
Þat al was sipen in his hond	And hwan he took þe grete lamprey
His þat hauelok was þe name	Ful wel he coupe þe rithe wei
But or he hauede michel shame	To Lincolne þe gode boru
Michel sorwe and michel tene	Ofte he yede it poru and poru
And yete he gat it al bidene	Til he hauede wol wel sold
Als ye shulen now forthward lere	And perfore þe penies told
Yf þat ye wilē perto here	Þanne he com pēne he were blipe
In humber grim bigā to lende	For hom he brouthe fele sipe
In lindeseye rith at þe north ende	Wastels, simenels with þe horn
Þer sat his ship upon þe sond	His pokes fulle of mele and korn
But grim it drou up to þe lond	Netes flesh, shepes and swines
And pere he made a litel cote	And hemp to maken of gode lines
To him and to hise flote	And stronge ropes to hise netes
Bigā he pere for to erþe	In þe se werē he ofte setes
A litel hus to maken of erþe	Þusgate Grim him fayre ledde
So þat he wel pore were	Him and his genge wel he fedde
Of here herboru herborwed pere	Wel twelf winter oper more
And for þat grim þat place aute	Hauelok was war þat grī swāk sore
Þe stede of grim þe name laute	For his mete and he lay at hom
So þat grimesbi it calleth alle	Þouthe Ich am now no grom
Þat peroffe speken alle	Ich am wel waxē and wel may etē
And so shulē mē callē it ay	More pā euere Grim may geten
Bitwene þis and Domesday	Ich ete more bi god on liue
Grim was fishere swiþe god	Þan grim an hise children fiue
And mikel coupe on þe flod	It nemay nouth ben þus lōge
Mani god fish þer īne he tok	Goddot! I wile with hem gange
Boþe with neth and withhok	For to leren sū god to gete.
He tok þe sturgiun and þe qual	Swinken ich wolde for my mete
And þe turbut and lax withal	It is no shame for to swinken
He tok þe sele and þe hwel	Þe mā þat may wel etē and drīkē
He spedde ofte swiþe wel	Þar nouth ne haue but on swink lōg
Keling he tok and tumberel	To liggē at hom it is ful strong
Hering and þe makerel	God yelde him þer I ne may
Þebutte þe schulle þe þornebake	Þat haueth me fed to þis day
Gode paniers dede he make	Gladlike I wile þe paniers bere
On til him and oþer prinne	Ich woth ne shal it me nouth dere
Til hise sones to beren fishe inne	Þey þer be īne a birpene gret
Up o londe to selle and fonge	Also heui als a neth
Forbar he neyþer tun ne gronge	Shal ich neere lengere dwelle
Þat he ne to yede with his ware	Tomorwē shal ich forth pelle
Kam he neuere hom hand bare	On þe morwen hwan it was day

Further reading

As we've seen, early Middle English is a period of great change. You might want to read one of the works that argues that the changes are so fast due to extreme language contact. One example of this is McWhorter's work of which I give one of his 2015 blogposts below.

The following texts could be used to supplement the texts in this chapter and the next and the grammatical depth. Mossé's 1952 *Handbook of Middle English* provides an (85-page) outline of Middle English grammar with verbal and nominal paradigms, complex sentences, and word order, and Fulk's 2012 *An Introduction to Middle English* a (70-page) one. Both of these also contain sample texts with notes. Fischer's 200-page 1992 chapter on syntax in *The Cambridge History of the English Language* is most helpful. It provides an in-depth analysis of the noun phrase, the verb phrase, tense, aspect, modality, word order, and complex clauses. Mustanoja's 1960 *A Middle English Syntax* provides an interesting supplement by going deeper into certain questions and, especially, into exceptions. The book doesn't provide the basic paradigms but instead points out differences with Old English and certain peculiarities of the Middle English system.

Fischer, Olga (1992), 'Syntax', in Norman Blake (ed.), *The Cambridge History of the English Language, Volume II: 1066–1476*, Cambridge: Cambridge University Press, pp. 207–408.
Fulk, Robert (2012), *An Introduction to Middle English: Grammar and Texts*, Peterborough: Broadview Press.
McWhorter, John (2015), 'English Is Not Normal', *Aeon*, 13 November, <https://aeon.co/essays/why-is-english-so-weirdly-different-from-other-languages> (last accessed 9 May 2017).
Mossé, Fernand (1952), *Handbook of Middle English*, Baltimore: Johns Hopkins University Press.
Mustanoja, Tauno [1960] (2016), *A Middle English Syntax*, Amsterdam: John Benjamins.

Notes

1. 'The Anglo-Saxon Chronicle. Part 1: A.D. 1–748, Online Medieval and Classical Library Release #17', *The Online Medieval and Classical Library*, available at <http://omacl.org/Anglo/part1.html> (last accessed 9 May 2017).
2. 'The Owl and the Nightingale ca. 1210', *Bibliotheca Augustana*, available at <http://www.hs-augsburg.de/~Harsch/anglica/Chronology/13thC/Owl/owl_text.html> (last accessed 9 May 2017).
3. 'The Owl and the Nightingale', *Wessex Parallel WebTexts*, available at <http://www.southampton.ac.uk/~wpwt/trans/owl/owltrans.htm> (last accessed 9 May 2017).
4. 'Arundel 292 f. 4', *Catalogue of Illuminated Manuscripts*, British Library, available at <http://www.bl.uk/catalogues/illuminatedmanuscripts/ILLUMIN.ASP?Size=mid&IllID=7560> (last accessed 9 May 2017).

5. 'The Psalter, or Psalms of David and certain canticles. Rolle, Richard, of Hampole, tr. 1290?–1349, Bramley, Henry Ramsden, ed. 1833–1917', *Corpus of Middle English Prose and Verse*, available at <http://quod.lib.umich.edu/c/cme/AJF7399.0001.001/1:2.2?rgn=div2;view=fulltext> (last accessed 9 May 2017).
6. Available at <http://bodley30.bodley.ox.ac.uk:8180/luna/servlet/view/search?QuickSearchA=QuickSearchA&q=Havelok&search=Search> (last accessed 9 May 2017).
7. See also 'Havelok the Dane', in *Four Romances of England: King Horn, Havelok the Dane, Bevis of Hampton, Athelston*, ed. Ronald B. Herzman, Graham Drake and Eve Salisbury, 1997, *TEAMS Middle English Texts Series*, available at <http://d.lib.rochester.edu/teams/text/salisbury-four-romances-of-england-havelok-the-dane> (last accessed 9 May 2017).

5

Late Middle and Early Modern English 1300–1600

This chapter stretches from 1300 to 1600 with the texts presented in chronological order. The beginning of the chapter considers texts from the Late Middle English period, i.e. after 1300. That period includes writers such as the Gawain poet, Chaucer, and Margery of Kempe. It sees the printing press introduced in England (in 1476). After the printing press is established, we continue to have handwritten letters and other documents, as the samples by Henry Machyn and Princess Elizabeth I show, and this is true up to today!

The script varies from Gothic to secretary hand to italic. The latter is still popular today. Figure 5.1 gives the letters of the secretary (or chancery or court) hand and Figure 5.2 of the italic hand.

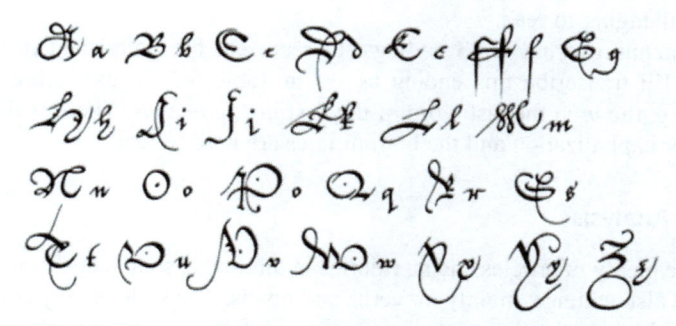

FIGURE 5.1. The secretary hand (from <http://genealogy.about.com/od/paleography/ig/old_handwriting/Secretary-Hand.htm>, last accessed 4 June 2017)

FIGURE 5.2. The italic hand (from <http://www.fountainpennetwork.com>, last accessed 4 June 2017)

142   *Analyzing Syntax through Texts*

Stylistically, the English we see in this chapter is complex, with many embeddings, as will be pointed out. I will also comment on analytic and synthetic features, both of which increase, as was also pointed out in Chapter 1.

Section 5.1 presents the late fourteenth-century poem *Cleanness* attributed to the Gawain poet from the Northwest Midlands. Section 5.2 examines Chaucer's *Astrolabe*, a set of instructions written in late fourteenth-century London English. Section 5.3 studies *The Book of Margery of Kempe*, an early fifteenth-century East Midlands text and section 5.4 investigates the only printed text in this book, namely Caxton's 1485 printing of Malory's *Morte d'Arthur*. Its printed text is very similar to the Gothic script popular at the time. Section 5.5 presents two sixteenth-century writers, one a merchant and the other a later monarch. Section 5.6 is a brief conclusion.

5.1   Cleanness

Cleanness is one of four alliterative poems in the Cotton Nero manuscript, the other ones being *Pearl, Patience*, and *Sir Gawain and the Green Knight*. As usual, these titles do not appear in the manuscript which was written in the late fourteenth century in the Northwest Midlands. The *Linguistic Atlas of Late Mediaeval English* identifies the place as Cheshire. *Cleanness* is a didactic poem, retelling the story of the flood, Sodom and Gomorrah, and the fall of Belshazzar. It starts by explaining the need for cleanness.

5.1.1   The text

The image in Figure 5.3 is from the British Library Cotton Nero A X manuscript. A fascimile edition is also avalable as Gollancz (1923). Wright (1960: 15) characterizes the handwriting as 'individualistic small, sharp, angular character'; it is quite challenging to read.

The manuscript has -(e)3 endings, to represent the plural and third person present. I'll transcribe this ending as -ez in Table 5.1. It also abbreviates the nasals, e.g. the *m* in the last word of the first line, *comende*. There is little punctuation or capitalization and the bottom lines are hard to read.[1]

5.1.2   Analysis

There are plenty of articles and auxiliaries in this stage, so it is fairly analytic, but there are also endings, mainly on verbs and nouns. The style is very complex, as we see right from the first sentence.

The first 17 words (from *clannesse* to *askez*) are the subject of the main clause and are repeated as *he*. The first word *clannesse* is the object of the verb *comende* 'to commend' and has been preposed. It looks as if *clannesse* is the subject (with a relative clause following) but that is not the case. Rather, the relative *who* is the subject on its own of *cowpe comende* and the entire clause is the subject of the main clause with the verbs *my3t* and *find*.

(1)   **Clannesse who so kyndly cowpe comende 7 rekken vp alle þe resounz pat ho by ri3t askez** fayre formez my3t **he** fynde in for[þ]ering his speche 7 in þe contrare kark 7 combraunce huge

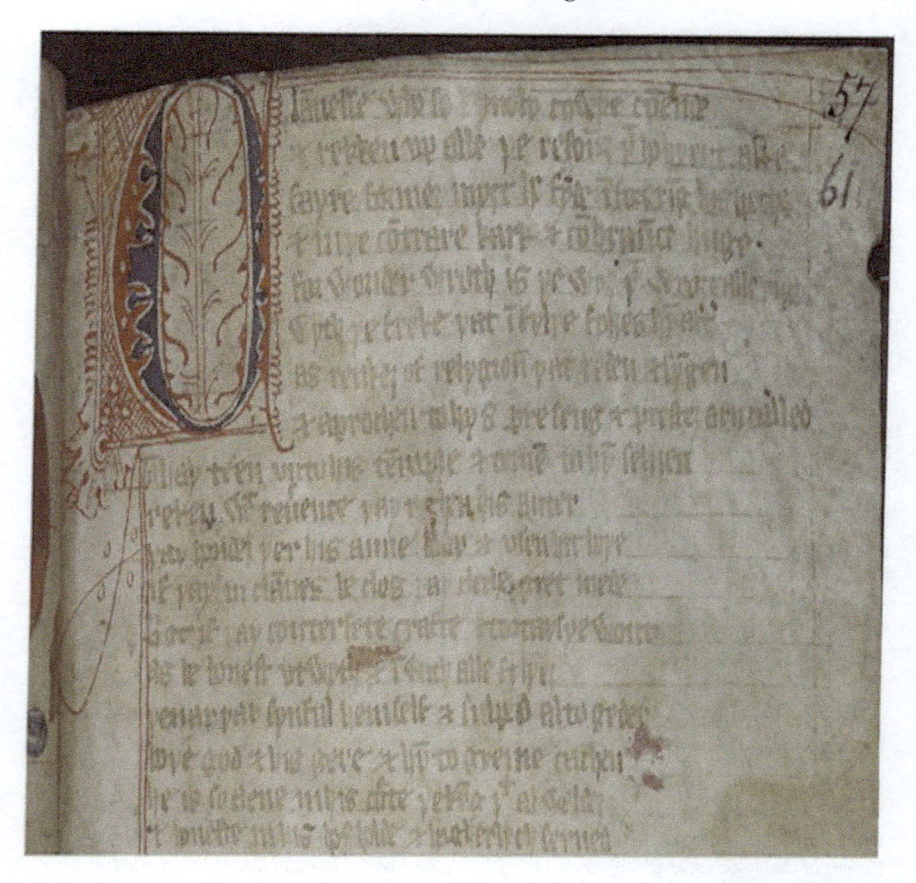

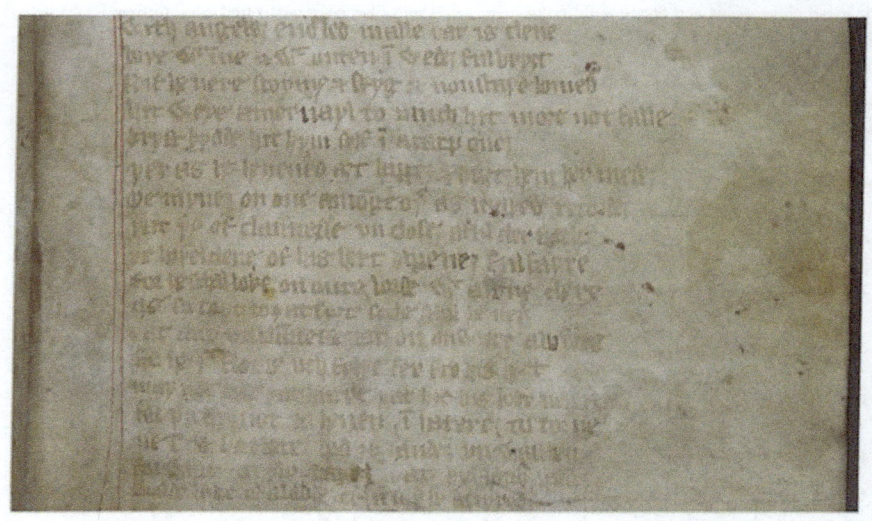

FIGURE 5.3. *Cleanness* (Cotton Nero A X, leaf 57. Reproduced with permission from the British Library Board)

TABLE 5.1. Transcription and word-by-word gloss of *Cleanness*, lines 1–36

Clānesse who so kyndly cowpe cōende 7 rekken vp alle þe resoūz þat ho by ri3t askez fayre formez my3t he fȳd ĩ forerĩg his speche 7 in þe cōtrare kark 7 cōbrañce huge.	Cleanness who so kindly could commend and reckon up all the reasons that she by right demands fair forms might he find in furthering his discourse and in the reverse trouble and difficulty huge.
for wonder wroth is þe wy3 þat wro3t alle pĩges wyth þe freke þat in fylpe fol3es hȳ aftĩ	For very angry is the being that made all things with the men in filth follow him after.
as renkez of relygioñ þat reden 7sȳgen 7 aprochen to hys presens 7 prestez arn called	As men of religion who read and sing and approach into his presence and priests are called
Thay teen vnto his tēmple 7 temen to hȳ seluen reken wt reurence þay rychen his auter þay hondel þer his aune body 7 vsen hit boþe if þay in clānes be clos þay cleche gret mede	They proceed to his temple and belong to themselves think with reverence they enrich his altar they handle there his own body and use it also if they in cleanness are close they obtain great reward
Bot if þay conterfete crafte 7 cortaysye wont as be honest vtwyth 7 ĩwith alle fylpez þen ar þay synful hemself 7 sulped altogeder boþe god 7 his gere 7 hȳ to greme cachen	But if they counterfeit craft and goodness lack as honest outward and inside all filth then are they sinful themselves sully both God and his sacraments. and him to anger drive
he is so clene in his courte þe kȳg þt al weldez 7 honeste in his hosholde 7 hagherlych serued with angelez enorled inalle þat is clene boþe wtĩne 7 wtouten ĩ wedez ful bry3t nif he nere scoymus 7 skyg 7 nonscape louied hit were ameruayl to much hit mo3t not falle	He is so clean in his court, the king that all rules and honest in his household scrupulously served by angels surrounded in all that is clean both inside and out in clothing very bright Not.if he not.was fastidious and fussy and not evil loved it were a marvel very much it will not happen
kryst kydde hit hym self ĩ a carp onez per as he heuened a3t happez 7 hy3t hem her medez me mynez on one amōge oþr as maþew recordez þat pus of clannesse vnclosez aful cler speche þe haþel clene of his hert haþenez ful fayre for he schal loke on oure lorde wt aboue chere As so saytz to þat sy3t seche schal he neuer þat any vnclānesse hatz on auwhere abowte for he þat flemus vch fylpe fer fro his hert may not byde þat burre þat hit his body ne3en forþy hy3 not to heuen ĩ haterez totorne ne ĩ þe harlatez hod 7 handez vnwaschen for what vrply haþel þat hy3honour haldez wolde lyke if aladde com lyperly attyred	Christ announced it himself in a speech. He extolls eight virtues and explains them their rewards I think on one among these, as Matthew records that thus cleanness discloses a full clear discourse The noble clean of his heart (will) find good fortune for he will look upon our Lord with good cheer As so says, to that sight seek shall he never that any uncleanness has on, anywhere about for he that banishes each filth far from his heart may not tolerate that shock that it his body nears Therefore hurry not to heaven in clothes torn nor in the beggarly hood and hands unwashed for what earthly nobleman that high honor holds would like if a man came wretchedly attired

'whoever can commend cleanness fittingly and reckon up all the reasons that she by right demands might find excellent terms to further his arguments and great difficulty in supporting the opposite view.'

The embedding of one clause in another is done through syntactic means, i.e. using the relativizers *who* and *þat*. What makes the clause a challenge is not so much the embeddings but the preposing of both *clannesse* and also of *fayre formez*. If we consider the long subject (*clannesse* to *askez*) as one position and count the preposed object *fayre formez*, the word order is V3.

Late Middle and Early Modern English 1300–1600   145

As for the morphology, it is very characteristic of the Gawain poet to use the *-(e)z* nominal plurals and the same third person singular ending. The plural verbal endings typical for a Midlands text are *-en*. Note the frequent definite articles and the continued use of the feminine *h-* pronoun *ho*.

The next sentence is an adverbial to the previous one if we consider *for* as 'because'. It has an emphatic sense, however, more like 'indeed', and can therefore be seen as independent.

(2) for wonder wroth <u>is</u> **þe wy3** [þat wro3t alle þinges] wyth þe freke [þat in fylþe fol3es hym after] [as renkez of relygioun [þat reden 7 syngen 7 aprochen to hys presens] 7 prestez arn called]
'because (indeed) the being that made all things gets incredibly angry with the men who follow him when they are wallowing in filth, as men of religion who read and sing and approach into his presence and are called priests.'

If we take the sentence as an independent clause, the word order of the main clause is again V3. There are three relative clauses that have V2 and most objects follow the verb. Note the object of *after* preceding it.

The verbs have *-es* and *-en* endings, depending whether they are singular or plural, and the verb 'to be' is represented by a singular *is* and a plural *arn*. The latter is a passive auxiliary; its accompanying participle *called* lacks the earlier *ge-* or *i-* prefix. The plural nouns show either *-es* or *-ez* endings, as before. Note that the adverb *wonder* lacks the *-ly*.

In (3), we start with a set of coordinated verbs, with the verb *temen* listed in the MED as 'of a pagan temple: to be dedicated (to the devil)'. The line ends and starts with a lower case letter on *reken* whose subject may have been left out. Then, another line follows. I show the beginning of the three lines in a snip and the reader may disagree with my paratactic analysis.

(3) **Thay** <u>teen</u> vnto his temmple 7 temen to hym seluen
reken with reuerence [þay rychen his auter]
Þay <u>hondel</u> þer his aune body 7 vsen hit boþe
'they proceed to his temple and are dedicated. They approach with reverence as to enrich his altar; they handle there his own body and use it both.'

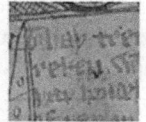

The word order is SV with pronominal objects following the verbs, e.g. *hit* after *vsen*.

There are a number of forms for third person plural pronouns: *thay*, *þay*, and *hym*. The nominative pronoun has the *th/þ* form but the accusative is *h*-initial. This is typical of a Midlands text. The verbal plural endings are *-en*. Note the reflexive *seluen*, which is still separate from the pronoun.

In (4), we see a few loosely connected clauses. Since there are no periods, we could pay attention to the capitals, e.g. what *bot* looks like.

This word starts a new line and has a capital so I assume it starts a new sentence.

(4) [if þay in clannes be clos] **pay** <u>cleche</u> gret mede Bot [if þay conterfete crafte 7 cortaysye wont] [as be honest vtwyth & inwith alle fylþez] Þen<u>ar</u> **pay** synful hemself 7 sulped altogeder boþe god 7 his gere 7 hym to greme cachen
'if they in cleanness are close, they obtain great reward. However, if they counterfeit craft and lack goodness and are honest outward and all filth inside, then are they sinful themselves and sully both God and his sacraments and drive him to anger.'

If the *if*-clause is an adverbial to the first main clause, the main clause has SV order. The sentence starting with *bot* is a V2 clause and includes three coordinated clauses. The last one of these is V-last. In this sentence, the reflexive is one word *hemself* and no longer has a plural *-en*, as in (3). A number of the plural verbs lack *-en*, e.g. *cleche* and *conterfete*.

The next sentence has a subject *he* that is later repeated in more detail. The main verb is *is* which is complemented by a series of adjectives, i.e. *clene*, *honeste*, and *serued*. There are two relative clauses introduced by *þat*.

(5) **he** <u>is</u> so clene in his courte **þe kyng [þat al weldez]** 7 honeste in his housholde 7 hagherlych serued with angelez [enourled in alle [þat is clene]] boþ withine 7 withouten in wedez ful bry3t
'he is so clean in his court, the king who rules all and (is) honest in his household, scrupulously served by angels, surrounded by all that is clean both inside and out in very bright clothing.'

The word order is SV in the main clause but V-last in the first relative clause. The order of the last three words is unusual from a modern perspective because the noun *wedez* precedes the adverb *ful* and adjective *bry3t*.

Sentence (6) starts with a negative contracted with the conjunction *if* and another contracted negative and auxiliary *nere* result in negative concord. I have analyzed the last embedded sentence as modifying *to much*: 'so much that it will not happen'.

(6) [nif he nere scoymus 7 skyg 7 non scape louied] **hit** <u>were</u> a meruayl to much [hit mo3t not falle]
'if he wasn't fastidious and fussy and loved the good, it were a marvel so much that it will not happen.'

In (7), the word order in the main clause is SV and objects follow the verbs. I assume the conjunction *Þer as* is subordinating.

(7) **kryst** <u>kydde</u> hit hymself in a carp onez [Þer as he heuened a3t happez 7 hy3t hem her medez]
'Christ announced it himself in a speech once where he raises eight virtues and explains them their rewards.'

Hymself is an emphatic this time. The plural third person pronouns are *hem* and *her* and the plural nouns have *-ez* endings.

In (8), we see an impersonal verb *mynez*, separated by an adverbial from its object clause starting with *Þat*.

(8) me mynez on one amonge oper [as mapew recordez] [Þat pus clannness vnclosez a ful cler speche]
'I refer to one among these, as Matthew records, that thus cleanness discloses in a fully clear manner.'

The third person singular endings on the verbs are all *-ez*.

The next sentence explains what is in the *speche* of (8), i.e. that certain things will happen to the nobleman, with the verb *hapenez* again impersonal.

(9) Þe hapel clene of his hert hapenez ful fayre [for he schal loke on oure lorde with a bone chere]
'the noble (one) with a clean heart (will) find good fortune for he will look upon our Lord with good cheer.'

The word order in the main clause is unclear as there is no subject but solidly SV in the subordinate one.

In (10), there is a subject pronoun missing if we look at it from a modern point of view. The sentence is structurally complex. The object clause starts with a preposed part (a verb phrase), *to pat sy3t seche*, and includes a relative and an adverbial, which in turn has a relative. The last relative clause is V-last.

(10) as so saytz [to pat sy3t seche schal he neuer [Þat any vnclannesse hatz on auwhere abowte] [for he pat flemus vch fylpe fer fro his hert may not byde pat burre [pat hit his body ne3en]]]
'which is to say: he that has any uncleanness will never seek for that sight, because he that banishes each (piece of) filth far from his heart may not tolerate that shock when it nears his body.'

The first part of the next passage is a simple imperative, and tells the reader 'not to hasten to heaven in torn clothes and with unclean hands'. The last part is an adverbial clause explaining why one needs to be clean.

(11) forpy hy3not to heuen in haterez totorne Ne in pe harlatez hod 7 handez vnwaschen [for what vrply hapel [pat hy3 honour haldez] wolde lyke [if a ladde com lyperly attired]
'therefore hurry not to heaven in clothes torn nor in the beggarly hood and hands unwashed for what earthly nobleman, who holds high honor, would like it if a man came wretchedly attired.'

The adverb *forpy* is a remnant from Old English with an instrumental demonstrative added to *for*, and a V-last relative clause (*pat hy3 honour haldez*) reinforces the archaic character.

5.1.3 Status and dialect

The word order is still varied compared, for instance, with the last text of Chapter 4. I summarize a few of the possibilities in (12), of which (12e) is the only such example.

(12) a. Þen<u>ar</u> **pay** synful (4) V2
'then they are sinful.'
b. **who** ... formez <u>my3t</u> **he** fynde (1) V3
'who might find terms.'
c. **hit** <u>were</u> a meruayl (6) SV
'it were a marvel.'
d. **þat** hy3 honour <u>haldez</u> (11) V-last
'that holds high honor.'
e. **þat** al <u>weldez</u> (5) pre-V object pronouns
'that rules all.'

There are reflexive pronouns, articles, relative markers in the shape of *who* and *that*, and many conjunctions. These grammatical function words make the language quite analytic. The style is quite complex in parts, e.g. because of multiple preposings.

As for the endings, nouns do not show case but pronouns do, and third person verbs – the only ones we have encountered – have endings, the singular ones in *-ez* or *-es* and the plural ones varying between *-en* and *-e*.

These plural verbal endings are typical for the Midlands. The use of *ho* confirms this origin and suggests that it is West Midlands, as does the use of *hem* and *thay*. On the basis of some lexical characteristics, Fulk (2012: 334) argues that it is the Northwest Midlands.

5.2 Chaucer's *Astrolabe*

Chaucer's *Astrolabe* is an instruction manual for using the astrolabe, an instrument to make astronomical measurements. The reader may want to check a description on the web or in an encyclopedia. It is Chaucer's original composition (though we have no manuscripts in his own hand) with instructions on the use of this instrument supposedly written for his son around 1391. It is based on an Arabic manual translated into Latin.

5.2.1 The text

The text can be found in thirty-two manuscripts and the pictures in Figures 5.4 and 5.5 are taken from MS Eng 920, dated around 1400, housed in the Houghton Library at Harvard University. There are clear (reddened) capital letters after a sentence final break, as in the snip.[2]

The scribe uses a Gothic hand whose thorn has lost the upper line, which I have shown in the transcription. As usual, there are some abbreviations.

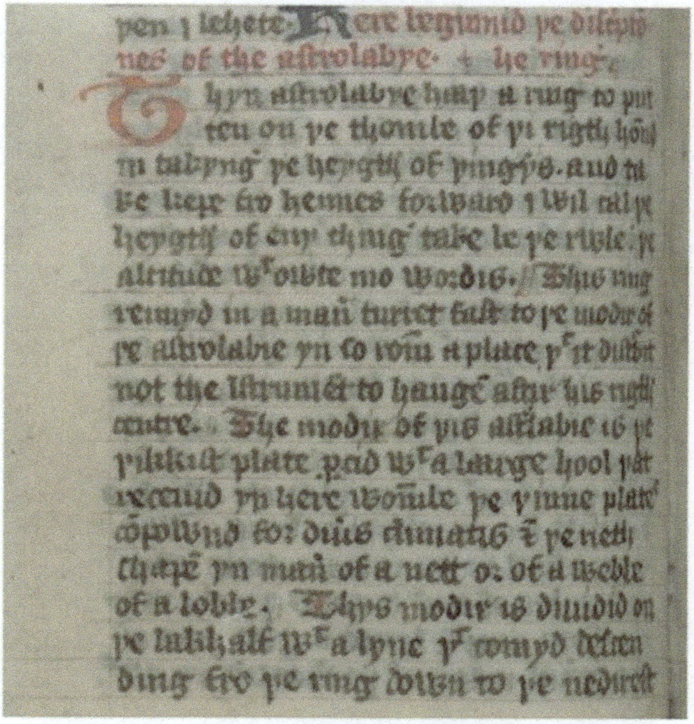

FIGURE 5.4. Chaucer's ***Astrolabe***, MS Eng 920, f. 5v (Houghton Library. Reproduced with permission from Harvard University)

TABLE 5.2. Transcription and translation of the first page of the *Astrolabe*

Here beginnid þe discpt	Here begins the description
nes of the astrolabye. the ring	of the astrolabe and the ring.
Thyn astrelabie haþ a ring to put	Your astrolabe has a ring to put
ten on þe thombe of þi riȝth hõnd	on the thumb of your right hand
in takyng þe heygty of þingys. and ta	when taking the height of things. And take care,
ke kepe fro from hennes forward I wil call þe	because from now onwards, I will call the
hepgtij of eny thing take be þe riȝle. þe	height of anything taken by the rule as the
altitude wtowte mo wordis. This ring	altitude without any more words. This ring
rennyd in a mañ turret fast to þe modir of	goes through a kind of ring fastened to the body
þe astrelabie yn so rõm a place þt it distrbit	of the astrolabe in so large a place that it doesn't
not the instrumẽt to hangẽ aftir his rigtij	disturb the instrument to hang
centre. The modir of þis astr(o)labie is þe	right down. The body of this astrolabe is the

(Continued)

TABLE 5.2. *Continued*

pikkist plate. prcd wt a large hool þat receiud yn here wombe þe pynne plates copownd for dius climatis 7 þe rieth shapẽ yn mañ of a nett or of a webbe of a lobbe. Thys modir is diuidid on þe bakhalf wt a lyne þt comyd descending fro þe ring down to the nedirest	thickest plate and is pierced with a large hole that receives the thin plates made for diverse celestial 15 zones and the reet shaped like a net or web of a spider. This body is divided on the back with a line that descends from the ring down to the lowest

FIGURE 5.5. Chaucer's *Astrolabe*, MS Eng 920, f. 6 (Houghton Library. Reproduced with permission from Harvard University)

Late Middle and Early Modern English 1300–1600   151

TABLE 5.3. Transcription and translation of the second page of the *Astrolabe*

bordure. þe whiche lyne fro þe forseide rĩg		border. The which line from the mentioned ring
vn to the centre of the large hole amydde ys clepid þe sowth lyne . or ellis þe line m(er)idional. and þe oþ deel of þe line dow̃		to the center of the large hole in the middle is called the south line or else the line meridional and the other part of the line down
to þe bordure is clepyd þe norplyne or ell þe lyne of mydnigti. Ouerdwart þe forseyde loñge lyne þr crosseþ hym a noþ̃ lyne of þe same length fro þe East to þe West. Of þe whyche lyne fro a lytil cos in þe bordur vnto þe centre of þe large is y clepid þe Eastlyne . or ell þe lyne Oriental and þe remenañt of this lyne fro the forsayde centre vnto þe bor dure is clepid þe west lyne or ellis the lyne Occidental. Now hast þ here the fou3r qrters of þin astrelabie diuidit aft þe four principal plagis 7 q̃rteris of þe firmamẽt.	5 10 15	to the border is called the north line or else the line of midnight. Across the mentioned long line there crosses itself another line of the same length from the East to the West of the which line from a little cross in the edge to the center of the large is called the eastline or else the line oriental and the remainder of this line from the mentioned center to the edge is called the west line or else the line occidental. Now have you here the four quarters of your astrolabe divided like the four principal zones and quarters of the firmament.
7 for þe mo re informa cioun loo heere a figure.	20	and for more information see here a figure.

5.2.2 Analysis

Chaucer's language is relatively simple compared with that of the previous text, analytic with few endings.

The beginning is a simple V2 sentence with a finite verb that ends in a *-d*, where other manuscripts have *-th*.

(13) Here <u>beginnid</u> **þe discpt nes of the astrolabye**.
'here begins the description of the astrolabe.'

In (14), the word order is SV and the finite verb has a *-th* ending, which is typical for third person singulars in Chaucer.

(14) **Thyn astrelabie** <u>haþ</u> a ring [to putten on þe thombe of þi ri3th hond [in takyng þe heygty of þingys]. and take kepe [fro from hennes forward I wil call þe heþgtij of eny thing [take be þe ri3le]. þe altitude withowte mo wordis].

'your astrolabe has a ring to put on the thumb of your right hand when taking the height of things. And take care, because from now onwards, I will call the height of anything taken by the rule as the altitude without any more words.'

The infinitive *putten* has an *-en* ending, also rather typical, of this time and region. After Chaucer's time, the ending simplifies to *-e*.

The next sentence has SV order again with a verb ending in *-d*, where other versions have *-th*.

(15) **This ring** <u>rennyd</u> in a man(er) turret fast to þe modir of þe astrelabie yn so rowm a place [þ(at) it dist(r)bit not the instrume(n)t [to hange(n) aftir his rigtij centre]].
'this ring goes through a kind of ring fastened to the body of the astrolabe in so large a place that it doesn't disturb the instrument to hang right down.'

It includes two embedded adverbials with SVO and SV order, respectively. Note that the lexical verb *dist(r)bit* (still) precedes the negative *not*, which will continue to occur until 1600. The neuter form of the possessive is *his* rather than *its*.

Sentence (16) starts as SV and has a non-finite reduced relative clause which itself contains a finite relative. There are two other reduced relatives or adjectives, in the form of *compownd* and *shapen*.

(16) **The modir of þis astr(o)labie** <u>is</u> þe pikkist plate. [p(e)rcd w(i)t a large hool [þat receiud yn here wombe þe pynne plates co(m)pownd for dius climatis] 7 þe rieth shape(n) yn man(er) of a nett or of a webbe of a lobbe].
'the body of this astrolabe is the thickest plate, pierced with a large hole that receives the thin plates made for diverse celestial zones and the reet shaped like a net or web of a spider.'

Nothing about the word order is surprising and the abundance of articles and prepositions makes the stage analytic.

I see the next section as consisting of two sentences, both with an SV order. You could also argue that the second sentence is embedded in the first as a relative.

(17) **Thys modir** <u>is</u> diuidid on þe bakhalf w(i)t a lyne [þt comyd descending fro þe ring down to the nedirest bordure . **þe whiche lyne fro þe forseide ring vn to the centre of the large hole amydde** <u>ys</u> clepid þe sowth lyne . or ellis þe line meridional. and þe op deel of þe line downe to þe bordure is clepyd þe norplyne or elles þe lyne of mydnigti.
'this body is divided on the back with a line that descends from the ring down to the lowest border. The one line from the mentioned ring to the center of the large hole in the middle is called the south line or else the line meridional and the other part of the line down to the border is called the north line or else the line of midnight.'

This passage has many words of location e.g. *bakhalf, nedirest, fro, vn to*, and *amydde*. Note the *ge/y*-less version of the participle *clepid*.

Late Middle and Early Modern English 1300–1600 153

The next portion can again be seen as two sentences, the first of which contains an existential *pr* 'there' with SV order, and the second is also SV.

(18) Ouerdwart þe forseyde longe lyne **pr** <u>crosseþ</u> hym a nop(er) lyne of þe same length fro þe East to þe West. **Of þe whyche lyne fro a lytil cros in þe bordure vnto þe centre of þe large** <u>is</u> y clepid þe Eastlyne . or elles þe lyne Oriental and þe remenant of this lyne fro the forsayde centre vnto þe bordure is clepid þe west lyne or ellis the lyne Occidental.
'across the mentioned long line there crosses itself another line of the same length from the East to the West. Of this line from a little cross in the edge to the center of the large is called the eastline or else the line oriental and the remainder of this line from the mentioned center to the edge is called the west line or else the line occidental.'

This time the participle is preceded by the prefix, as a snip shows clearly. y clepid. The reflexive *him* is used without its modern *-self*.

The last sentence of the page is V2.

(19) Now <u>hast</u> **þ(ow)** here the fou3r q(ua)rters of þin astrelabie diuidit aft(er) þe four principal plagis 7 q(ua)rteris of þe firmament. 7 for þe more informacioun loo heere a figure.
'now have you here the four quarters of your astrolabe divided like the four principal zones and quarters of the firmament. And for more information see here a figure.'

I see *hast* as an auxiliary to the lexical verb *diuidit*. The meaning is not that of a present perfect but more of a resultative which was its original meaning in Germanic.

5.2.3 Status and dialect

Chaucer's style is relatively non-embedded and his word orders are the typical late Middle English SV and V2, as in (20).

(20) a. **Thyn astrelabie** <u>haþ</u> a ring   (14) SV
     b. Here <u>beginnid</u> **þe discpt nes**   (13) V2

The language is analytic with numerous articles and prepositions. Auxiliaries in this passage are restricted to future *wil* in (14), *have* in (19), and *be* in (17) and (18), and do not occur in combinations of two or more.

The present participle *taking* in (14) is modern in its *-ing* ending and the past participle occurs once with the older *y-* prefix in (18) and twice without it in (17) and (18). The third person singular present tense ends in a variety of dentals, e.g. *-d* in (13) and 15), *-th* in (14), (15), and (18), and second person singular verbs end in *-st* in (19). Finally, *-en* infinitives still occur. Thus, although the language is analytic, it is also synthetic in its verbal endings.

The dialect characteristics are not very obvious. The third person singular *-th* shows it to be southern text but we have no plural verbs to check between Midlands and southern endings.

5.3 Margery of Kempe

Margery of Kempe was a fourteenth-century mystic from Norfolk, in the Northeast Midlands, who dictated her work. The text is preserved in one manuscript, discovered by Hope Allen in a private library, but now held in the British Library and known as Add MS 61823.

5.3.1 The text

Figure 5.6 is taken from the British Library and the edited text from the TEAMS edition.[3] I have used Triggs (1995) for the translation. The script represents secretary or court hand. The manuscript has markings that seem to indicate breaks, e.g. in line 7.

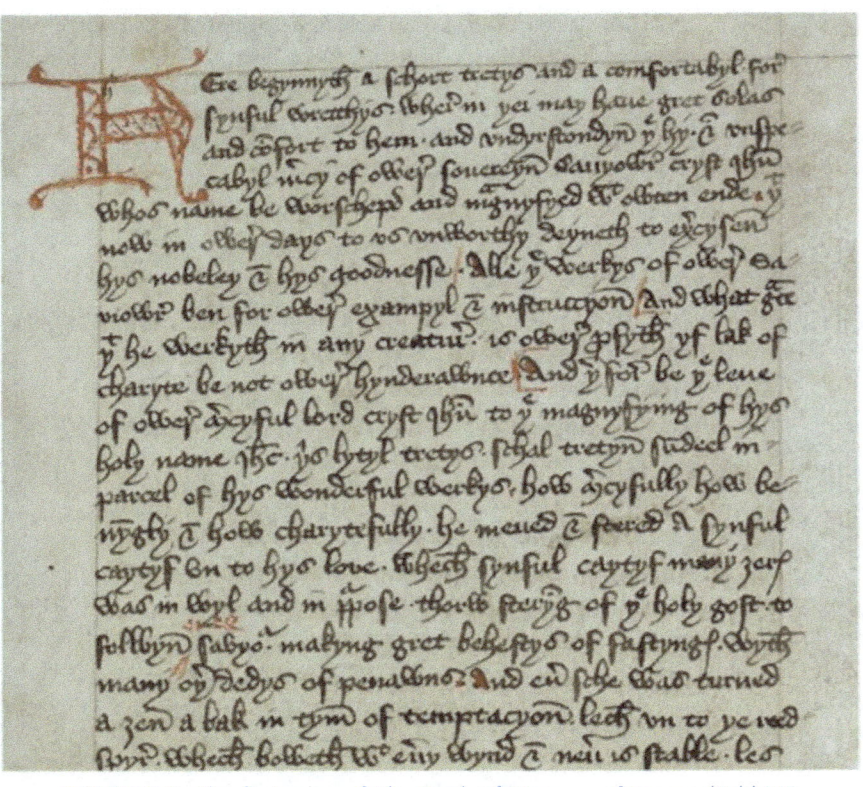

I have sometimes followed these but not always, e.g. not in (22), (24), and (25). There are also abbreviations, e.g. 'therefore' in line 10.

FIGURE 5.6. The first page of *The Book of Margery of Kempe* (Add MS 61823, f. 1. Reproduced with permission from the British Library Board)

(Continued)

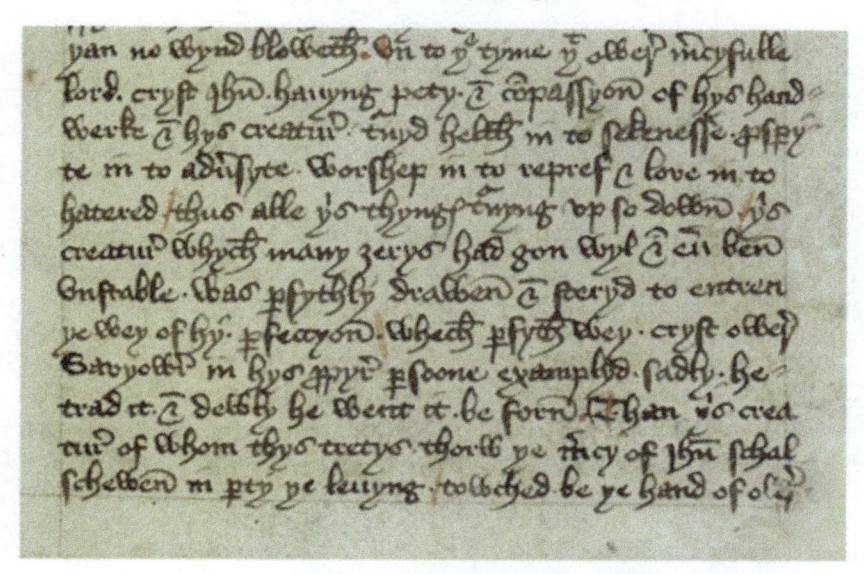

Late Middle and Early Modern English 1300–1600 155

FIGURE 5.6. *Continued*

In the transcription in Table 5.4, I have added the remainder from the next manuscript page in order to make the last sentence understandable. I have used 'th' for the ⟨þ⟩ symbol, 'g' for the ⟨ȝ⟩, and added the abbreviated text.

5.3.2 Analysis

The text is fairly analytic, but verbs still have numerous endings. The writing is complex in structure and punctuation is not always indicative of sentence boundaries. In the translation of the sentences, I have been more literal than Triggs, given in Table 5.4.

Sentence (21) starts very simply, with an initial adverb and a finite verb making it a V2 word order.

(21) Here begynnyth a schort tretys and a comfortabyl for synful wrecchys [wherin thei may have gret solas and comfort to hem . and undyrstondyn the hy and unspecabyl mercy of ower sovereyn savyowr cryst jhesu [whos name be worschepd and magnyfyed wythowten ende [that now in ower days to us unworthy deyneth to exercysen hys nobeley and hys goodnesse]]].
'here begins a short study and a comfortable one for sinful wretches wherefrom they may get great consolation and comfort to them and understanding of the high and unspeakable mercy of our sovereign savior Christ Jesus whose name should be worshipped and praised forever for in our own lifetime he has deigned to show us his majesty and goodness in spite of our unworthiness.'

The entire remainder of the sentence after *begynnyth* is the subject with numerous embeddings. The first two embedded clauses are relatives and the last is an adverbial. This sentence ends in the manuscript with a clear period.

TABLE 5.4. Transcription and translation from *The Book of Margery of Kempe*

Here begynnyth a schort tretys and a comfortabyl for synful wrecchys wherin thei may have gret solas and comfort to hem . and undyrstondyn the hy and unspe cabyl mercy of ower sovereyn savyowr cryst jhesu whos name be worschepd and magnyfyed wythowten ende that now in ower days to us unworthy deyneth to exercysen hys nobeley and hys goodnesse. Alle the werkys of ower sa viowr ben for ower exampyl and instruccyon and what grace that he werkyth in any creatur is ower profyth yf lak of charyte be not ower hynderawnce. And therfor be the leve of ower mercyful lord cryst jhesu to the magnyfying of hys holy name Jhesu . this lytyl tretys schal tretyn sumdeel in	Here begins a short study that offers sinful wretches great reassurance, consolation and comfort to them and understanding of the high and unspeakable mercy of our sovereign Savior Christ Jesus. May his name be worshipped and praised forever for in our own lifetimes he has deigned to show us his majesty and goodness in spite of our unworthiness. All our savior's works are for our instruction and guidance and the favor he shows to any of his created souls brings benefit to all who have the grace to respond. To the glory of his holy name our merciful Lord JC has therefore allowed this little treatise to be set down.
parcel of hys wonderful werkys how mercyfully how be nyngly and how charytefully . he meved and stered a synful caytyf unto hys love . whech synful caytyf many yerys was in wyl and in purpose thorw steryng of the holy gost to folwyn oure savyour makyng gret behestys of fastyngys wyth many other dedys of penawns.	It will touch on some of his wonderful works on how mercifully, kindly and lovingly he stirred and incited a wicked wretch like me to love him and how at the prompting of the holy spirit I then spent many years doing my best to follow our saviour, with vows of fasting and other penances.
And evyr sche was turned a gen abak in tym of temptacyon lech unto the reed spyr which boweth wyth every wynd and nevyr is stable . les than no wynd bloweth . On to the tyme that ower mercyfulle lord cryst jhesu havyng pety and compassyon of hys hand werke and hys creatur turnyd helth in to sekenesse prosper te in to adversyte . Worshep in to repref and love in to hatered.	In times of temptation I was constantly suffering setbacks; I was like a reed that bends with every breath of wind and only stays upright when all is calm. This was the case until our merciful lord JC took pity on me. Out of compassion for his handiwork and his creation, he turned my health into sickness, my success into failure, the good opinion of others to blame and their love into hatred.
Thus alle this thyngys turnyng up so down this creatur whych many yerys had gon wyl and evyr ben unstable . Was parfythly drawen and steryd to entren the wey of hy perfeccyon . whech parfyth wey . cryst ower Savyowr in hys propyr persoone examplyd. Sadly . he trad it	For many years I had gone my own uncertain way but all these reverses inescapably drew and incited me to follow the way of his perfection – the way which Christ our savior had exemplified in his own person, having duly followed the path before us and trodden it with dignity. By the mercy of Jesus this

(Continued)

TABLE 5.4. *Continued*

and dewly he went it beforn. Than this creatur of whom thys tretys thorw the mercy of jhesu schal schewen in party the levyng towched be the hand of owyr ...	study will show you something of my way of life. It will show how the hand of our lord touched my body with
lord wyth grett bodyly sekenesse wher thorw sche lost reson and her wyttes a long tym tyl ower Lord be grace restoryd her ageyn, as it schal mor openly be schewed aftyrward.	serious illness, causing me to go out of my mind and suffer a lengthy spell of insanity. It lasted until our lord, by his grace, made me well again, as I shall reveal more fully below.

The morphology shows third person singular *-th* in *begynnyth* and *deyneth*, *-yn/-en* as an infinitive marking on *undyrstondyn* and *exercysen*, and the passive subjunctive *be worschepd*. The third person pronoun shows both *thei* and *hem*, and the relatives are *whos* and *wherin* rather than *that*.

In (22), the word order is SV and there is a relative clause and adverbial clause with SV orders as well.

(22) **Alle the werkys of ower saviowr** <u>ben</u> for ower exampyl and instruccyon and what grace [that he werkyth in any creatur] is ower profyth [yf lak of charyte be not ower hynderawnce].
'all the works of our savior are for our example and instruction and what favor he shows to any of his creatures is to our profit if lack of grace doesn't hinder us.'

The plural *ben* shows a Midlands influence, and the singular *-th* on *werkyth* is compatible with that. The *be* in the adverbial clause is a subjunctive. It is a light verb that together with the noun *hynderawnce* renders the modern English 'to hinder'.

(23) is an SV sentence but with a coordinating *and* and three initial adverbials coming before the subject and verb: *therfor*, the PP starting with *be the leve of ower mercyful lord cryst jhesu*, and the PP adverbial *to the magnyfying of hys holy name Jhesu* .

(23) And therfor be the leve of ower mercyful lord cryst jhesu to the magnyfying of hys holy name Jhesu. **this lytyl tretys** <u>schal</u> tretyn sumdeel in parcel of hys wonderful werkys how mercyfully how benyngly and how charytefully . [he meved and stered a synful caytyf unto hys love] . whech synful caytyf many yerys was in wyl and in purpose thorw steryng of the holy gost to folwyn **oure** savyour makyng gret behestys of fastyngys wyth many other dedys of penawns.
'and therefore with the permission of our merciful Lord to magnify the name Jesus, this little treatise shall treat on some of his wonderful works, on how mercifully, kindly and lovingly he moved and stirred a wicked wretch like me to love him and how at the prompting of the holy spirit I then spent many

years doing my best to follow our savior, with vows of fasting and other penances.'

In the manuscript, it is obvious that *oure* has later been added before *savyour.* The verbal endings are standard for the simple past. The *-ly* on the adverbs *mercyfully*, *benyngly*, and *charytefully* is clearly marked.

The next passage shows SV in the main clause and has two finite relative clauses which I have bracketed. The first relative has an adverbial starting with *les than* and the second relative has a non-finite clausal modifier *havyng pety and compassyon of hys hand werke and hys creatur*.

> (24) And evyr **sche** was turned a gen abak in tym of temptacyon lech unto the reed spyr [which boweth wyth every wynd and nevyr is stable . [les than no wynd bloweth]] . On to the tyme [that ower mercyfulle lord cryst jhesu [havyng pety and compassyon of hys hand werke and hys creatur] turnyd helth in to sekenesse prosper te in to adversyte . Worshep in to repref and love in to hatered].
> 'and always she was turned back again in time of temptation like the reed which bends with every wind and is never stable except when no wind blows. Until the time that our merciful lord Jesus Christ, having pity and compassion for his handiwork and his creature, turned health into illness and success into failure, worship into blame and love into hatred.'

The verbal endings are past for *was* and *turnyd* and present for the habituals *boweth, is,* and *bloweth*.

The next subject is complicated. For modern readers, there is no obvious subject to the main verb group *was drawen and steryd.* The *creatur* that seems the object of *turnyng* is also the subject of the main verb.

> (25) Thus alle this thyngys [turnyng up so down this creatur [whych many yerys had gon wyl and evyr ben unstable]] . Was parfythly drawen and steryd [to entren the wey of hy perfeccyon . [whech parfyth wey . cryst ower Savyowr in hys propyr persoone examplyd]].
> 'thus all these things happening, which for many years had gone well though always had been unstable, drew this creature in and steered it to enter the way of high perfection, which perfect way Christ our Savior exemplified in his own person.'

The passage also has two relative clauses, both of which start with a *wh-* pronoun, and there is an infinitival adverbial. The progressive participle ends in *-yng*, the infinitive in *-en*, and the simple past in *-d*. There is also a past perfect *had gon ... and ... ben*.

The last part of the page has an initial adverb *sadly* and then SV and a parallel coordinate with an adverb *dewly* and SV order. The second sentence is either not finite or has an implicit auxiliary *was* to go with *towched*. It contains two relatives and two adverbials, all finite clauses.

> (26) Sadly . **he** trad it and dewly he went it beforn. Than this creatur of [whom thys tretys thorw the mercy of jhesu schal schewen in party the levyng] towched be the hand of owyr
> ...

lord wyth grett bodyly sekenesse [wher thorw sche lost reson and her wyttes a long tym [tyl ower Lord be grace restoryd her ageyn, [as it schal mor openly be schewed aftyrward.]]]

'firmly, he followed it and duly went before us. Now this creature, about whom this treatise through the mercy of Jesus shall show the living, touched by the hand of our lord with great bodily illness through which she lost reason and her mind for a long time until our lord restored her again, as it will more clearly be shown afterwards.'

The preposition *beforn* follows its pronominal object *it*, a remnant from older times. The inflection is past tense on *trad* 'trode', *went*, and *restoryd* and has an *-en* after the first modal *schal*. (26) also has a sequence of two auxiliaries in *schal ... be schewed*.

5.3.3 Status and dialect

As before, the language has lots of pronouns, auxiliaries, and prepositions, which make it analytic, but it also keeps verbal endings and is therefore synthetic as well. The style is fairly complex and sentence boundaries are not always marked.

The word order is predominantly SV with one V2; there are sometimes quite a number of adverbials preceding the subject, unlike later English. These are repeated in (27).

(27) a. Here begynnyth **a schort tretys** (21) V2
b. **Alle the werkys of ower saviowr** ben for ower exampyl. (22) SV
c. AP PP PP **this lytyl tretys** schal tretyn sumdeel (23) ... SV

The pronouns include *sche, he, thei,* and *hem*. The plural *thei* as well as *hem* reveal a Midlands origin. Relative pronouns are varied in form: *whos, wherin, whom,* and *which/which*. There are a modal and passive auxiliaries and participles lack an *i-* prefix, as (21), (24), and (25) show. Finite verbs show a third person plural *ben* and a singular *-th*, again compatible with an (East) Midlands dialect.

5.4 Caxton's *Morte d'Arthur*

William Caxton brought movable print to England and translated many works into English before printing them. Movable print meant individual letters could be arranged into a frame by a compositor who then rolled ink over the frame and pressed paper onto it. In Chapter 2, we saw the printed page of Shakespeare's First Folio. A folio means that two pages are printed on one side of a sheet which then is folded once.

As shown in Figures 5.7 and 5.8, the type in early printed texts resembles the Gothic writing we have seen in the manuscripts. It also follows other conventions such as irregular punctuation and capitalization (from our point of view) and the use of abbreviations. To aid the binders, there are sometimes letters and numbers at the bottom right of the page, e.g. 'a' in Figure 5.7. Caxton uses various punctuation marks, e.g. capitals, space / ℂ.

5.4.1 The text

The images in Figures 5.7 and 5.8 of Malory's *Morte d'Arthur* as printed by Caxton are taken from the *Rylands Medieval Collection*[4] and the book dates from 1485. Its transcription follows the one at *Corpus of Middle English Prose and Verse*.[5]

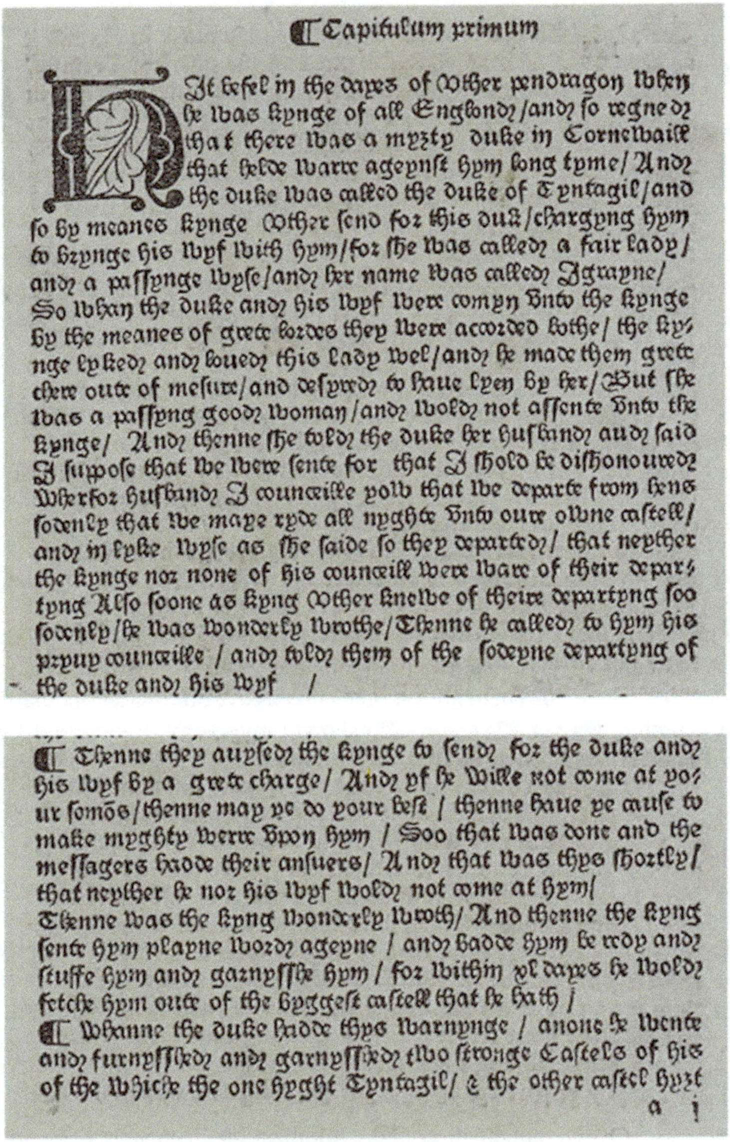

FIGURE 5.7. The first page of the first chapter of Malory's *Morte d'Arthur* as printed by Caxton (from *Rylands Medieval Collection*, University of Manchester)

Late Middle and Early Modern English 1300–1600 161

> Terrabyl / So his wyf Dame Igrayne he putte in the castell of Tyntagil / And hym self he putte in the castel of Terrabyl the whiche had many yssues and posternes oute / Thenne in all haste came Other with a grete hoost / and leyd a syege aboute the castel of Terrabil / And ther he pyght many pauellons / and ther was grete warre made on bothe partyes / and moche peple slayne / Thenne for pure angre and for grete sorue of fayr Igrayne the kyng Other felle seke / So came to the kynge Other Syre Vlfius a noble knyght / and asked the kynge why he was seke / I shall telle the said the kynge / I am seke for angre and for loue of fayre Igrayne that I may not be hool / wel my lord said Syre Vlfius / I shal seke Merlyn / and he shalle do som remedy that youre herte shalbe pleasyd / So Vlfius departed / and by auenture he mette Merlyn in a beggars aray / and ther Merlyn asked Vlfius whom he soughte / and he said he had lytyl ado to telle hym / Well saide Merlyn / I knowe whome thou sekest / for thou sekest Merlyn / therfore seke no ferther / for I am he / and yf kynge Other wille rewarde me / and be sworne vnto me to fulfille my desyre that shall be his honour & profite more thā myn for I shalle cause hym to haue alle his desyre / Alle this wyll I vndertake said Vlfius that ther shalle be nothyng resonable / but thow shalt haue thy desyre / Well said Merlyn / he shall haue his entente and desyre / And therfore saide Merlyn / ryde on your wey / for I wille not be long behynde

FIGURE 5.8. The second part of the first chapter of Malory's *Morte d'Arthur* as printed by Caxton (from *Rylands Medieval Collection*, University of Manchester)

5.4.2 Analysis

I have not separated all sentences in (28) to (34). Many times, the divisions are less clear than they are in Modern English. Because the language is quite modern, I have not provided a translation underneath.

The first sentence is clearly marked in the layout of the printed page as ending on line 8. It starts with an expletive subject *hit* making the sentence SV in order, the impersonal verb *befall* not having a real subject of its own. There is an additional expletive, *there*.

> (28) **HIt** befel in the dayes of Vther pendragon [when he was kynge of all Englond / and so regned] [that there was a my3ty duke in Cornewaill [that helde warre ageynst hym long tyme / And the duke was called the duke of Tyntagil] / and so by meanes kynge Vther send for this duk / [chargyng hym to brynge his wyf with hym / [for she was called a fair lady / and a passynge wyse / and her name was called Igrayne]]

All finite verbs are past tense (*befell, was, regned, was, helde, was, send, was,* and *was*) and there is a present participle ending in *-yng* and an infinitive in *-e*.

TABLE 5.5. Transliteration and translation from Caxton's *Morte d'Arthur*

HIt befel in the dayes of Vther pendragon when he was kynge of all Englond / and so regned that there was a my3ty duke in Cornewaill that helde warre ageynst hym long tyme / And the duke was called the duke of Tyntagil / and so by meanes kynge Vther send for this duk / chargyng hym to brynge his wyf with hym / for she was called a fair lady / and a passynge wyse / and her name was called Igrayne /	IT happened in the days of Uther Pendragon, when he was king of all England, and so reigned, that there was a mighty duke in Cornwall that waged war against him for a long time. And the duke was called the Duke of Tintagil. And so by means King Uther sent for this duke, charging him to bring his wife with him, for she was called a fair lady, and a passing wise one, and her name was called Igraine.
So whan the duke and his wyf were comyn vnto the kynge by the meanes of grete lordes they were accorded bothe / the ky nge lyked and loued this lady wel / and he made them grete chere out of mesure / and desyred to haue lyen by her / But she was a passyng good woman / and wold not assente vnto the kynge / And thenne she told the duke her husband and said I suppose that we were sente for that I shold be dishonoured Wherfor husband I counceille yow that we departe from hens sodenly that we maye ryde all nyghte vnto oure owne castell /	So when the duke and his wife had come unto the king, by the means of great lords they were accorded both. The king liked and loved this lady well, and he made them great cheer out of measure, and desired to have lain by her. But she was a passing good woman, and would not assent unto the king. And then she told the duke her husband, and said, I suppose that we were sent for that I should be dishonoured; wherefore, husband, I counsel you, that we depart from hence suddenly, that we may ride all night unto our own castle.
and in lyke wyse as she saide so they departed / that neyther the kynge nor none of his counceill were ware of their departyng Also soone as kyng Vther knewe of theire departyng soo sodenly / he was wonderly wrothe / Thenne he called to hym his pryuy counceille / and told them of the sodeyne departyng of the duke and his wyf /	And in like wise as she said so they departed, that neither the king nor none of his council were aware of their departing. So, as soon as King Uther knew of their departing so suddenly, he was wonderly angry. Then he called to him his privy council, and told them of the sudden departing of the duke and his wife.
Thenne they auysed the kynge to send for the duke and his wyf by a grete charge / And yf he wille not come at your somōs / thenne may ye do your best / thenne haue ye cause to make myghty werre vpon hym / Soo that was done and the messagers hadde their ansuers / And that was thys shortly / that neyther he nor his wyf wold not come at hym /	Then they advised the king to send for the duke and his wife by a great force; and if he will not come at your summons, then may ye do your best, then you have cause to make mighty war upon him. So that was done, and the messengers had their answers; and that was this shortly, that neither he nor his wife would not come at him.
Thenne was the kyng wonderly wroth / And thenne the kyng sente hym playne word ageyne / and badde hym be redy and stuffe hym and garnysshe hym / for within xl dayes he wold fetche hym oute of the byggest castell that he hath /	Then was the king wonderly wroth. And then the king sent him plain word again, and bade him be ready and stuff him and garnish him, for within forty days he would fetch him out of the biggest castle that he hath.

(Continued)

TABLE 5.5. *Continued*

Whanne the duke hadde thys warnynge / anone he wente and furnysshed and garnysshed two stronge Castels of his of the whiche the one hyght Tyntagil / & the other castel hy3t Terrabyl / So his wyf Dame Igrayne he putte in the castell of Tyntagil / And hym self he putte in the castel of Terrabyl the whiche had many yssues and posternes oute / Thenne in alle haste came Vther with a grete hoost / and leyd a siege a boute the castel of Terrabil / And ther he pyght many pauelyons / and there was grete warre made on bothe partyes / and	When the duke received this warning, anon he went and furnished and garnished two strong castles of his, of the which the one hight Tintagil, and the other castle hight Terrabil. So he put his wife Dame Igraine in the castle of Tintagil, and he put himself in the castle of Terrabil, which had many issues and posterns out. Then in all haste came Uther with a great host, and laid a siege about the castle of Terrabil. And there he ... many pavilions, and there was great war made on both parties, and much people slain.
moche peple slayne / Thenne for pure angre and for grete loue of fayr Irayne the kyng Vther felle seke / So came to the kynge Vther Syre Vlfius a noble knyght / and asked the kynge why he was seke / I shall telle the said the kynge / I am seke for angre and for loue of fayre Igrayne that I may	Then for pure anger and for great love of fair Igraine the king Uther fell sick. So came to the king Uther Sir Ulfius, a noble knight, and asked the king why he was sick. I shall tell thee, said the king, I am sick for anger and for love of fair Igraine, that I may not be whole.
not be hool / wel my lord said Syre Vlfius / I shal seke Merlyn / and he shalle do yow remedy that youre herte shalbe pleasyd / So Vlfius departed / and by aduenture he mette Merlyn in a beggars aray / and ther Merlyn asked Vlfius whome he soughte / and he said he had lytyl ado to telle hym / Well saide Merlyn / I knowe whome thou sekest / for thou sekest Merlyn / therfore seke no ferther / for I am he / and yf kynge Vther wille wel rewarde me / and be sworne vnto me to fulfille my desyre that shall be his honour & profite more thā myn for I shalle cause hym to haue alle his desyre / Alle this wyll I vndertake said Vlfius that ther shalle be nothyng resonable / but thow shalt haue thy desyre / well said Merlyn / he shall haue his entente and desyre / And therfore saide Merlyn / ryde on your wey / for I wille not be long behynde	Well, my lord, said Sir Ulfius, I shall seek Merlin, and he shall do you remedy, that your heart shall be pleased. So Ulfius departed, and by adventure he met Merlin in a beggar's array, and there Merlin asked Ulfius whom he sought. And he said he had little ado to tell him. Well, said Merlin, I know whom thou seekest, for thou seekest Merlin; therefore seek no farther, for I am he; and if King Uther will well reward me, and be sworn unto me to fulfil my desire, that shall be his honour and profit more than mine; for I shall cause him to have all his desire. All this will I undertake, said Ulfius, that there shall be nothing reasonable but thou shalt have thy desire. Well, said Merlin, he shall have his intent and desire. And therefore, said Merlin, ride on your way, for I will not be long behind.

The word order in (29) is SV throughout. The passage seems to consist of four sentences, one starting with *so*, one with *the kynge*, with *but*, and *wherefore*.

(29) So [whan the duke and his wyf were comyn vnto the kynge by the meanes of grete lords] **they** were accorded bothe / **the kynge** lyked and loued this lady

wel / and he made them grete chere out of mesure / and desyred [to haue lyen by her] / But **she** <u>was</u> a passyng good woman / and wold not assente vnto the kynge / And thenne she told the duke her husband and said [I suppose [that we were sente [for that I shold be dishonoured]]] Wherfor husband **I** <u>counceille</u> yow [that we departe from hens sodenly [that we maye ryde all nyghte vnto oure owne castell]]

The combination of *were comyn* is with the auxiliary 'be'; Modern English would have *had come*. There are several other auxiliaries, passive *were*, the modals *wold*, *shold*, and *maye*, and a perfect infinitive (*to haue lyen*). Many finite verbs are past tense. Interesting from a pragmatic point of view is that Igraine uses the polite plural *yow* to address her husband.

The next section consists of three sentences, all with SV word order, which is indicated through the underlined verbs and bolded subjects.

(30) and in lyke wyse [as she saide] so **they** <u>departed</u> / [that neyther the kynge nor none of his counceill were ware of their departing] Also [soone as kyng Vther knewe of theire departyng soo soddenly] / **he** <u>was</u> wonderly wrothe / Thenne **he** <u>called</u> to hym his pryuy counceille / and told them of the sodeyne departyng of the duke and his wyf /

Verbal endings are restricted to past tense and there is a *none* in a negative context where later English would use *any*. All adverbs have endings, e.g. *soddenly* and *wonderly*, and the accusative plural pronoun is now *them*.

The next sentence is clearly marked by a paragraph mark ⁋. I have divided it into four sentences but there could be more. The first two are SV and the last two V2.

(31) Thenne **they** <u>auysed</u> the kynge [to send for the duke and his wyf by a grete charge / And [yf he wille not come at your somōs] / thenne may ye do your best / thenne haue ye cause to make myghty werre vpon hym] / Soo **that** <u>was</u> done and the messagers hadde their ansuers / And that was thys shortly / that neyther he nor his wyf wold not come at hym / Thenne <u>was</u> **the kyng** wonderly wroth / And thenne **the kyng** <u>sente</u> hym playne word ageyne / and badde hym [be redy and stuffe hym and garnysshe hym] / [for within xl dayes he wold fetche hym oute of the byggest castell [that he hath]]

The verbal endings are as expected and many auxiliaries appear: *wille*, *may*, *was*, and *wold*. The king uses the plural *ye* and *your* because he addresses more than one person.

Another paragraph mark starts the next group of sentences, which again show a mix of SV and V2 in the main clause.

(32) [Whanne the duke hadde thys warnynge] / anone **he** <u>wente and furnysshed and garnysshed</u> two stronge Castels of his of the whiche the one hyght Tyntagil / & the other castel hy3t Terrabyl / So his wyf Dame Igrayne **he** <u>putte</u> in the castell of Tyntagil / And hym self he putte in the castel of Terrabyl the whiche had many yssues and posternes oute / Thenne in alle haste <u>came</u> **Vther** with a grete hoost / and leyd a syege aboute the castel of Terrabil / And ther he pyght many pauelyons / and there was grete warre made on bothe partyes / and moche peple slayne /

Late Middle and Early Modern English 1300–1600 165

This passage shows preposings of objects such as *his wyf Dame Igrayne* and *hym self*. Most embeddings use *wh-* pronouns. Two *there* pronouns appear but it is not clear if they are locative or expletive. Lexically, there is a remnant of *hetan* 'to be called' in *hyght*.

The next passage has a number of sentences that are lightly connected, with a variety of SV and VS orders.

(33) Thenne for pure angre and for grete loue of fayr Irayne **the kyng Vther** felle seke / So came to the kynge Vther Syre Vlfius **a noble knyght** / and asked the kynge [why he was seke] / **I** shall telle the said the kynge / **I** am seke for angre and for loue of fayre Igrayne [that I may not be hool] / wel my lord said **Syre Vlfius** / [I shal seke Merlyn / and he shalle do yow remedy that youre herte shalbe pleasyd] / So **Vlfius** departed / and by aduenture he mette Merlyn in a beggars aray / and ther Merlyn asked Vlfius [whome he sought] / and he said [he had lytyl ado to telle hym]

This passage contains one of the first copula uses of *fall*. It also contains a dialogue in which the use of the second person pronouns *the* and *yow* indicate status of speaker and addressee: the familiar *the* from the king and the polite *yow* to the king.

The last part consists of five sentences, some of which are quite embedded.

(34) Well saide **Merlyn** / [I knowe [whome thou sekest / [for thou sekest Merlyn]]] / therfore seke no ferther / [for I am he / and yf kynge Vther wille wel rewarde me / and be sworne vnto me to fulfille my desyre [that shall be his honour & profite more thā myn [for I shalle cause [hym to haue alle his desire]]]] / Alle this [wyll I vndertake] said **Vlfius** [that ther shalle be nothyng resonable / but thow shalt haue thy desire] / well said **Merlyn** / [he shall haue his entente and desire] / And therfore saide **Merlyn** / [ryde on your wey / [for I wille not be long behynde]]

This time, Merlin uses *thou* and *your* to the same person. The case after a copula is nominative in 'I am he' and modals are abundant.

5.4.3 Status and dialect

Both SV and VS occur, as shown in (35), and long initial adverbials and object preposings, as in (36), are frequent.

(35) a. Thenne **they** auysed the kynge (31) SV
 b. So came to the kynge Vther Syre Vlfius **a noble knight** (33) VS
(36) **So [his wyf Dame Igrayne]** he putte in the castell of Tyntagil.

There are expletives (*there* and *hit*) and third person feminine and plural *she* and *they*, indicating a late text. The use of *yee* and *thou* indicates some social differences between speech participants.

The text is analytic in its use of auxiliaries and prepositions; there are no present tense verbs so we can't check the third person singular *-th* endings typical of texts before 1600.

166 *Analyzing Syntax through Texts*

The text doesn't show specific dialect features, but is clearly a rendering of a late Middle English text. Caxton often prefaces his books with a comment on the use of his English, so that we know it was from Kent.

5.5 Henry Machyn and Queen Elizabeth

This section covers informal writing. Henry Machyn kept a chronicle from 1550 to 1563 and Queen Elizabeth wrote letters throughout her long life. I have combined the analysis, status, and dialect into one section.

5.5.1 The texts

Machyn's notes are from Bailey et al. (n.d.). The writing is secretary hand.

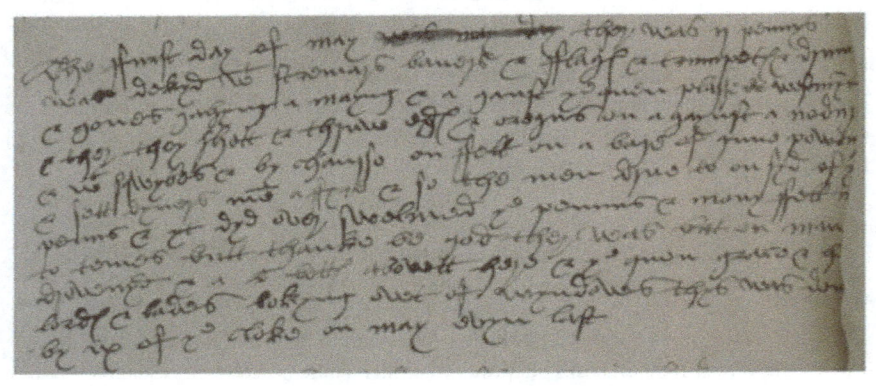

FIGURE 5.9. Machyn, 1 May 1559

The transcription follows as Figure 5.10 from Bailey et al. (n.d.).

The ffurst day of may ~~waſ may day~~ ther waſ ij pennyſ
waſ dekyd wt stremarſ banerſ & fflag{s} & trumpett{s} & drums
& gones gahyng a mayng & a ganst ye quen plasse at westmẏter
& ther they shott & thruw eg{s} & oregnſ on a gaynst a nodur
& wt sqwybeſ & by chansse on ffell on a bage of gune powdur e
& sett dyuerſ mē affyre & so the men drue to on syd of ye
penuſ & yt dyd over swelmed ye pennuſ & mony ffell in
to temeſ butt thanke be god ther waſ but on man
drownyd & a c bott{s} abowtt here & ye quen grace & her
lord{s} & ladeſ lokyng owt of wyndowſ thyſ waſ done
by ix of ye cloke on may evyn last

The first day of May there was two pinnaces
was decked with streamers, banners, flags, trumpets and drums
and guns going a-Maying and against the Queen's place at Westminster
And there they shot and threw eggs and oranges, one against another
and with squibs. And by chance, one fell on a bag of gunpowder
and set divers men afire. And so the men drew to one side of the pinnace,
and it did overwhelm the pinnace. And many fell in
to Thames. But, thanks be God, there was but one man
drowned. And a hundred boats about her. And the Queen's Grace and her
lords and ladies looking out of windows. This was done
by nine o'clock on May eve last.

FIGURE 5.10. Machyn, 1 May 1559 transcription and translation (from Bailey et al. n.d.)

Late Middle and Early Modern English 1300–1600   167

Elizabeth's letter from 1554 was written when she was a princess kept under house arrest. Her handwriting is in italic. Developed in Italy, the handwriting was popular with, for example, Roger Ascham who was Elizabeth's tutor. Silent -*e* symbols abound, the spellings of *wiche*, *might*, and *thogth* are pretty consistent, and most nasals are abbreviated on the preceding vowel, which is shown in Figure 5.11. More on Elizabeth's writing style can be found at *The National Archives*.[6]

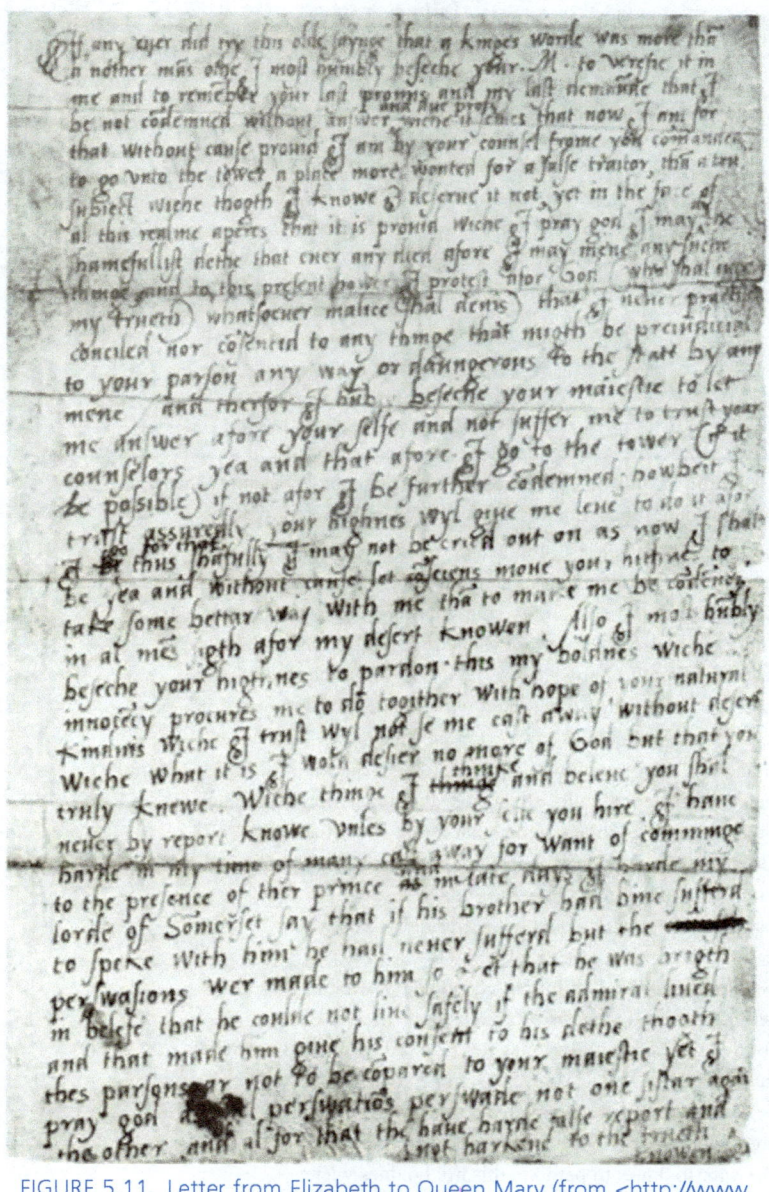

FIGURE 5.11. Letter from Elizabeth to Queen Mary (from <http://www.luminarium.org/renlit/elizabib.htm>, last accessed 4 June 2017)

(Continued)

FIGURE 5.11. *Continued*

TABLE 5.6. Transcription of Elizabeth's letter

If any euer did try this olde sayinge that a kinge's worde was more thã a nother mãs othe I most humbly beseche your . M. to verefie it in	
me and to remẽber your last promis and my last demaũde that I be not cõdemned without answer and due profe wiche it semes that I now am for that without cause prouid I am by your counsel frome you commanded to go unto the tower, a place more wanted for a false traitor, thã a tru subiect wiche thogth I knowe I deserue it not, yet in the face of all this realme aperes that it is proud wiche I pray god I may die the shamefullest dethe that euer any died afore I may mene any suche thinge and to this present hower I protest afor God (who shal iuge my trueth) whatsoeuer malice shal deuis) that I neuer practiced conciled nor cõsented to any thinge that migth be preiudicial to your parson any way or daungerous to the state by any mene / and therefor I hũbly beseche your maiestie to let me answer afore your selfe and not suffer me to trust your councelors yea and that afore I go to the tower (if it be possible) if not afor I be further cõdemned; howbeit I trust assuredly your highnes wyl giue me leue to do it afor I go for that thus shamefully I may not be cried out on as I now shal be yea and without cause let cõsciens moue your highnes to to take some bettar way with me thã to make me be cõdẽned in al mẽs sigth afor my desert knowen. Also I most hũbly beseche your hightnes to pardon . this my boldnes wiche innocẽcy procures me to do togither with hope of your natural kindnis wiche I trust wyl not se me cast away without desert	5 10 15 20 25

(Continued)

TABLE 5.6. Continued

wiche what it is I wold desier no more of God but that you truly knewe . Wiche thinge I thinke and beleue you shal neuer by report knowe vnles by your selfe you hire. I haue harde in my time of many cast away for want of comminge to the presence of ther prince and in late days I harde my lorde of Somerset say that if his brother had bine sufferd	30
to speke with him he had neuer sufferd but the perswasions wer made to him so gret that he was brogth in belefe that he coulde not liue safely if the admiral liued and that made him giue consent to his dethe thoath	
thes parsons ar not to be cōpared to your maiestie yet I pray God ... perswasiōs perswade not one sistar again the other and al for that the haue harde false report and not harkene to the trueth knowen	35
therefor, ons again with hūblenes of hart, bicause I am not sufferd to bow the knees of my body I humbly crave to speke with your higthnis wiche I wolde not be so bold as to desier if I knewe not my selfe most clere as I know my selfe most tru. and as for the traitor. Wiat he migth perauentur writ	40
me a lettar but on my faith I neuer receued any from him and as for the copie of my lettar sent to the frēche kinge I pray God cōfoūd me eternally if euer I sent him word, message tokē or lettar by any menes, and to this my truth I wyl stande in to my debbe.	45
I humbly craue but only one worde of answer frō your selfe.	50
Your highnes most faithful subiect that hathe bine from the beginninge, and wylbe to my ende. Elizabeth	

5.5.2 Analysis, status, and dialect

The note by Machyn is more challenging than Caxton's printed page because of spelling freedom, so I will add a translation again. Elizabeth's hand is clear as is her syntax so I will comment in general, not sentence by sentence.

Machyn

In (37), two main sentences are combined without punctuation separating them, and a reduced relative starting with *waſ dekyd* is also not set off by punctuation. The word order is solidly SV, with the expletive *ther* ensuring that order.

(37) **The ffurst day of may** waſ may day **ther** waſ ij pennyſ [waſ dekyd wt stremarſ banerſ & fflag{s} & trumpett{s} & drums & gones gahyng a mayng] & a ganst ye quen plasse at westmÿter

'the first day of May there was two pinnaces – was decked with streamers, banners, and flags and trumpets and drums and guns going a-Maying – and against the Queen's place at Westminster.'

The original thorn in *ye* has changed shape and the nasal is still marked on the previous vowel in *westmÿter*. The present participle shows variation in the prefix *a*, not present in *gahyng* but present in *a mayng*.

The next sentence, (38), is very long with many coordinations. I have kept it as one passage with the last sentence added.

(38) & ther **they** shott & thruw eg{s} & oregnſ on a gaynst a nodur & wt sqwybeſ & by chansse on ffell on a bage of gune powdur e & sett dyuerſ mē affyre & so the men drue to on syd of ye penuſ & yt dyd over swelmed ye pennuſ & mony ffell in to temeſ butt thanke be god ther waſ but on man drownyd & a c bott{s} abowtt here & ye quen grace & her lord{s} & ladeſ lokyng owt of wyndowſ thyſ waſ done by ix of ye cloke on may evyn last

'and there they shot and threw eggs and oranges, one against another, and with squibs and by chance, one fell on a bag of gunpowder and set divers men afire and so the men drew to one side of the pinnace, and it did overwhelm the pinnace and many fell into Thames but, thanks be God, there was but one man drowned and a hundred boats about her and the Queen's Grace and her lords and ladies looking out of windows. This was done by nine o'clock on May eve last.'

The difficulty for modern readers is caused by the spelling. The dummy auxiliary *dyd* is used before a verb with a participle ending (*over swelmed*). Other auxiliaries include the passive *was*.

Machyn's style is paratactic as one would expect from a journal. It is modern in word order and verbal endings and doesn't display obvious dialect characteristics.

Elizabeth

As mentioned, I will make general comments about her syntax and morphology. The word order is solidly SV, as exemplified in (39).

(39) **I** most humbly beseche your . M. to verefy it   SV

Third person endings on present tense verbs are *-s*, as in *semes*, *aperes*, and *procures*, although she uses *-th* in other writings. There are subjunctives, e.g. *be not cõdemned*. Auxiliaries are many: *wyl*, *schal*, and *might*, and *may*, and combinations, as in *had bine suffered*. The auxiliary *do* is still emphatic, as in (40a), and not necessarily used in negatives or questions, as (40b) shows.

(40) a. If any euer **did** try this olde saying.
     b. I deserue it **not**.

The typical negative is the uncontracted *not*, which occurs thirteen times, whereas *neuer* appears four times, as in (41). Evans (2013: 92) notes that multiple negation still occurs in her other writings.

(41) that I **neuer** practiced

Late Middle and Early Modern English 1300–1600

Finally, multi-syllable adjectives can have superlatives ending in *-est*, as in *shamefullest*. This synthetic form is on the increase in this period over analytic ones, such as *most shameful*.

As for pronouns, the relatives become specialized, *who* for God and humans and *wiche* for non-humans, as (40) shows. Elizabeth's personal pronouns show a generalized *you(r)*.

(42) a. God ... **who** shal iuge.
    b. kindnis **wiche** I trust.

Elizabeth's English is solidly late sixteenth century, with emphatic *do*, subjunctives, and present tense *-s*. The style is quite embedded – see the sentence starting in the middle of the second line which continues to line 14. As in the case of Machyn, it is hard to discern specific dialect features.

5.6 Conclusion

This chapter has discussed a variety of text types, poems, manuals, and prose. It includes manuscripts, printed material, and letters. The language used is diverse. Although all texts have analytic characteristics, all show synthetic endings on verbs. The texts also alternate between being paratactic and having complex embeddings.

Exercises

A The Paston Letters provide some insight into the affairs of a (well-to-do) family. Some letters are drafts, some written by the actual authors, and some are dictated to secretaries. The letters contain wills, recipes, and other information.[7] Agnes Paston might have been the author although the hand used is similar to that of a secretary in the household (Davis 1971: 26).
Look at Figure 5.12, transcribed in Table 5.7, from Davis (1971), who adds punctuation. Which words do you recognize?

B Which letter shapes are typical for the secretary hand shown in Figure 5.1?

C Comment on the syntax and morphology.

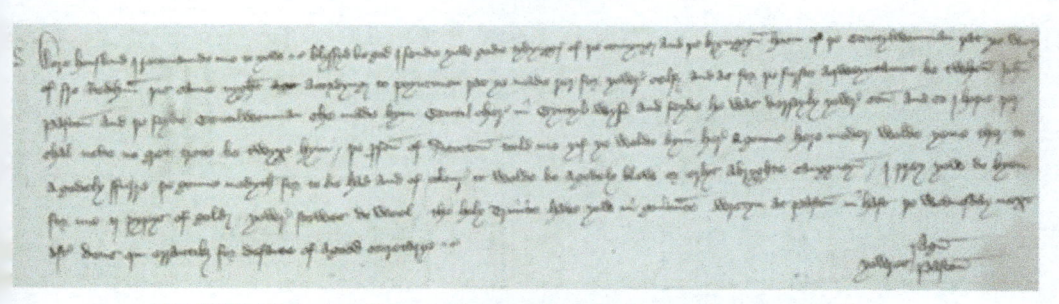

FIGURE 5.12. Letter 13, seemingly written by Agnes Paston, 1440 (from <http://britishlibrary.typepad.co.uk/digitisedmanuscripts/2015/04/the-paston-letters-go-live.html>, last accessed 4 June 2017. Reproduced with permission from the British Library Board)

TABLE 5.7. Transcription of Agnes Paston's letter

Dere housbond, I recomaunde me to yow, &c. Blyssyd be God, I sende yow gode tydynggys of þe comyng and þe brynggyn hoom of þe gentylwomman þat ye wetyn of fro Redham þis same nyght, acordyng to poyntmen þat ye made þer-for yowre-self. And as for þe furste aqweyntaunce be-twhen John Paston and þe seyde gentilwomman, she made hym gentil chere in gyntyl wyse and seyde he was verrayly yowre son. And so I hope þer shal nede no gret treté be-twyxe hym. þe parson of Stocton toold me yif ye wolde byin here a goune, here moder wolde yeue ther-to a godely furre. þe goune nedyth for to be had, and of coloure it wolde be a godely blew or ellys a bryghte sanggueyn. I prey yow do byen for me ij pypys of gold. Yowre stewes do weel. The Holy Trinité have yow in gouernaunce. Wretyn at Paston in hast þe Wednesday next after Deus qui errantibus, for defaute of a good secretarye, &c. Yowres, Agnes Paston.

D The printing of the English translation of Cicero's *De senectute* is from 1481. Its translator is unknown. This is what Caxton says about it at the end: 'Thus endeth the boke of Tulle of olde age translated out of Latyn in to Frenshe by Laurence de Primo Facto ... and enprynted by me symple persone William Caxton in to Englysshe at the playsir solace and reuerence of men growyng in to olde age the xii day of August the yere of our Lord. M. CCCC. lxxxi.'
Try to read the left-hand column in Figure 5.13.

E What period does the language belong to? Justify your answer.

FIGURE 5.13. Caxton's rendering of Cicero's *De senectute*[8]

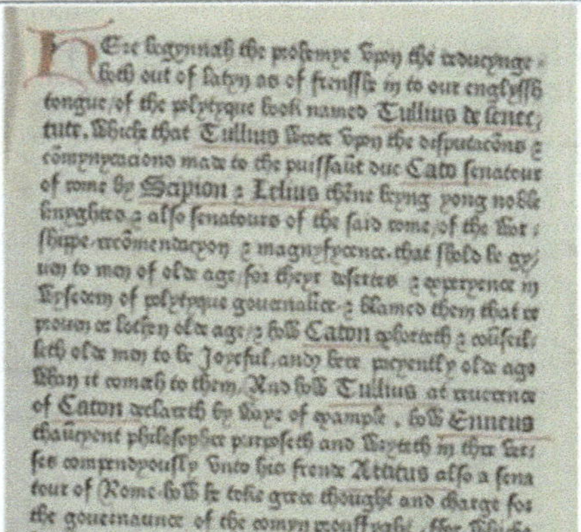

HEre begynneth the prohemye vpon the reducynge both out of latyn as of frensshe in to our englyssh tongue of the polytyque book named Tullius de senec: tute. whiche that Tullius wrote vpon the disputacōns ɛ cōmynycacions made to the puissaūt duc Cato senatour of rome by Scipion ɛ Lelius thēne beyng yong noble knyghtes ɛ also senatours of the said rome / of the wor: shippe / recōmendacyon ɛ magnyfycence. that shold be gy uen to men of olde age / for theyr desertes ɛ experyence in wysedom of polytyque gouernaūce / ɛ blamed them that re prouen or lothen olde age / ɛ how Caton exhorteth ɛ coūseil leth olde men to be loyeful / and bere pacyently olde age whan it cometh to them / And how Tullius at reuerence of Caton declareth by waye of example. how Enneus thaūcyent philosophre purposeth and wryteth in thre ver: ses compendyously vnto his frende Attitus also a sena tour of Rome / how he toke grete thought and charge for the gouernaunce of the comyn prouffyght / ffor whiche he deserued grete lawde and honoure in preferryng the same named in latyn Res Publica kepyng the Ro maynes prosperous / ɛ defendyng them fro theyr aduersa ryës and rebelles / whiche book was translated and thystoryes openly declared. by the ordenaunce ɛ desyre of the noble Auncyent knyght Syr Iohan Fastolf of the countee of Norfolk banerette. lyuyng the age of four score yeres. excercisyng the warrys in the Royame of Fraunce and other countrees / ffor the diffence and vnyuersal welfare of bothe royames of englond and ffraunce by fourty yeres enduryng / the fayte of armes

Further reading

Rissanen (1999) and Nevalainen (2006) provide more information on the grammar of Early Modern English. Evans (2013) discusses some linguistic features of Queen Elizabeth's English. A resource with texts of 'Everyday English' from the period 1500–1700 is Cusack (1998).

The writing varies and an online course is available at <http://www.english.cam.ac.uk/ceres/ehoc/> for the years 1500–1700 (last accessed 9 May 2017). Other paleographic sites are <http://paleo.anglo-norman.org/empfram.html>, <http://isites.harvard.edu/fs/docs/icb.topic453618.files/Central/editions/paleo.html>, and <http://medievalwriting.50megs.com/exercises/flexercise.htm> (all last accessed 9 May 2017).

Cusack, Bridget (1998), *Everyday English 1500–1600*, Ann Arbor: University of Michigan Press.
Evans, Mel (2013), *The Language of Queen Elizabeth I: A Sociolinguistic Perspective on Royal Style and Identity*, Chichester: Wiley Blackwell.
Nevalainen, Terttu (2006), *An Introduction to Early Modern English*, Oxford: Oxford University Press.
Rissanen, Matti (1999), 'Syntax', in Roger Lass (ed.), *The Cambridge History of the English Language, Volume III: 1476–1776*, Cambridge: Cambridge University Press, pp. 187–330.

Notes

1. For the translation, the version at *Eleusinianm* has been helpful; see 'Religious verse: Cleanness', *Eleusinianm*, available at <http://www.eleusinianm.co.uk/blueWellow/bof24cleanness.html> (last accessed 9 May 2017).
2. For a translation and edition of the entire *Astrolabe*, see *Chaucer's Astrolabe Treatise*, ed. James E. Morrison, available at <http://www.chirurgeon.org/files/Chaucer.pdf> (last accessed 9 May 2017).
3. 'The Book of Margery Kempe: Book I, Part I', in *The Book of Margery Kempe*, ed. Lynn Staley, 1996, *TEAMS Middle English Texts Series*, available at <http://d.lib.rochester.edu/teams/text/staley-book-of-margery-kempe-book-i-part-i> (last accessed 9 May 2017).
4. *Rylands Medieval Collection*, University of Manchester, available at <http://johannes.library.manchester.ac.uk:8181/luna/servlet/media/book/showBook/Man4MedievalVC~4~4~698705~142656> (last accessed 9 May 2017).
5. 'Le Morte Darthur, Syr Thomas Malory, William Caxton, H. Oskar Sommer', *Corpus of Middle English Prose and Verse*, available at <http://quod.lib.umich.edu/c/cme/MaloryWks2/1:3.1?rgn=div2;view=fulltext> (last accessed 9 May 2017).
6. 'Document 1: A letter dated 16 March 1554 from Elizabeth I, as princess, to her sister Queen Mary I (Catalogue reference: EXT 11/25)', in *Palaeography, The National Archives*, available at <http://www.nationalarchives.gov.uk/palaeography/doc1/default.htm> (last accessed 9 May 2017).

7. See Paston Family (1993), 'Paston letters and papers of the fifteenth century, Part I', *Corpus of Middle English Prose and Verse*, available at <http://quod.lib.umich.edu/c/cme/Paston?rgn=main;view=toc> (last accessed 9 May 2017).
8. Image available at <http://lcweb2.loc.gov/cgi-bin/displayPhoto.pl?path=/service/rbc/rbc0001/2009/2009rosen0562&topImages=0353r.jpg&topLinks=0353v.jpg,0353u.tif,0353a.tif,0353.tif&displayProfile=0>; transcription available at <http://quod.lib.umich.edu/e/eebo/A69111.0001.001/1:1?rgn=div1;view=fulltext> (both last accessed 9 May 2017).

Appendix I

Summary of All Grammatical Information

This Appendix provides in one place information on Old and Middle English grammar that is discussed in Chapters 2, 3, and 4. It retains the original numbering of the tables.

I.1 Syntax in general; dialect

TABLE 2.2. Word order in Old English

main clause	finite verb = V2 non-finite verb(s) = V-final
	subject position is variable though often before or after the finite verb
	object position is variable but often after the finite verb and before the non-finite verb
subordinate	all verbs = V-final
	subject and object before V
pronouns	relatively early
questions	*wh*-element and the verb are fronted

TABLE 2.13. Middle English dialect characteristics

	North	Midlands	South
Sound and spelling			
	no change:	mixed:	change to:
palatalization of velars	[k]; [g], e.g. *frankis, egg*	[k]; [g] or [tʃ]; [j]	[tʃ]; [j], e.g. *French, eye*
long [a] > [ɔ]	[a], e.g. *ham*	mainly [ɔ]	[ɔ], e.g. *hom*
short *on-an*	*on*, e.g. *mon*	*on* and *an*	*an*, e.g. *man*
voicing of initial fricatives	[f]; [s], e.g. *father, sea*	[f]; [s]	[v]; [z], e.g. *vather, zea*
hw-/qu- spelling	*qu-*, e.g. *quere* 'where'	*hw-*	*hw-*, e.g. *hwere* 'where'
fronting of [ʃ] to [s]	[s], e.g. *sal* 'shall, Inglis'	[s] or [ʃ]	[ʃ], e.g. *shal, English*

(Continued)

TABLE 2.13. *Continued*

	North	Midlands	South
Morphology and syntax			
	change to:	mixed:	no change:
third plural pronoun	*they/them*	*they/hem*	*hi/hem*
feminine third NOM S	*she*	*she/heo*	*heo*
verbal present tense	*-(e)s*	mixed	like Old English
present participle	*-ande*	*-ende*	*-ing/inde*
past participle	no prefix	*y-/i-*	*y-/i-*
word order	V-second (V2)	V2 and V3	V2 and V3
infinitive marker	occasionally *at*	only *to*	only *to*
preposition *till*	yes	only later	only later

1.2 Nominal, adjectival, and pronominal inflections

TABLE 2.3. Some Old English (strong) noun endings

		stan (M) 'stone'	word (N) 'word'	lufu (F) 'love'	sunu (M) 'son'
singular	NOM	stan	word	lufu	sunu
	GEN	stanes	words	lufe	suna
	DAT	stane	worde	lufe	suna
	ACC	stan	word	lufe	sunu
plural	NOM	stanas	word	lufa	suna
	GEN	stana	worda	luf(en)a	suna
	DAT	stanum	wordum	lufum	sunum
	ACC	stanas	word	lufa	suna

TABLE 3.3. The *-an* declension for the noun *tima*

	singular	plural
NOM	se tima	þa timan
GEN	þæs timan	þara timena
DAT	þæm timan	þæm timum
ACC	þone timan	þa timan

TABLE 3.4. The definite adjective declension

	singular	plural
NOM	egeslica	egeslican
GEN	egeslican	egeslicra
DAT	egeslican	egeslicum
ACC	egeslican	egeslican

Summary of All Grammatical Information

TABLE 3.5. Indefinite declensions of *halig* 'holy'

	Smasc	Pmasc	Sfem	Pfem	SNeuter	Pneuter
NOM	halig	halge	halgu	halga	halig	halgu
GEN	halges	haligra	haligre	haligra	halges	haligra
DAT	halgum	halgum	haligre	halgum	halgum	halgum
ACC	haligne	halge	halge	halge	halig	halgu

TABLE 2.9. Old English personal pronouns

		singular	dual	plural
first	NOM	ic	wit	we
	GEN	min	uncer	ure
	DAT	me	unc	us
	ACC	me, mec	unc, uncit, uncet	us, usic
second	NOM	þu	git	ge
	GEN	þin	incer	eower
	DAT	þe	inc	eow
	ACC	þe, þec	inc, incit	eow, eowic
third	NOM	he/heo/hit	–	hi, hie, heo
(M/F/N)	GEN	his/hire/his	–	hira, hiera
	DAT	him/hire/him	–	him
	ACC	hine/hi(e)/hit	–	hi, hie

TABLE 2.10. Late Middle English pronouns

		singular	plural
first	NOM	ic	we
	GEN	min	ure/our
	DAT/ACC	me	us
second	NOM	thou	ye(e)
	GEN	thi(n)	your
	DAT/ACC	thee	you
third	NOM	she/he/it	they
	GEN	her/his/it	their
	DAT/ACC	her/him/it	them

TABLE 2.11. Demonstratives in Old English

	masculine	feminine	neuter	plural
NOM	se	seo	þæt	þa
GEN	þæs	þære	þæs	þara
DAT	þæm	þære	þæm	þæm
ACC	þone	þa	þæt	þa

TABLE 4.4. Proximal demonstratives in Old English

	masculine	feminine	neuter	plural
NOM	þes	þeos	þis	þas
GEN	þisses	þisse	þisses	þissa
DAT	þissum	þisse	þissum	þissum
ACC	þisne	þas	þis	þas

1.3 Verbal inflections

TABLE 2.4. An Old English strong verb

			indicative	subjunctive	imperative
present	1S	ic	drife	drife	
	2S	þu	drifest	drife	drif
	3S	he/heo/hit	drif(e)ð	drife	
	PL	we/ge/hi	drifað	drifen	drifað
past	1S	ic	draf	drife	
	2S	þu	drife	drife	
	3S	he/heo/hit	draf	drife	
	PL	we/ge/hi	drifon	drifen	
participles	drifende, (ge)drifen			

TABLE 2.5. An Old English weak verb

		indicative		subjunctive	imperative
present	1S	ic	fremme	fremme	
	2S	Þu	frem(e)st	fremme	freme
	3S	he/heo/hit	frem(e)þ	fremme	
	PL	we/ge/hi	fremmaþ	fremmen	fremmaþ
past	1S	ic	fremede	fremede	
	2S	Þu	fremedest	fremede	
	3S	he/heo/hit	fremede	fremede	
	PL	we/ge/hi	fremedon	fremeden	
participles	fremende, (ge)fremed			

TABLE 2.6. The Old English forms of the verb *beon* 'to be'

		indicative	subjunctive	imperative
present	ic	eom	sie/beo	
	þu	eart	sie/beo	wes/beo
	he/heo/hit	is	sie/beo	
	PL	sint/sindon	sien/beon	wesaþ/beoþ
past	ic	wæs	S wære	
	þu	wære		
	he/heo/hit	wæs		
	we/ge/hi	wæron	PL wæren	
future	ic	beom		
	þu	bist		
	he/o	biþ		
	we/ge/hi	beoþ		
participles		wesende, beonde, gebeon		

TABLE 2.7. Late Middle English verbal inflection

		indicative	subjunctive	imperative
present	1S	ic find(e)	S find(e)	
	2S	thou findes(t)		find
	3S	he/heo/hit findeþ/findes		
	PL	we, ye(e), thei findeþ/en	find(en)	findeþ/es
past	S	found(e)	founde	
	PL	found(en)	founde(n)	
participles		findende, (y)founden		

TABLE 2.8. The modal paradigm for *sculan* 'be obliged to'

		indicative		subjunctive	
present		ic	sceal	S	scyle
		þu	scealt		
		he/heo/hit	sceal		
	PL	sculon		PL	scylen
past		ic	sceolde	S	sceolde
		þu	sceoldest		
		he/heo/hit	sceolde		
		we/ge/hi	sceoldon	PL	sceolden

Appendix II

Background on the Old English Texts That Are Discussed, Alphabetically

II.1 Old English

Beowulf. Mixed dialect Northumbrian/West Saxon; manuscript from c. 1000 but based on an earlier, oral version (cf. Bjork and Obermeier 1997). Edition: Klaeber (1922); Zupitza (1959); Bjork and Niles (1997). For a good side-by-side version, see <http://www.heorot.dk/beowulf-rede-text.html> (last accessed 9 May 2017).

Boethius. Early West Saxon; ascribed to King Alfred. Edition: Sedgefield (1899).

Caedmon's Hymn. A short poem composed by Caedmon, known through the inclusion by Bede in his history. Many Old English versions survive from different time periods and dialect areas. Edition: Miller (1890).

Exeter Book. Early poetry; contains *Riddles*, *Wulf and Eadwacer*, *The Wanderer*, and *The Seafarer*. Edition: Krapp and Kirk Dobbie (1936); Mackie (1934).

Gregory's Pastoral Care. Early West Saxon, late ninth century; ascribed to King Alfred. Image available at <http://parkerweb.stanford.edu/parker/actions/page_turner.do?ms_no=12> (last accessed 9 May 2017). Edition: Sweet (1871), who provides both Cotton and Hatton versions side by side, as well as a gloss.

Homilies, by Aelfric. West Saxon, c. 1000. Edition: *Catholic Homilies I*: electronic edition available at *Dictionary of Old English*, <http://tapor.library.utoronto.ca/doecorpus/> (last accessed 9 May 2017); *Catholic Homilies II*: Godden (1979); *Supplementary Homilies*: Pope (1967–8).

Homilies, by Wulfstan. West Saxon of the late tenth and early eleventh centuries; survive in eighteen manuscripts. Manuscript available at <http://parkerweb.stanford.edu/parker/actions/page_turner.do?ms_no=419> (last accessed 9 May 2017). Edition: Bethurum (1957).

Junius Manuscript. Written between the seventh and tenth centuries (some argue partly by the *Caedmon* poet); compiled towards the late tenth century; contains *Genesis*, *Exodus*, *Christ and Satan*. Images of Junius 11 available at the Bodleian Library, <http://image.ox.ac.uk/show?collection=bodleian&manuscript=msjunius11> (last accessed 9 May 2017). Edition: Krapp (1931).

Lindisfarne Gospels. Northumbrian interlinear gloss, c. 950. Images available at <http://www.bl.uk/manuscripts/FullDisplay.aspx?ref=Cotton_MS_Nero_D_IV> (last accessed 9 May 2017). Edition: Skeat ([1881–7] 1970) but see Campbell (1959: 360 ff.) for more recent references on this.

Orosius. Early West Saxon; ascribed to King Alfred. Image available at <http://www.bl.uk/manuscripts/Viewer.aspx?ref=add_ms_47967_fs001r> (last accessed 9 May 2017). Edition: Bately (1980).

Rushworth Glosses. Interlinear gloss, c. 970. *Matthew* is Mercian; *Mark*, *Luke*, and *John* are Northumbrian. Image available at <http://digital.bodleian.ox.ac.uk> (last accessed 9 May 2017). Edition: Skeat ([1881–7] 1970) but see Campbell (1959: 362–3) for background.

West Saxon Gospels. Skeat's ([1881–7] 1970) edition provides the transcription of two West Saxon Gospels: one is from Corpus Christi College, CXL, and the other from the Hatton MS, Bodleian. Chapter 3 uses the former. Images available at <http://parkerweb.stanford.edu/parker/actions/page_turner.do?ms_no=140> (last accessed 9 May 2017). Edition: Skeat ([1881–7] 1970).

II.2   Early Middle English

Anglo-Saxon Chronicle. Many versions; one composed in Peterborough that continues to 11, 54, known as the *Peterborough Chronicle* from the East Midlands, and another referred to as *Parker*. Peterborough images available at <http://bodley30.bodley.ox.ac.uk:8180/luna/servlet/view/all/what/MS.+Laud+Misc.+636?pgs=250> (last accessed 9 May 2017). Edition: Thorpe (1861).

Havelok. Northeast Midlands, early thirteenth century. Edition: Herzman et al. (1997).

Katherine Group (e.g. *Katerine*, *Margarete*, *Juliene*, *Hali Meidhad*, and *Sawles Warde*, but also *Ancrene Wisse* and some other texts). Bodley 34 MS: Southwest Midlands, early thirteenth century. Titus MS: slightly more northern and eastern than Bodley. Edition: d'Ardenne (1977); Einenkel (1884). Facsimile: Ker (1960).

Layamon's *Brut*. Caligula and Otho manuscripts, now both considered to be from the second half of the thirteenth century, (North) Worcestershire. Edition: Brook and Leslie (1963).

Ormulum. East Midlands, twelfth century. See <http://www.orrmulum.net/orrmulum_site.html> for additional information (last accessed 9 May 2017).

The Owl and the Nightingale. Southeastern, from the thirteenth century. Edition: Ker (1963).

II.3   Later Middle English and Early Modern

Roger Ascham. Sixteenth-century scholar who served as tutor to Queen Elizabeth; most famous for *The Scholemaster*. Facsimile: Ascham ([1570] 1967).

Ayenbite of Inwyt. Kent, mid-fourteenth century. Edition: Gradon (1965).

Chaucer's *Astrolabe*. Southern, late fourteenth century. Images available at <http://pds.lib.harvard.edu/pds/view/7400889?n=1&imagesize=1200&jp2Re

s=.25&printThumbnails=no> (last accessed 9 May 2017). Edition: Benson (1987).

Cursor Mundi. Various manuscripts from the early fourteenth century: Cotton and Göttingen are northern; Fairfax and Trinity are more southern. Edition: Morris (1874–93).

Elizabeth I. Lived 1533–1603 and was queen from 1558 to her death. Some work is available at <http://www.luminarium.org/renlit/elizabib.htm> (last accessed 9 May 2017).

Gawain and the Green Knight, St. Erkenwald, Pearl, Cleanness, and *Patience*. Assumed to be by the 'Gawain Poet'. Northwest Midlands, mid-fourteenth century. Edition: Andrew and Waldron (1978); Gardner (1965).

Margery of Kempe. Northeast Midlands, fourteenth century. See <http://www.bl.uk/manuscripts/FullDisplay.aspx?ref=Add_MS_61823> (last accessed 9 May 2017). Edition: Meech et al. (1961).

Henry Machyn. London, kept a Chronicle in the mid-sixteenth century. Edition: Bailey et al. (n.d.).

Morte d'Arthur. East Midlands, late fourteenth century. Facsimile: Caxton ([1485] 1976).

Richard Mulcaster. Sixteenth-century educator, most famous for his *Elementarie*. Facsimile: Mulcaster ([1582] 1970).

The Paston Letters. Letters from a family in Norfolk, fifteenth century. Edition: Davis (1971).

The Physiologus. Also known as *The Bestiary*. Northeast Midlands, from 1300. See 'Arundel 292 f. 4', *Catalogue of Illuminated Manuscripts*, British Library, available at <http://www.bl.uk/catalogues/illuminatedmanuscripts/ILLUMIN.ASP?Size=mid&IllID=7560> (last accessed 9 May 2017). Edition: Wirtjes (1991).

William Shakespeare. Lived 1564–1616. First Folio edition from 1623. Image available at <http://www.folger.edu/first-folio-tour> (last accessed 9 May 2017). Facsimile: Kökeritz (1954).

Appendix III

Keys to the Exercises

Chapter 1

A   Accusative case marks the object; an example is 'him' in 'I saw him'.

B   **The National Weather Service** <u>has</u> issued an excessive heat warning for Tuesday and Wednesday. **Much of south-central and southwestern Arizona** <u>will</u> (no visible agreement though) see hotter temperatures over the next two days. **The area in Arizona covered by the warning** <u>stretches</u> from Yuma and other communities along the Colorado River eastward into the Phoenix area and the Pinal County communities of Casa Grande, Coolidge and Florence. **Officials** <u>say</u> **the temperature** <u>is</u> expected to climb to between 112 and 115 degrees on both days. **The warning** <u>is</u> in effect from 11 a.m. until 8 p.m. both days. **Residents who** <u>work or play</u> outdoors <u>face</u> a greater risk of heat-related illness. **The Weather Service** <u>is</u> advising people to drink more water than usual, wear a hat outside and take rest breaks in air-conditioned places.

C   This text has a few hypotactic, or embedded clauses, an object clause to 'say', a relative clause for 'residents', and an object clause to 'advising'. The first two sentences are very paratactic.

D   Synthetic means having lots of endings on nouns and verbs where analytic means few endings. Endings may be lost and prepositions and auxiliaries may replace them.

E   Highly analytic.

Chapter 2

A   I'll pick one, V2. Verbs in main clauses often occur as the second constituent. For instance, in the text below, *se wæs Wine haten* has the finite verb *wæs* in second position.

B   Then, at last, the king, who only knew the Saxon language, became tired of the bishop's foreign speech and then invited into Wessex another bishop who knew the king's language. That bishop was called Wine and had been consecrated in Gaul. The king then divided his kingdom into two dioceses and gave Wine a bishopseat in Winchester.

C   The verbs are: *cuðe, wæs, aðroten, aspon, cuðe, wæs, haten, wæs, gehalgod, todælde*, and *gesealde*. The three instances of *wæs* are passive auxiliaries, the others are lexical. The first sentence starts with two adverbials, then the long subject and then the verb group *wæs aðroten* so is V4. The relative inside is V-last. The second sentence starts without a subject so is V1 with the relative again V-last. As mentioned under A, the next sentence is V2 with the lexical verb last and the same is true in the next sentence. The last sentence is a coordinated one with the verb *todælde* reasonably early but *gesealde* after the indirect and before the direct object.

D   The personal pronouns are *he* and *his*; the demonstratives *se* and *þæm*; and relative markers are the demonstrative *se* followed by *ðe*.

E   The relative is subordinating and *ond* coordinating. We'd have to look at the manuscript to be sure.

F   *se* is nominative, masculine, singular; *aspon* past tense; *se* again nominative, masculine singular; *gehalgod* a participle; and *þæm* a dative demonstrative.

G   Hypotactic.

Chapter 3

The transcription and free translation (based on Sweet 1871) of the exercise appears in Table III.1.

A   *ALFRED* should be easy and *cyning*.
B   The *f* in *lufliche* is low; the *r* has a long tail.
C   The first sentence has an initial adverbial, which makes it V3, then V2 and V-last. Both finite verbs have past tense plural endings and the infinitive shows *-enne*.
D   It is fairly hypotactic with an initial V2 and an embedded V2 as well. The adverbial clause starts with *forþam* and a preposed adjectival subject predicate with another preposing in the coordinate. The present tense

TABLE III.1. Transcription and translation of exercise

Alfred cyning hateð gre	King Alfred greets ...
tan his wordum luflice 7 freondlice	with his words lovingly and friendly
7 ðe cyðan hate ðæt	and you let know that
me com swiðe oft onge mynd	it came to my mind
hwelce wiotan io wæron geond ang	very often which wise (men) formerly (there) were
gel cyn ægðer ge godcundra hada	throughout England, either religious monks
ge weoruld cundra. 7 hu gesælig	or worldly and how happy
lica tida ða wæron geond angelcynn	times they were throughout England
7 hu ða cyningas ðe ðone onweald	and how the kings who had that power
hæfdon ðæs folces gode 7 his arend	obeyed the people's God and his messengers.
wrecum hiersumedon. 7 huhie	and how they
ægðer gehiora sibbe gehiora sido	kept the peace inside
gehiora anweald innanbordes	and also outside their realm prospered.
geheoldon. 7 eac ut hiora edel [rymdon]	

endings on the first, third, and last verbs are standard, the subjunctive on the second as well. The text is late West Saxon; it is from *Ælfric's Colloquy* (Garmonsway 1947).

Chapter 4

A   *æn3lalande* in line 1, *da3um* in line 2. From line 8 on, the *ge-* prefix is rendered as 3e rather than 3; in general the second half has fewer abbreviations.

B   There are endings, e.g. *-um*, *-a*, and *–e*, so it is synthetic.

C   Very similar in style; very similar in variety although this text has an additional *y-* on *y wuste* in line 10 of the first column.

D   The page starts with two negatives, *ne* and *neuere*, but in other instances, a simple *ne* appears. The use of definite and indefinite articles is common, e.g. lines 2 and 3. The word order is relatively free but subjects precede their verbs.

E   Analytic. By the way, *Havelok* is from the Midlands. Linguistic evidence for this is the use of *michel* as well as *mikel, hem, til,* and *haveth*.

TABLE III.2. Translation of *Havelok* (adapted from <http://wwww.sfsu.edu/~medieval/romances/havelok_rev.html>, last accessed 9 May 2017)

When they were but a mile from land the wind began to rise out of the north and drove them to England, which would be Havelok's. But first he would have much shame, sorrow and pain, yet he got it all, as you will learn if you are willing to listen. Grim landed in Humber, at the north end of the district of Lindsey. The ship sat on the sand, but Grim drew it onto the land, and he built a small cottage for his group. He made a little house of earth so that they were well protected. Because Grim lived there, the place was called Grimsby and will be until doomsday. Grim was an excellent fisherman and caught many good fish, both with net and hook. He took sturgeon, turbot, salmon, eel, cod, porpoise, seal and whale, flounder, herring, mackerel, halibut and many others. He made good baskets, one for himself, and one for each of his sons for carrying the fish to sell and trade. He went to every town and farm with his wares, and never came home empty-handed without bread and grain; his work was not wasted. When he caught the great lamprey, he knew the way to the borough of Lincoln. He went through the town until he sold everything and counted his pennies. They were happy when he came home, bringing fine breads and meat of cattle, sheep and swine, as well as hemp to make strong ropes for the nets he set. In this way, Grim fed his household well for twelve years or more. Havelok was aware that he lay at home while Grim worked hard to feed him. 'I am no longer a boy,' he thought. 'I am grown and may eat more than Grim can get; by God, I eat more than Grim and his five children! This cannot go on. I will go with them to learn how to be useful and work for my food. There is no shame in working; to eat and drink without working is wrong. God reward him who has fed me to this day! I will gladly bear baskets, which will not harm me even if the burden they contain is as heavy as an ox. I will no longer stay at home, but hurry forth tomorrow.' In the morning, when it was day

Chapter 5

A   *[handwritten]* is *Dere housbond*.
B   In the above, the *h*, *o*, *u*, and *b* are; the *r* is different.
C   The language is analytic with definite articles and prepositions. The language is Midlands because of the use of plural *hym* in: *[handwritten]* and the plural *wetyn*. Other characteristics are the use of polite plural nominative *ye* and accusative *you*. There is a *þat* relative.
D   The printing uses Gothic letters but is much easier than the secretary hand.
E   Early Modern English. Case endings have disappeared and auxiliaries are frequent. The present tense *-th* still occurs and there is a *whiche that* (line 4), which classify it as early.

Glossary

This Glossary tries to be somewhat comprehensive, and lists key terms, abbreviations, and some common terminology not used in this book but perhaps used elsewhere, e.g. 'attributive adjective'. If the definitions in the Glossary do not suffice, check the Index.

accusative case The case of the direct object or prepositional object, only visible on pronouns in English, e.g. *me*, in *He saw me*; also called the objective case.
active A sentence in which the doer of the action is the subject, as in *I saw an elephant*.
adjective A word which often describes qualities, e.g. *proud, intelligent*, or physical characteristics, e.g. *short, strong*.
AdjP = Adjective Phrase: group of words centered around an adjective, e.g. *very happy*.
adjunct Term not used in this book; alternative for 'adverbial'; see there.
adverb E.g. *proudly*; it is similar to an adjective but it modifies a verb, adjective, or other adverb, whereas an adjective modifies a noun.
adverbial A function at sentence level providing the background on where, when, how, and why the event described in the VP takes place.
AdvP = Adverb Phrase: group of words centered around an adverb, e.g. *extremely happily*.
affix Cannot stand on its own, e.g. an ending such as *-ing*.
agreement Ending on the verb that 'agrees' with the subject, e.g. *-s* in *She walks*.
alliteration A poetic device that uses the same initial sound in different words.
ambiguity/ambiguous Word (lexical ambiguity) or sentence (structural ambiguity) with more than one meaning.
analogy Something, e.g. a verbal ending, may be compared to another similar ending and changed to make it more similar.
analytic Of a language, grammatical information comes in the form of separate words, not of endings on nouns and verbs.
antecedent What a pronoun refers to, e.g. the noun that a relative pronoun such as *who* refers to in *The man who(m) I saw*. Antecedent is used more generally though for any pronoun that refers to a noun.

apposition The second part of *Tegucigalpa, the capital of Honduras*. It rephrases the first and provides extra information; similar to a non-restrictive relative clause.

article *A, an, the* in English.

aspect When the character of the action is emphasized, as in *He is reading*, rather than when the action took place.

attributive adjective An adjective that modifies a noun inside an NP.

auxiliary A 'verb' that cannot stand on its own, but that 'helps' (combines with) another verb, e.g. *have* in *They have seen a riot*.

bare infinitive Infinitive without a *to*, e.g. *leave* in *I saw her leave*.

case In English, case is only visible on pronouns. Thus, *she* in *She saw me* has nominative case, i.e. is used in subject position, and *me* has accusative or objective case, i.e. is used in object position.

clause Unit containing a lexical verb; see also main clause, subordinate clause.

comparative Forms such as *greater* that compare one situation or entity with another.

complement Complements to verbs are divided into direct and indirect object, subject predicate, object predicate, prepositional, and phrasal object. Nouns, adjectives, and prepositions can have a single complement.

complementizer E.g. *that, if, whether*. Connects two clauses, one subordinate to the other.

complex transitive A verb with a direct object and an object predicate.

conjunction A general term to describe a word that joins two or more words or phrases or sentences together. There are subordinating (*that*) and coordinating (*and*) conjunctions.

consonant Sound, such as *b, k, p, s, t, v*, made by modifying the airstream in some way.

constituent A group of words that form a unit, typically a phrase.

contraction A word that is shortened, e.g. *he's* for *he has*.

coordination Connecting two phrases or clauses that are equal to each other by means of, e.g., *and*.

coordinating conjunction Same as coordinator; see there.

coordinator Connects two phrases or clauses that are equal to each other, e.g. *and, or*.

copula A verb with a subject predicative, typically *to be* or *to become*.

dative The case of the indirect object; in Modern English, the same form as the accusative.

declarative A neutral sentence that is a statement, not a question or command.

declension Variation in the noun, pronoun, and adjective to show the number, case, and gender.

degree adverb Adverbs that indicate degree, e.g. *very, too, so, more, most, quite, rather*.

deontic modal Modal with a meaning of permission, obligation, or ability.

Glossary

descriptivism Describing what language users really say, as opposed to what they 'should' say.

determiner Word that points or specifies, e.g. *the*.

direct object Object of a verb such as *eat, see, enjoy*, e.g. *him* in *They saw him*.

ditransitive Verb that has both a direct and an indirect object, e.g. *tell, give*.

dummy A word used to fulfill a grammatical requirement; see dummy *do* and dummy subject.

dummy *do* If no auxiliary is present in a sentence, *do* is used with questions and negatives.

dummy subject If a subject is not present, *it* or *there* is used; also called expletive subject.

-ed participle See past participle.

elided/elision Word or phrase left out to avoid repetition, e.g. in *He wrote a poem and painted a picture*, the subject of *painted* has been left out.

ellipsis Word or phrase left out to avoid repetition.

embedded sentence/clause A sentence or clause inside another phrase or sentence/clause.

emphasizer Words such as *even* and *just* that are used to emphasize a phrase; also called focusser.

epistemic modal Modal with a meaning of possibility or likelihood.

expletive Different name for 'dummy subject'; see there.

extraposed/extraposition When an embedded clause (usually in subject position) is placed at the end of the sentence, e.g. *It was nice [that he left]*. A dummy subject *it* is put in the original position.

facsimile An exact copy of a document.

finite clause A clause with a finite verb (see there) and a nominative subject.

finite verb A verb expressing agreement and tense (past or present).

formal language Language used in formal situations such as ceremonies, formal lectures, meeting a government official.

fragment An incomplete sentence, e.g. one missing a finite verb.

functions Phrases (and clauses) have functions, such as subject and direct object, at the level of the sentence. There are also functions inside the phrase, namely as determiner, modifier, and complement.

genitive case The case that a possessive has, e.g. *Catweazle's* in *Catweazle's book*.

gerund A verbal noun that ends in *-ing*.

grammar The rules to form and understand language.

grammatical A sentence (or word) that native speakers consider acceptable.

grammatical category Word with little meaning, e.g. article or auxiliary.

hypotactic Style that uses embedding or subordination.

imperative A command, e.g. *Go away!, Shut up!*

impersonal verb A verb that need not have a subject.

indicative A 'normal' sentence, i.e. not asking a question, indicating a wish or command. Declarative is also used.
indirect object Object that can be preceded by *to* or *for*, e.g. *Doris* in *Clovis gave Doris a flower*.
infinitive Form such as *to go, to be, to analyze*; it is one of the non-finite constructions.
inflection Change in the form of a word to express a function or agreement.
informal language Language used in informal situations such as casual conversation. In/formality depends on the situation, the participants, the topic.
ing- participle See present participle.
innate faculty Enables us to acquire language.
interrogative pronoun Pronouns that start a *wh-*question, e.g. *who* in *Who left?*
intransitive A verb without an object, e.g. *laugh, swim*.
irregular verbs The past tense and past participle of these verbs are not formed by adding *-ed* to the present, as in the case of regular verbs, e.g. *go, went, gone; see, saw, seen; write, wrote, written*.

lexical category Word with lexical meaning, such as a Noun, Verb, Adjective, Adverb, and Preposition.
lexical verb Verb that can stand on its own, e.g. *see, walk*.
light verb Verbs such as *make, do, take* with a very general meaning that combine with nouns, such as *take a walk*. They can be replaced by verbs, e.g. *walk*.
linguistic knowledge Knowledge about linguistic notions and rules that we have in our heads, e.g. consonants and vowels, structure, question formation.
linguistics The study of language.

main clause Independent clause, i.e. a sentence that can stand on its own, minimally containing a subject and a predicate and not embedded within another clause.
main verb The verb that contributes verbal meaning to the clause; alternative for lexical verb.
minim A short vertical stroke, such as the ones that form the letter *n*.
modal Auxiliary that expresses necessity, uncertainty, or possibility, e.g. *must, will, would, can, could*.
modifier An element whose function is to modify another element, e.g. *purple* in *purple sage*.
modify Describe the quality of something.
morphology Rules for how to build words, e.g. *formal + ize*.

negation/negative E.g. *not* or *n't* or a negative word such as *nothing*.
negative concord When two or more negative words (*not, nobody*) occur in the same clause with a negative meaning, e.g. *I didn't eat nothing*.
negative contraction Where a negative marker is pronounced/written together with another word, e.g. *nis* in Old English stands for *ne* and *is*.
nominative case The case of the subject, only visible on pronouns, e.g. *she* in *She left early*.

non-finite verb or clause A verb or clause that lacks tense and a nominative subject, e.g. *To be or not to be*.

non-linguistic (or social) knowledge Knowledge of social rules.

non-restrictive relative clause A clause that provides background information to the noun it modifies; it is often set apart from the rest of the sentence through commas or comma intonation.

noun A word such as *table, freedom, book, love*.

NP = Noun Phrase: group of words centered around a noun, e.g. *a happy person*.

numeral A word such as *one, two*.

objective or accusative case In English, case is only visible on pronouns, e.g. *him*, in *Hermione saw him*. Objects typically get this case, hence the name objective.

P = Preposition: a word making a noun relate to other parts of the sentence, e.g. *of, to, under*.

paradigm Set of forms that are related, e.g. all present tense verb endings.

paradigm leveling Reduction in the forms that differ in a paradigm.

paratactic Juxtaposing clauses without subordinating one to the other.

participle Either accompanied by an auxiliary or on its own heading a non-finite clause, e.g. *discussed, discussing*.

particle Similar in form to prepositions and adverbs, but only used together with a verb.

passive A construction where what looks like an object is functioning as a subject, e.g. *she* in *She was arrested*.

passive auxiliary A form of *to be* used together with a past participle, e.g. *was* in *She was arrested*.

past participle Typically follows auxiliary *to have* to form a perfect, or *to be* to form a passive. It can function on its own in a non-finite clause. The participle ends in *-ed/-en* (*walked, written, chosen*) or may be irregular, e.g. *gone, swum, begun, learnt*.

perfect auxiliary *To have* when used together with a past participle, e.g. *have* in *I have done that already*.

phonology The structure of the sound system.

phrasal verb A verb that is always combined with a preposition-like element but which has a special meaning, e.g. *look up* does not mean 'see upwards', but 'go to the library and check on something'.

pied piping Taking the preposition along in a relative clause or a question, as in *the man [to whom] I talked*.

possessive E.g. *his* or *Catweazle's* in *his book* or *Catweazle's book*.

PP = Preposition Phrase: group of words belonging to the preposition, e.g. *in the garden*.

predicate Says something about the subject, typically a VP, e.g. *saw him* in *Hermione saw him*.

predicative adjective Term not used in this book; an adjective that heads an AP with the function of subject predicate or object predicate.

preposing Moving a word or phrase to a position towards the beginning of a sentence.

preposition A word indicating location (in place and time), e.g. *at, in, on*; direction, e.g. *to, into, towards*; or relationship, e.g. *with, between, among, of.*

preposition stranding Leaving the preposition behind in a relative clause or a question, as in *the man who I talked to.*

prescriptivism A rule typically learned in school, e.g. *don't split an infinitive* or *don't use multiple negation.*

present participle Forms that end in *-ing*, e.g. *walking*, used after a progressive auxiliary, as in *He is walking*, or on its own in a non-finite clause, as in *Walking along the street, I saw a fire.*

progressive Indicating that the action is or was going on.

pronoun Words such as *he, she, it, me* that refer to an NP; pronouns replacing PPs (*there*), AdjPs (*so*), AdvPs (*thus*), or VPs (*do so*) are called either pronoun or pro-form.

proper noun A noun used for names, e.g. *Bertha, Arizona.*

quantifier Words such as *all, some, many, each*; they are either like determiners or adjectives, or occur before determiners.

question See *wh*-question and *yes/no* question.

regular verbs Verbs formed by adding *-ed* to the present to form the past tense and the past participle, as in the case of regular verbs such as *walk, walked, walked.*

relative clause A clause/sentence that typically modifies a noun, e.g. *The tree which I see from the window.*

relative pronoun pronoun such as *who, whose* that introduces relative clauses. The same set is used in questions and then they are called interrogative pronouns.

semantics The linguistic aspects to meaning.

semi-modal Auxiliary such as *dare (to), need (to), used to, ought to, have to.* They have properties of both main verbs and modal verbs.

sentence/clause A unit that contains at least a verb. The subject may or may not be expressed.

specify Point to something, i.e. a determiner's function in a phrase.

split infinitive Separating the *to* from the verb, e.g. as in *To boldly go ...*

strong verbs Originally, a term for a verb that had a different vowel for the present, the past, and the past participle, e.g. *swim, swam, swum*. Now the term is often used for any kind of irregular verb, e.g. *be, was, been.*

subject In Modern English, the subject agrees with the verb in person and number and the pronoun has nominative case.

subject predicate An AdjP, PP, or NP that says something about the subject and is connected to it through a copula verb.

subject verb agreement Finite verbs agree with subjects in English. Evidence for it is fairly limited, e.g. the *-s* on *She walks.*

subjunctive Expressing a wish, intention, or necessity, e.g. *go* is a subjunctive verb in *It is important that he go there.* In Modern English, most of these are replaced by modal verbs.

subordinate clause Dependent clause, or clause embedded in another by means of a complementizer such as *that, because, if*.
subordinating conjunction Same as complementizer; see there.
superlative An adjective such as *greatest*.
synonym A word with an almost identical meaning, e.g. *often* and *frequently*.
syntax Rules for how words are combined into phrases and sentences.
synthetic Of a language, grammatical information is marked by means of endings on nouns and verbs rather than as separate words.

tag-question A repetition of the subject and the auxiliary, as in *She has been there before, hasn't she?*
tense Indicating past or present time.
transitive Verb with one object, e.g. *see*.
tree A representation of the units/phrases of a sentence by means of branches and nodes.

Universal Grammar Grammatical properties shared by all languages but now more and more replaced by general cognitive abilities; see Chapter 1.

verb A lexical category often expressing a state, act, event, or emotion.
vowel Sounds such as *a, e, i, o, u*, made by not blocking the airstream.
VP = Verb Phrase: group of words centered around a verb, e.g. *ate an apple*.

weak verbs A verb that has a past with *-ed*, such as *walked*.
wh-question A question that starts with *who, what, how, why, when*, or *where*.
word order Linear sequencing of words and phrases.

Yes/No question A question for which the appropriate answer would be 'yes', 'no', or 'maybe/perhaps'.

References

Allen, Cynthia (1995), *Case Marking and Reanalysis*, Oxford: Oxford University Press.
Allen, Hope Emily (ed.) (1931), *The English Writings of Richard Rolle*, Oxford: Clarendon Press.
Andersen, Henning (1973), 'Abductive and Deductive Change', *Language* 49:4, 765–93.
Andrew, M. and R. Waldron (1978), *The Poems of the Pearl Manuscript*, Exeter: University of Exeter Press.
Ascham, Roger [1570] (1967), *The Scholemaster*, Menston: Scolar Press.
Bailey, Richard W., Marilyn Miller and Colette Moore (n.d.), *A London Provisioner's Chronicle, 1550–1563, by Henry Machyn: Manuscript, Transcription, and Modernization*, <http://quod.lib.umich.edu/cgi/t/text/text-idx?c=machyn;cc=machyn;view=text;idno=5076866.0001.001;rgn=div2;node=5076866.0001.001%3A8.10> (last accessed 9 May 2017).
Baker, Peter (2007), *Introduction to Old English*, 2nd edn, Oxford: Blackwell.
Bately, Janet (ed.) (1980), *The Old English Orosius*, Oxford: Oxford University Press.
Benson, L. (1987), *The Riverside Chaucer*, Boston: Houghton Mifflin.
Bethurum, Dorothy (1957), *The Homilies of Wulfstan*, Oxford: Oxford University Press.
Bjork, Robert E. and John D. Niles (eds) (1997), *A Beowulf Handbook*, Lincoln, NE: University of Nebraska Press.
Bjork, Robert E. and Anita Obermeier (1997), 'Date, Provenance, Author, Audiences', in Robert E. Bjork and John D. Niles (eds), *A Beowulf Handbook*, Lincoln, NE: University of Nebraska Press, pp. 13–34.
Blake, Norman (ed.) (1992), *The Cambridge History of the English Language, Volume II: 1066–1476*, Cambridge: Cambridge University Press.
Bosworth, Joseph and N. T. Toller (1898), *An Anglo-Saxon Dictionary, Edited and Enlarged*, Oxford: Clarendon Press, <http://beowulf.engl.uky.edu/~kiernan/BT/Bosworth-Toller.htm> (last accessed 9 May 2017).
Bramley, H. R. (ed.) (1884), *The Psalter or Psalms of David and Certain Canticles with a Translation and Exposition in English by Richard Rolle of Hampole*, Oxford: Clarendon Press.

Brook, G. and R. Leslie (eds) (1963), *Layamon: Brut*, Oxford: Oxford University Press, EETS 250.
Campbell, Alastair (1953), *The Tollemache Orosius*, Copenhagen: Rosenkilde and Bagger.
Campbell, Alastair (1959), *Old English Grammar*, Oxford: Clarendon Press.
Caxton, William [1485] (1976), *Morte d'Arthur*, London: Scolar Press.
Chambers, R.W., Max Förster and Robin Flower (eds) (1933), *The Exeter Book of Old English Poetry*, London: Humphreys.
Chomsky, Noam (1957), *Syntactic Structures*, The Hague: Mouton.
Chomsky, Noam (1975), *Reflections on Language*, New York: Pantheon Books.
Chomsky, Noam (1986), *Knowledge of Language*, New York: Praeger.
Chomsky, Noam (1995), *The Minimalist Program*, Cambridge, MA: MIT Press.
Chomsky, Noam (2007), 'Approaching UG from Below', in Uli Sauerland and Hans-Martin Gärtner (eds), *Interfaces + Recursion = Language?*, Berlin: Mouton de Gruyter, pp. 1–29.
Chomsky, Noam (2015), 'Problems of Projection: Extensions', in Elisa Di Domenico, Cornelia Hamann and Simona Matteini (eds), *Structures, Strategies and Beyond*, Amsterdam: John Benjamins, pp. 3–16.
Clark, Cecily (1970), *The Peterborough Chronicle 1070–1154*, 2nd edn, Oxford: Clarendon Press.
Clark Hall, John R. (1894), *A Concise Anglo-Saxon Dictionary*, Cambridge: Cambridge University Press.
Clemens, Raymond and Timothy Graham (2007), *Introduction to Manuscript Studies*, Ithaca, NY: Cornell University Press.
Cole, Marcelle (2014), *Old Northumbrian Verbal Morphosyntax and the (Northern) Subject Rule*, Amsterdam: John Benjamins.
Curtiss, Susan (1977), *Genie: A Psycholinguistic Study of a Modern-Day 'Wild Child'*, San Francisco: Academic Press.
d'Ardenne, S. (1977), *The Katherine Group*, Paris: Les Belles Lettres.
Davis, Norman (1971), *Paston Letters and Papers of the Fifteenth Century*, Oxford: Clarendon Press.
Dekeyser, Xavier (1986), 'Relative Markers in the Peterborough Chronicle: 1070–1154', *Folia Linguistica Historica*, 7:1, 93–105.
Denholm-Young, Noel (1964), *Handwriting in England and Wales*, Cardiff: University of Wales Press.
Einenkel, E. (ed.) (1884), *The Life of Saint Katherine*, London: Trübner, EETS 80.
Evans, Mel (2013), *The Language of Queen Elizabeth I: A Sociolinguistic Perspective on Royal Style and Identity*, Chichester: Wiley Blackwell.
Farquharson, Joseph (2013), 'Jamaican', in Susanne Michaelis, Philippe Maurer, Martin Haspelmath and Magnus Huber (eds), *The Survey of Pidgin and Creole Languages, Volume I: English-Based and Dutch-Based Languages*, Oxford: Oxford University Press, pp. 81–91.
Fischer, Olga (2007), *Morphosyntactic Change*, Oxford: Oxford University Press.
Fischer, Olga, Ans van Kemenade, Willem Koopman and Wim van der Wurff (2000), *The Syntax of Early English*, Cambridge: Cambridge University Press.

Fleischer, Jürg (2009), 'Paleographic Clues to Prosody', in Roland Hinterhölzl and Svetlana Petrova (eds), *Information Structure and Language Change*, Berlin: Mouton de Gruyter, pp. 161–89.
Freeborn, Dennis (1998), *From Old English to Standard English*, 2nd edn, Ottawa: Ottawa University Press.
Fulk, Robert (2012), *An Introduction to Middle English: Grammar and Texts*, Peterborough: Broadview Press.
Gardner, John (1965), *The Complete Works of the Gawain Poet*, Chicago: University of Chicago Press.
Garmonsway, G. N. (ed.) (1947), *Aelfric's Colloquy*, London: Methuen.
van Gelderen, Elly (2011), *The Linguistic Cycle*, Oxford: Oxford University Press.
van Gelderen, Elly (2014), *A History of the English Language*, rev. edn, Amsterdam: John Benjamins.
Godden, Malcolm (1979), *Ælfric's Catholic Homilies*, 2nd series, London: Oxford University Press.
Gollancz, Israel (1923), *Pearl, Cleanness, Patience and Sir Gawain: Reproduced in Facsimile from the Unique MS. Cotton Nero A.x in the British Museum*, London: Oxford University Press for the Early English Text Society.
Gradon, Pamela (1965), *Dan Michel's Ayenbite of Inwyt*, Oxford: Oxford University Press.
Herzman, Ronald B., Graham Drake and Eve Salisbury (eds) (1997), *Four Romances of England: King Horn, Havelok the Dane, Bevis of Hampton, Athelston*, Kalamazoo, MI: Medieval Institute Publications.
Hogg, Richard (ed.) (1992a), *The Cambridge History of the English Language, Volume 1: The Beginnings to 1066*, Cambridge: Cambridge University Press.
Hogg, Richard (1992b), 'Introduction', in Richard M. Hogg (ed.), *The Cambridge History of the English Language, Volume 1: The Beginnings to 1066*, Cambridge: Cambridge University Press, pp. 1–25.
Jespersen, Otto (1931), *A Modern English Grammar*, Part IV, London: George Allen & Unwin.
van Kemenade, Ans and Bettelou Los (2006), *The Handbook of the History of English*, Oxford: Blackwell.
Ker, N. R. (1960), *Facsimile of MS Bodley 34: St. Katherine, St. Juliana, Hali Meidhad, Sawles Warde*, London: Oxford University Press.
Ker, N. R. (1963), *The Owl and the Nightingale: Facsimile of the Jesus and Cotton Manuscripts*, London: Oxford University Press, EETS o.s. 251.
Klaeber, Fr. (1922), *Beowulf*, Boston: Heath.
Klima, Edward (1965), *Studies in Diachronic Transformational Syntax*, PhD dissertation, Harvard University.
Kline, A. S. (2007), *Sir Gawain and the Green Knight*, <http://www.poetryintranslation.com/PITBR/English/GawainAndTheGreenKnight.htm> (last accessed 9 May 2017).
Kökeritz, Helge (1954), *Mr. William Shakespeares Comedies, Histories and Tragedies*, facsimile edition of the First Folio of 1623, New Haven, CT: Yale University Press.
Krapp, G. P. (1931), *The Junius Manuscript*, New York: Columbia University Press.

Krapp, G. P. and E. V. Kirk Dobbie (1936), *The Exeter Book*, New York: Columbia University Press.
Kroch, Anthony and Anne Taylor (1997), 'Verb Movement in Old and Middle English: Dialect Variation and Language Contact', in Ans van Kemenade and Nigel Vincent (eds), *Parameters of Morphosyntactic Change*, Cambridge: Cambridge University Press, pp. 297–325.
Kytö, Merja and Päivi Pahta (2016), *The Cambridge Handbook of English Historical Linguistics*, Cambridge: Cambridge University Press.
Lass, Roger (1994), *Old English: A Historical Linguistic Companion*, Cambridge: Cambridge University Press.
Lightfoot, David (1979), *Principles of Diachronic Syntax*, Cambridge: Cambridge University Press.
Los, Bettelou (2005), *The Rise of the To-Infinitive*, Oxford: Oxford University Press.
Mackie, W. S. (1934), *The Exeter Book, Part II*, London and Oxford: Oxford University Press.
Marsden, Richard (2004), *The Cambridge Old English Reader*, Cambridge: Cambridge University Press.
Meech, Sanford, Hope Emily Allen and W. Butler-Bowdon (eds) (1961), *The Book of Margery Kempe*, Oxford: Oxford University Press.
Miller, Thomas (1890), *The Old English Version of Bede's Ecclesiastical History of the English People*, London: Oxford University Press.
Mitchell, Bruce (1985), *Old English Syntax*, 2 vols, Oxford: Clarendon Press.
Morris, Richard (1874–93), *Cursor Mundi*, 7 Parts. London: K. Paul, Trench, Trübner & Co. for the Early English Text Society.
Mulcaster, Richard [1582] (1970), *Elementarie*, Menston: Scolar Press.
Napier, Arthur (1883), *Wulfstan: Sammlung der Ihm Zugeschriebenen Homilien Nebst Untersuchungen über Ihre Echtheit*, Halle: Max Niemeyer.
Nevalainen, Terttu and Elizabeth Closs Traugott (eds) (2012), *The Oxford Handbook of the History of English*, Oxford: Oxford University Press.
Orchard, Andy (2001), *A Critical Companion to Beowulf*, Cambridge: Boydell & Brewer.
Pope, John (ed.) (1967–8), *Homilies of Aelfric: A Supplemental Collection*, 2 vols, London: Oxford University Press.
Quirk, Randolph and Christopher Wrenn (1958), *An Old English Grammar*, London: Methuen.
Roberts, Jane (2005), *Guide to Scripts*, London: British Library.
Sedgefield, Walter John (ed.) (1899), *King Alfred's Old English Version of Boethius*, Oxford: Clarendon Press.
Skeat, Walter (ed.) [1881–7] (1970), *The Gospel According to St. Matthew, St. Mark, St. Luke and St. John*, Darmstadt: Wissenschaftliche Buchgesellschaft.
Suárez-Gómez, Cristina (2009), 'On the Syntactic Differences between OE Dialects: Evidence from the Gospels', *English Language and Linguistics* 13:1, 57–75.
Sweet, Henry (1871), *King Alfred's West-Saxon Version of Gregory's Pastoral Care*, London: Oxford University Press.
Szmrecsanyi, Benedikt (2016), 'An Analytic-Synthetic Spiral in the History of

English', in Elly van Gelderen (ed.), *Cyclical Change Continued*, Amsterdam: John Benjamins, pp. 93–112.
Thorpe, Benjamin (1861), *Anglo-Saxon Chronicle I and II*, London: Longman.
Triggs, Tony (1995), *The Book of Margery Kempe: A New Translation*, Tunbridge Wells: Burns & Oats.
Whitelock, Dorothy (1954), *The Peterborough Chronicle: The Bodleian Manuscript Laud Misc. 636*, Copenhagen: Rosenkilde and Bagger.
Wirtjes, Hanneke (ed.) (1991), *The Middle English Physiologus*, Oxford: Oxford University Press.
Wright, C. E. (1960), *English Vernacular Hands*, Oxford: Clarendon Press.
Zupitza, Julius (1959), *Beowulf, Reproduced in Facsimile*, 2nd edn, EETS 245.

Index

abbreviation, v, xiii, 4, 47, 56, 97, 148, 154, 159, 185
adjective, 9, 56, 60–3, 86–9, 91, 124, 146, 152, 171
adverb, 6, 15, 37, 73, 75, 87, 89–92, 111, 116, 130, 133, 145–7, 155, 158, 164
adverbial, 4–6, 16, 18–20, 37, 48, 51, 61–4, 77, 86–7, 102–4, 110–12, 116–18, 122, 124, 131, 145–7, 152, 157, 159, 165, 184
Aelfric, 5–6, 28, 45, 72, 180, 185, 196–7
agreement, 4, 6–8, 10, 12, 23, 79, 129, 183
Aldred, 65
Alfred, 29, 47, 93, 180–1, 184, 197
Allen, Cynthia, 22
Allen, Hope Emily, 125, 154
alliteration, 16, 142
analogy, 110
analytic, 2–4, 7–10, 12, 15, 24, 30, 32, 37, 42, 55, 71, 74, 76–7, 79, 107, 113, 119, 125, 130–2, 133, 135, 138, 142, 148, 151–3, 159, 165, 171, 183, 185–6
Andersen, Henning, 8
article, 2, 10, 15–17, 25, 28–32, 37, 43, 55, 61, 64, 71, 74, 79–80, 93, 100–1, 105–7, 110, 112–13, 119, 121–5, 129, 133, 137, 142, 145, 148, 152–3, 185–6
Ascham, Roger, 21, 167, 181
aspect, 2, 6–8, 21, 23, 25, 55, 139
auxiliary, 2–3, 7, 9–10, 15–17, 20–1, 23, 26–8, 42, 49, 51–2, 55, 64, 72, 75, 77, 87, 94, 110, 118, 122, 124, 133, 142, 145–6, 153, 158–9, 164–5, 170, 183–4, 186
Ayenbite of Inwit, 20, 41, 118, 181, 196

Baker, Peter, 80
Bately, Janet, 42, 52, 55

Bean, Marian, 43
Bech, Kristin, 43
Bede, 2, 15, 42, 180, 197
Beowulf, 6, 18–19, 21, 24–5, 27–31, 33, 37, 39, 46, 60, 180
Bestiary, 96, 119–24, 182
Bosworth, Joseph, 11

Caedmon's Hymn, 14–15, 37, 39, 180
Campbell, Alastair, 47, 61
Canale, Michael, 43
capitalization, 47, 142, 159
Carolingian, 45–7, 96
case, 2, 4–6, 12, 15–17, 21–3, 30, 32, 55, 60–1, 69, 72–5, 77, 79, 89–90, 92, 104, 110, 112, 121, 125, 129, 148, 165, 183, 186
Caxton, William, 96, 142, 159–66, 172
Chaucer, 24, 27, 148–53, 173, 181
Chomsky, Noam, 8–9
cleanness, 142–7, 182
code switching, 56
Cole, Marcelle, 65
compositor, 36, 159
compound, 52, 60, 85–8, 91, 116
conjunction, 8, 18, 32–3, 35–7, 42, 47, 55, 89, 105, 107, 111–12, 117–18, 125, 131–2, 146, 148
contraction, 17, 38, 51, 87, 91–3, 110, 116, 146, 170
copula, 5, 55, 60–3, 64, 91, 109, 123, 165
creole, 12
Cursor Mundi, 39, 71, 182
Curtiss, Susan, 8
cycle, 10

Danelaw, 97
d'Ardenne, S., 107

demonstrative, 10, 16–17, 21–3, 25, 28–32, 42, 53, 55, 60–4, 70–9, 88–9, 93, 97, 100–4, 106–7, 110, 116–17, 123, 133, 147, 184
Denholm-Young, Noel, 36
dialect, 1, 14, 37–41, 43, 55, 64–5, 71, 78–9, 92–3, 102, 106–7, 110, 112, 116, 118, 124, 132–3, 147, 153, 159, 165–6, 169–71, 175
dual, 30–1
dummy auxiliary, 20–1, 112, 170
dummy subject, 24, 52, 55, 116, 119, 124

Einenkel, Eugen, 107, 110
Elizabeth(an), 36, 141, 167–71, 182
Evans, Mel, 170, 173
existential, 124, 153
expletive, 111, 131, 133, 161, 165, 169
external change, 9–10, 14
extraposed/extraposition, 19, 49, 51–5, 62–3, 75, 77, 86, 92, 102, 110

Farquharson, Joseph, 12
feminine gender, 22, 60, 63–4, 74, 86–9, 92, 101, 106–9, 112, 116
feminine pronoun, 29–32, 40, 48, 116, 119, 145, 165
Fischer, Olga, xiii, 43, 139
Fleischer, Jürg, xiii
fragment, 87, 131

Gawain, 16, 142, 145, 182
Gelderen, Elly van, 10, 13
gender, 11, 30, 32, 60, 63, 104
Gothic script, 45, 96, 107, 113, 119, 125, 141–2, 148, 159, 186
grammaticalization, 10, 32, 51

Havelok, 41, 137–8, 181, 185
Henry Machyn, 166, 169–71, 182
Herzman, Ronald, 138
Hogg, Richard, 13, 27, 82
hypotactic, 8, 12, 43, 112, 183–4

impersonal, 24, 56, 116–17, 123, 146–7, 161
infinitive, 7, 40, 53, 64, 88, 90, 103, 121–4, 152–3, 157–9, 161, 164, 184
instrumental, 70, 147
insular script, 45–7, 93, 96
internal change, 2, 42
italic script, 141, 167

Jespersen, Otto, 25

Katerine, 107–113, 181
Kemenade, Ans van, 43
Kent(ish), 37, 41, 166, 181
Ker, N. R., 107, 113, 136
Klima, Edward, 8
Komen, Erwin, 43
Kroch, Anthony, 43, 106

Lass, Roger, 85
Layamon, 23, 29, 35–6, 41, 181
light verb, 105, 157
Lightfoot, David, 8, 13
Lindisfarne, 46, 66–9, 75, 77–80, 181
linguistic cycle, 10
Los, Bettelou, 28, 43

Marckwardt, Albert, 43, 94
Margery of Kempe, 154–9, 182
masculine gender, 22, 29, 32, 60, 63, 72, 85–8, 91–2, 101, 104, 125
masculine pronoun, 21, 71
Mercian, 37, 45, 64–8, 71, 181
Midlands, 39–41, 96, 107, 109–12, 119, 125, 137, 142, 145, 148, 153–4, 157–9, 181–2, 185–6
Mitchell, Bruce, 60, 71
modal, 7, 10, 25–8, 52–5, 60–4, 88, 90–3, 122–4, 133, 159, 164–5
mood, 6–8, 23–8
Moore, Samuel, 43, 94
Mossé, Fernand, 43, 139
Mulcaster, Richard, 16
Mustanoja, Tauno, 43, 139

Napier, Arthur, 56
nasal abbreviation, 35, 47, 62–3, 67, 102, 125, 142, 167, 170
negative concord, 64, 91, 93, 112, 117–18, 122, 125, 146
negative contraction, 38, 87, 91–2
negative/negation, 10, 17, 56, 61–2, 87, 91–3, 106, 110, 118, 122–5, 137, 146, 152, 164, 170, 185
neuter gender, 22, 29, 32, 60, 63, 85–8, 92, 101, 104, 109–10, 116
neuter pronoun, 152
Nevalainen, Terttu, 173
northern dialect, 38–9, 41, 55–6, 75, 96, 106, 109, 112, 125, 129–33, 136
Northumbrian, 14, 37–8, 45, 65, 67–8, 71

Orchard, Andy, 33
Owl and Nightingale, 113–19

Index

paper, 11, 159
paratactic, 8, 12, 33, 35, 37, 43, 55, 65, 80, 100, 103, 107, 113, 116, 118–19, 123–4, 130, 133, 136, 145, 170–1, 183
parchment, 11
participle, 7, 24–6, 28, 40–1, 49, 51, 55, 63, 71, 75, 86, 89–90, 93, 109–12, 114, 116, 122, 124–5, 129–30, 133, 145, 152–3, 158–9, 161, 170, 184
particle, 25, 29, 61, 74, 80, 93, 105
passive, 8, 16, 25–6, 51, 55, 63, 145, 157, 159, 164, 170, 184
Pastoral Care, 6, 29, 93–4, 180
Peterborough Chronicle, 4–6, 11, 15, 18, 22, 25, 32, 34, 37, 47, 55, 97–106, 181
Physiologus, 119–25, 182
Pintzuk, Susan, 43
plural number, 6, 15, 22, 25, 53, 55–6, 60–4, 69–76, 78–9, 86–93, 101–4, 106, 110–12, 119, 123, 129–30, 132–3, 142, 145–6, 148, 153, 157, 159
plural pronoun, 29–32, 40–1, 48, 52, 56, 110, 114, 122, 129, 146, 159, 164–5
possessive, 15–16, 87, 89, 152
preposed, 49, 75, 105–6, 122, 124, 142, 144, 147
preposition, 2–6, 9–10, 15–19, 21–3, 32, 40, 49, 51, 63, 73, 78–9, 101–2, 116–17, 125, 130, 133, 152–3, 159, 165, 176, 183, 186
printing, 96, 141–2, 159, 172, 186
progressive, 2, 7–8, 25–6, 158
punctuation, 1, 32–7, 42, 47, 56, 84, 86, 92, 117, 122, 142, 155, 159, 169, 171

Quirk, Randolph, 11

reflexive, 29–30, 32, 42, 55, 110–12, 118–19, 122, 129, 133, 145–6, 148, 153
relative, 16, 28–30, 42, 56, 60–5, 70–1, 74, 76–8, 80, 86–9, 91, 93, 102–3, 106–7, 109–10, 112, 116, 122–3, 125, 129–33, 142, 145–8, 151–2, 155, 157–9, 169, 171
Richard Rolle, 125–32
riddle, 11, 26, 30, 180
Roberts, Jane, 94, 119
rune/runic, 11, 45
Rushworth, 18, 67, 73–80, 181

Scheffer, Johannes, 43
Secretary, 141, 154, 166, 171, 186

Shakespeare, 21, 36, 159, 182
singular, 4, 6, 22, 25, 29–32, 48, 56, 60–1, 64–5, 69, 72, 74, 76, 78, 85–92, 104, 107, 111–12, 116–19, 122, 125, 129, 133, 145, 147–8, 151, 153, 157, 159, 165
Skeat, Walter, 65, 67–8
southern dialect, 39, 41, 64, 69, 80, 93, 96–7, 106, 109, 112, 114, 119, 125, 129, 136, 153
spacing, 1, 47, 69, 87
strong verb, 23–4
Suárez-Gómez, Cristina, 80
subjunctive, 7, 21, 23–6, 28, 49, 52, 55, 62, 64, 88, 91, 93, 121, 123–5, 157, 170–1, 185
superlative, 61, 171
synthetic, 2–4, 8, 10, 12, 14–15, 21, 32, 37, 42, 55, 70, 72, 75, 77, 82, 92–3, 107, 114, 135, 138, 142, 153, 159, 171
Szmrecsanyi, Benedikt, 2–3

Taylor, Ann, 43, 106
tense, 2, 6–8, 12, 17, 21, 23, 27–8, 40, 53, 55, 64, 78, 85, 89–91, 103, 111, 113, 118, 129, 153, 159, 161, 164–5, 170–1
Toller, N. T., 11
Traugott, Elizabeth Closs, 43

Universal Grammar, 8–9

vellum, 11
V-final, 18–22, 28, 33, 35, 42, 51–6, 61–4, 78–9, 86–7, 92, 124
V-initial, 64, 86, 117
V-second (V2), 17–21, 28, 35, 37–8, 40–3, 49, 52–6, 61–4, 77–80, 85–6, 90, 92, 101–7, 110–13, 116, 118, 122–4, 129–30, 132, 183

weak noun, 22, 85–6, 88, 91, 93
weak verb, 23–4
West Saxon, 37–8, 45, 47, 55–6, 64–8, 70–1, 76–80, 92
Whitelock, Dorothy, 97
Wirtjes, Hanneke, 119, 125
Wrenn, Christopher, 11
Wright, C. E., 119, 142
Wulfstan, 5, 56–64, 180
Wurff, Wim van der, 43